# Progressive Heritage

## The Evolution of a Politically Radical Literary Tradition in Canada

# Progressive Heritage

## The Evolution of a Politically Radical Literary Tradition in Canada

James Doyle

**Wilfrid Laurier University Press**

WLU

This book has been published with the help of a grant from the Humanities and Social Sciences Federation of Canada, using funds provided by the Social Sciences and Humanities Research Council of Canada. We acknowledge the financial support of the Government of Canada through the Book Publishing Industry Development Program for our publishing activities.

## National Library of Canada Cataloguing in Publication Data

Doyle, James, 1937–
   Progressive heritage : the evolution of a politically radical literary tradition in Canada

Includes bibliographical references and index.
ISBN 0-88920-402-0 (bound)

1. Communism and literature—Canada—History—20th century.
2. Canadian literature (English)—20th century—History and criticism.
I. Title.

PS8101.P65D69 2002        C810.9'358        C2002-900011-4
PR9185.5.P64D69 2002

© 2002 Wilfrid Laurier University Press
Waterloo, Ontario, Canada N2L 3C5
www.wlupress.wlu.ca

Cover design by Leslie Macredie, using a painting
by Frederick B. Taylor entitled *Talking Union* (1950).
Reproduced courtesy of The Montreal Museum of Fine Arts, gift of the artist.
Photo: The Montreal Museum of Fine Arts.

The author and publisher have made every reasonable effort to obtain permission to reproduce the secondary material in this book. Any corrections or omissions brought to the attention of the Press will be incorporated in subsequent printings.

Printed in Canada

# Contents

# Acknowledgements

I wish to thank Wilfrid Laurier University for two short-term grants, in 1995 and 1998, which enabled me to complete the research for this book. I also extend appreciation to my student research assistants, Kathy Cawsey and Sarah Brophy, for their commitment to the often tedious work of searching bibliographies and catalogues, scanning microfilm sources, and performing other routine but essential tasks. My research was facilitated by librarians and archivists in the National Archives of Canada, the Public Archives of Ontario, and the rare books and special collections divisions of the libraries of Toronto, Manitoba, British Columbia and McMaster universities. The Communist Party of Canada readily granted me permission to consult restricted portions of the CPC/LPP papers in the National Archives.

Parts of this book have appeared in different form in various publications. An early version of my discussion of Joe Wallace's life and writings was published in *Canadian Poetry: Studies/Documents/ Reviews* 35 (1994). Some of my comments on Margaret Fairley appeared in an article in *Canadian Literature* 147 (1995). My first thoughts on the Communist poetry of Milton Acorn appeared in *Canadian Poetry: Studies/Documents/Reviews* 40 (1997). The discussion of Dyson Carter's life and work is adapted from an article I wrote for *Left History* 5 (1998). An early version of my comments on Canadian social and socialist realist short stories of the 1930s was published in *Dominant Impressions: Essays on the Canadian Short Story*, ed. Gerald Lynch and Angela A. Robbeson (1999).

# Introduction

In an essay entitled "Our Cultural Heritage" published in 1952, literary critic and anthologist Margaret Fairley identified the "progressive culture" of Canada as the "energetic expression of our life of social struggle, directed to positive, creative, fruitful ends" (2). As the reference to "social struggle" suggests, Fairley's ideas on the form and purpose of literature were shaped by leftist political loyalties. For almost forty years, since her arrival in Canada as an immigrant from England before the First World War, Fairley had been writing about literature, first as a non-revolutionary socialist and ultimately as a Marxist and a member of the Communist Party of Canada (CPC). Fairley was perhaps the most influential of the Marxist Communists who attempted in the twentieth century to establish a politically radical view of Canadian literary history. In the long run, however, this attempt has had little impact on the artistic, academic, and bureaucratic establishments that have supported the prevailing liberal bourgeois conception of the subject. Indeed, just a year before Fairley wrote "Our Cultural Heritage," radical Canadian literature was amiably but conclusively dismissed by a rising spokesman for cultural liberalism, Northrop Frye. "The poetry of social protest, during the thirties," wrote Frye in his annual review of "Letters in Canada,"

> was attached to a number of powerful supports: it had a philosophy in Marxism, a programme of action in the proletarian revolution, and a reading public among bourgeois intellectuals. It never achieved a really distinguished expression, but it spoke for a large and influential pressure group. *Nous avons changé tout cela*; the poet's heart is no longer so far on the left side, and the poetry of social protest has retreated into a disembodied anarchism, in some respects a reversion to the old artist-versus-society theme of earlier decades. (*Bush Garden* 7)

Frye's opinion would still be accepted as conclusive by many critics and historians of Canadian literature, but his sweeping judgement of politically leftist writing needs to be based on more evidence than he provided. A substantial body of poetry, fiction, drama, and discursive literary prose relevant to the traditions Frye mentions had appeared in Canada before 1929, and continued to be published after 1939. Some of it was badly written and deservedly ignored, but much of it was competently written and marginalized by Canadian literary historians and critics with pro-capitalistic conceptions of Canadian society and culture. Almost from the time of the establishment of the Communist Party of Canada in 1921, furthermore, Communist writers were anxious to establish their work as part of the national literary heritage by drawing lines of connection between themselves and Canadian writers they regarded as their predecessors. Post-1921 Communist commentators were especially interested in such connections because they were eager to demonstrate that Communism was not an alien importation, as right-wing politicians and police insisted, but a tradition as natural to Canada as it was to Russia or to any other country in the world. It was important to show how Marxist Communism was prefigured and eventually expressed in Canadian literature from its earliest beginnings through the twentieth century.

In emphasizing this continuity, Canadian Communists were following the dominant model of cultural history propagated within the international Communist movement. As James F. Murphy, among others, has demonstrated, a prolonged international debate was to arise among Communist writers and critics in the 1920s over the question of the relationship between the culture of the post-Revolutionary era and that of past ages, even though Karl Marx and V.I. Lenin had expressed themselves fairly decisively on this subject. Marx was a great admirer of literary tradition; his writing, and that of Frederick Engels, are filled with allusions to Shakespeare, Goethe, Molière, epic poetry, classical mythology, and the Christian Bible. Marx, Engels, and Lenin were well aware of the relevance of this tradition to revolutionary political thought, and never envisaged a detached, self-contained proletarian culture. As early as 1920 Lenin asserted in a draft resolution to the All-Russian Congress on Proletarian Culture that "Marxism has won its historic significance as the ideology of the revolutionary proletariat because, far from rejecting the most valuable achievements of the bourgeois epoch, it has, on the contrary, assimilated and refashioned everything of value in the more than two thousand years of the development of human thought and culture" (*Selected Works* 3: 485).

During the Stalinist era Soviet bureaucrats attempted to impose revised theories of aesthetics and literary history on Communist artists. But as Edward J. Brown has shown, these attempts produced not regimented submission but endless debates among artists and between artists and Party officials. Barbara Foley has accumulated an impressive amount of documentary evidence to demonstrate the same generalization about proletarian literature in the United States during the 1930s. Canadian Communists engaged in similar debates, although they tended on the whole toward the Leninist view of cultural history. Like non-Communist historians of Canadian literature, they were eager to demonstrate the existence of a continuous and culturally distinctive Canadian literary heritage. More specifically, Canadian Communists wanted to emphasize the theme of the "life of social struggle" of the working class against imperialistic and capitalistic power.

The concept of the class struggle implies that Marxists conceive of history in terms of a conflict between impersonal, abstract forces. But Marxist historians, literary critics, and literary artists have always been anxious to emphasize that they are talking about the free, imaginative thoughts and actions of human beings. According to Stanley

Ryerson, a Marxist historian and promoter of culture within the Communist Party of Canada,

> Contrary to an oft-repeated fallacy, Marxism is not "economic determinism." Marxism holds that it is the people who make history—their labor and their struggles and their dreams; and that these are understandable and have meaning when seen in their real setting: man's progressively extending mastery over the forces of nature, and the succession of social systems that have marked, one after another, the stages of his progression. (Postscript to *The Founding of Canada* 326)

The succession of social systems is brought about by periodic revolutions which may involve armed conflict, or a combination of violent and non-violent confrontation. In the historical record of European and European-derived societies, the most important revolutions have involved bourgeois struggles against feudalism and proletarian opposition to bourgeois industrial capitalism. The relatively brief three-hundred-year record of European settlement in Canada has mainly featured non-violent antagonism between the classes. The earliest armed revolts, in Upper and Lower Canada in 1837, were provoked by bourgeois ambitions to overthrow the last vestiges of British feudal power. The rebels of 1837, in spite of their failure, were perceived in terms of heroic mythology by Canadian political dissenters in the late nineteenth and early twentieth centuries. Their story was rewritten in specific Marxist terms by Stanley Ryerson in his *1837: The Birth of Canadian Democracy* (1937). Conceived in part as an expression of solidarity with the Republican fighters in Spain, Ryerson's book prefigured the later tendency in Canadian Marxist writing to transform the military failures of both the Spanish republicans and the rebels of 1837 into rhetorical rallying points in the appeal for the redoubled efforts needed to bring about the ultimate triumph promised in the Marxist view of history.

The title of Ryerson's history of the 1837 rebellion also indicates the importance that the word "democracy" took on in twentieth-century Marxist rhetoric. Unlike its usage in the bourgeois capitalist system, the word does not refer to parliamentary politics or representative government but to a broadly based participatory system such as that allegedly established in Soviet Russia in 1917. Ryerson's title involves another element of Marxist ideology that has important implications for the Communist view of Canadian literature. According to Karl Marx, struggles for national liberation from feudal and bourgeois power would be the preludes to what would eventually become a worldwide revolutionary movement. In Soviet Russia, tentatively under Lenin and more comprehensively under Stalin, the ideal of "socialism in one country" as a means of concentrating efforts on the struggle for the economic survival of the Soviet Union became the authorization for nationalistic revolutionary movements and for various forms of nationalistic expression within these movements. The adaptation of this tendency to Communist aesthetic theory was definitively articulated by the Hungarian-born literary critic Georg Lukács in the 1950s:

> Socialist art is, of its nature, *national* art....And the great realist works of art are a main factor in creating the intellectual and spiritual climate which gives human personality its specifically nationalistic character. The stronger a writer's ties with the cultural heritage of his nation, the more original his work will be. (Lukács, *Meaning* 103)

Lukács and the Russian Communists understood "nation" to mean a group of people bound by ties of language and ethnicity. Canadian Communists have expressed that meaning, especially when making distinctions between francophone and anglophone communities, but they also conceive "nation" in the sense of a community united by a centralized political system. Thus an important task for Communist writers and critics was to promote a literary heritage that would embody the humanistic, democratic, and nationalistic ideals of Marxism-Leninism within the distinctive context of Canadian society.

But literary scholars have rarely examined Marxist-Leninist Canadian literature, or even acknowledged it as a significant alternative to the dominant bourgeois view. One of the few attempts to evaluate Canadian creative writing inspired by leftist politics emerged just a few years after Northrop Frye made his dismissive comment on the subject. In his doctoral dissertation "Radicalism in English-Canadian Literature since Confederation" (1957), F.W. Watt was especially interested in the origins and early development of radical writing in Canada. Although he had limited access to source materials, he made an excellent beginning at demonstrating that socialistic, communistic, and revolutionary ideals influenced several important Canadian poets, essayists, and fiction writers in the late nineteenth and early twentieth centuries. In pursuing this tradition into the post-Russian Revolution decades, however, Watt concluded his thesis with a discussion of a limited selection of writers from the Depression era, thus supporting Frye's notion that Canadian literary radicalism was never very significant and after the 1930s went into a state of decline. Except for an article "Literature of Protest" that Watt distilled from his thesis for the first edition of the *Literary History of Canada* (1965), little scholarly attention has been devoted to the critical study of this country's radical literary heritage. Among the political historians of Communism in Canada, only Ivan Avakumovic mentions the CPC's cultural activities at all, and he goes into very little detail. For a while in the 1970s various authors and editors made some important efforts at reviving lost and forgotten texts. Dorothy Livesay's memoir/anthology *Right Hand Left Hand* (1977) reproduced many of the author's own poems, essays, and stories from the 1930s, unified by a narrative of her involvement with the Communist Party. Livesay was also instrumental in making available a new edition in 1973 of Irene Baird's long-neglected 1939 proletarian novel, *Waste Heritage*. Other significant reprints in the 1970s include Brian Davis's two volumes of the *Poetry of the Canadian People* (1976 and 1978) covering the years 1720-1950; and Donna Phillips's *Voices of Discord: Canadian Short Stories from the 1930s* (1979). Except for Davis's two volumes of poetry, these efforts concentrated on the 1930s, providing further support for Frye's impression of Canadian radical literature as an obsolete vestige of the Depression.

The close identification of Marxist-inspired literary activity with the 1930s is not an exclusively Canadian tendency. The same inclination is typical of scholarly studies of the much more abundant radical literary heritage of the United States, such as Daniel Aaron's *Writers on the Left: Episodes in American Literary Communism* (1961), James F. Murphy's *The Proletarian Moment: The Controversy over Leftism in Literature* (1991), and Barbara Foley's *Radical Representations: Politics and Form in U.S. Proletarian Fiction, 1929-1941* (1993). Alan M. Wald is perhaps the only American critic who has demonstrated, in *Writing from the Left* (1994), that a unified radical tradition of creative writing can be traced from nineteenth-century origins, through the Russian revolutionary era, the 1930s, and the decades following the Second World War. Among US-based scholars interested in the politically radical literary activity of the 1930s, Caren Irr has extended her studies of this activity to Canada in *The Suburb of Dissent: Cultural Politics in the United States and Canada during the 1930s* (1998). But while most of the US writers Irr discusses were Marxists active in the Communist Party and its affiliated literary movements, almost all her Canadian examples are drawn from the democratic socialist and liberal left. Of writers who were members or active sympathizers of the Communist Party of Canada in the 1930s, only Dorothy Livesay is discussed in any detail. So Irr goes further than Frye, by suggesting that even in the 1930s there were almost no Communist writers in Canada worth serious critical consideration.

Irr also ignores the historical roots and continuity of the Canadian radical literary tradition. Many writers in Canada, before 1917, expressed political and artistic ideas based on a critique of capitalism, although they usually had more extensive connections with eighteenth- and nineteenth-century notions of natural liberty or Victorian Protestant ideas of social reform than with scientific socialism. These writers include journalists such as William Lyon Mackenzie and Thomas MacQueen, poets such as Alexander McLachlan and Isabella Valancy Crawford, and the novelist Agnes Maule Machar. After the Second World War the Communist Party of Canada (renamed, from 1943 to 1959, the Labor-Progressive Party) became a vigorous champion of cultural activity that reflected left-wing political ideologies. The Party attracted, for varying periods, such promising young writers as Milton Acorn, George Ryga, and Patrick Anderson, and less well known but even more politically fervent writers like Dyson Carter, Louise Harvey, and Myrtle Bergren. After 1960 Communist sponsorship of literary activity decreased visibly, as the fortunes of the CPC waned under the force of such upheavals in the international Communist movement as Nikita Khrushchev's denunciation of Stalin, the Sino-Soviet split, and the rise of the New Left and its rejection of old Party lines. But many writers still affiliated with the old CPC or still loyal to much of the Marxist ideology it had promulgated, as well as writers inspired by the New Left, continued to produce politically radical literary work.

A great deal of research material relevant to Canadian leftist literary activity has become more readily accessible since F.W. Watt wrote his dissertation in 1957. Through the nineteenth and twentieth centuries, creative writers of radical political inclinations often placed their work with the publications of trades and labour unions and of various left-wing political parties. Many such limited circulation newspapers, magazines, and yearbooks survive in the library of the former federal Department of Labour, now Human Resources Development Canada, and much of this material is available on microfilm. The backfiles of the newspapers of the Communist Party of Canada—*The Worker* (1922-36), the *Daily Clarion* (1936-39) and the *Canadian Tribune* (1940-92), as well as many regional Communist papers, are likewise available on microfilm. The archives of the Communist Party—or at least, that part of their files the Party preserved and chose to release—have been deposited in the National Archives of Canada. These sources all contain a great deal of information about the lives and works of individual writers as well as about the Party's various arts clubs, writers' groups, and cultural commissions. Manuscript archives of various left-wing writers are available, including Margaret Fairley at the University of Toronto, Dyson Carter and Milton Acorn at the National Archives, and Dorothy Livesay at the University of Manitoba, to name only some of the more prominent. But a significant research gap in this subject is the limited opportunity to acquire first-hand information from some of the people who contributed to the Canadian radical literary tradition. The task has been left too long; as I write, there are almost no survivors from the 1920s and 1930s, and few enough from the 1940s and 1950s. I have found, furthermore, that among the latter memories have grown dim or personal recollections have merged with popular legend. However, I have regarded my primary task as the rediscovery and reading of the relevant published material: the fiction, poems, autobiographical narratives, critical essays, and reviews that constitute what Margaret Fairley called the "expression of our life of social struggle."

I have not attempted to deal with the substantial and fascinating story of radical left-wing theatre activity in Canada. Something of this story—again focussing on the 1930s—has been told in Richard Wright and Robin Endres's edition of *Eight Men Speak and Other Plays from the Canadian Workers' Theatre* (1976), and from a personal perspective by Toby Gordon Ryan in her *Stage Left* (1981). I am interested in literary rather than performance art, and have restricted myself to discussing plays as written texts, except where performance details seem relevant to my narrative. I must also admit to my neglect of literature written by progressive Canadians in languages other than English and French. Marxist and non-Marxist socialist newspapers, magazines, and literary periodicals have been published in Canada in many languages, most notably in Finnish, Ukrainian, and Yiddish, but very few of the resultant creative efforts are available in English translation. My treatment of French-Canadian literature is a bit more substantial, but still brief. As Ben-Z. Shek has demonstrated in detail, a tradition of social realism in Québecois fiction runs continuously from the late nineteenth century. I have drawn extensively on Shek's work to show how French-Canadian fiction has included criticism of the capitalist, imperialist, and federalist power that kept the Québecois people subjugated in the nineteenth and early twentieth centuries. But such works were seldom inspired by socialistic ideas until after 1960, when Marxist and other revolutionary theories emerged in the political and cultural action of the "Quiet Revolution." As Emile J. Talbot has demonstrated, even in the 1930s Quebec novelists and dramatists were much more likely to maintain the strong ultramontane Catholic influence and express anti-Communist sentiments. The organized Communist movement had comparatively little influence among Québecois artists and intellectuals, either before or after 1960, although the Party made a concerted effort in that province. Some of the literary consequences of this effort can be glimpsed in the backfiles of the Party newspapers *Clarté* (1935-39), under the co-editorship of Stanley Ryerson, and *Combat* (1947-60), edited by novelist Pierre Gélinas. Of particular importance are the achievements of Ryerson, for many years education director of the CPC/LPP, whose bicultural family heritage enabled him to make significant contributions to both anglophone and francophone literary circles.

As I have suggested, this survey of the Canadian radical literary heritage is organized primarily around the perspectives and experiences of members of the Communist Party. I am attracted by the argument of some historians, such as Michael Denning in *The Cultural Front* (1997), that the most significant politically radical cultural activity was the result of a broadly based and often collaborative effort of people with a variety of left-of-centre political commitments. Denning is referring to activity in the US in the 1930s and 1940s, and he is quite right in suggesting that historians have overemphasized the role of the Communist Party in this context. But I am writing about the heretofore neglected subject of radical Canadian culture from the 1920s to the 1960s, and I believe my subject needs a centre of focus to unify a variety of aesthetic and political developments. I have chosen to use the Communist Party as this centre because its substantial cultural commitment has been almost completely ignored, and because I believe that the most significant achievements in this tradition can be credited to Party members. I have, however, frequently taken into account where relevant the achievements of non-partisan Marxists and other socialists, including both sympathizers and opponents of the Party.

My basic intention is to write not a partisan defense of Communistic culture in Canada but a historical and critical evaluation of it. This seems to me a more rational response to what has been an undeniable part of Canadian cultural and social life than simply ignoring it, or dismissing it briefly, as too many other historians of Canadian literature have done. In the course of researching and writing this book, I have learned a great deal about Marxist Communism. I have learned, for instance, that its theoretical foundations and its historical expressions are far more intellectually rigorous and humanistic than its opponents are willing to admit, or take the time to discover. I have learned also that many of the Canadian writers who embraced Communism were intelligent, sincere, and talented people with an enviable faith in the perfectibility of humanity. The Marxist Communist belief in human perfectibility must often be distinguished from the clumsy attempts to apply theory to action. The Soviet Russian regime was badly stained by the bloody excesses and bureaucratic stupidity of Stalinism; in Canada, many of the Party's policies suffered from the stubborn refusal of its leaders to recognize Stalinism for what it was. But one could make similar charges against almost every other political and ideological movement in history. The British Empire in the nineteenth century and that would-be empire, the United States of America, have both wallowed in violent and corrupt excesses in pursuit of abstract ideals that sound highly laudable in theory. And in spite of such excesses, something of the ideals of great socio- political movements survive, especially in the imaginative literature that inspires and is inspired by these movements.

The ideals of the Communist movement were based on a complex and intellectually rigorous political ideology, and there is a commonly expressed notion in literary studies that ideology is antagonistic to creativity. As Barbara Foley has demonstrated in her study of American proletarian fiction of the 1930s, this notion was expounded especially by the so-called "New Critics" of the 1930s and 1940s, who assumed that art shows rather than tells, and deals with universal aspects of human nature rather than with historically localized ideas and experiences (Foley 3-4). With its perceived tendency to express dogmatic and deterministic conceptions of human thought and conduct, Marxist Communism has been seen by the New Critics and other literary scholars as especially hostile to art. As in all matters of aesthetic theory, these questions belong to a vast dialectical context that cannot be resolved by a total rejection of any one position in the debate. Many Communists, including Lenin, repeatedly warned against reducing the function of art to nothing but political propaganda. Other Party members and sympathizers have believed that all literature ultimately resolves thematically toward the class struggle. Sometimes the purposes of art are ill-served by the demands of political ideology; at other times, art and politics have blended well together. Art does not usually flourish in an environment of bureaucratic domination, although the efforts of bureaucracies to encourage art have not always been unsuccessful. Inflexible dogma can sometimes come into conflict with the narratological and rhetorical methods of creative literature, while at other times novels, poems, and plays can expound dogma with remarkable success.

But the imaginative literature inspired by Marxist Communist and other anti-capitalist ideologies is by no means significant only because of the political and economic theories that this literature advocates. As the expression of an element of a larger cultural community, it contributes to the communal self-revelation that Northrop Frye defines as one of the essential purposes of creative writing. In his "Conclusion" in Klinck's *The Literary History of Canada* (1965), Frye points out that "Canadian literature, whatever its inherent merits, is an indispensable aid to the knowledge of Canada. It records what the Canadian imagination has reacted to, and it tells us things about this environment that nothing else will tell us" (822). Although Frye is not prepared to acknowledge the fact, creative literature written from anti-capitalist and revolutionary perspectives must be regarded as an essential part of the revelations about the Canadian imagination and its environment.

The literary output of Canadian progressive writers also reveals something about the people who produced it. Besides all the formal and ideological aspects of this subject, I am interested in the human side of it, by which I mean the words, actions, beliefs, and artistic achievements of the individual people who were involved. I have devoted considerable attention to biographical detail, and have organized most of my chapters around the lives and literary careers of individual writers. This biographical emphasis is especially appropriate to a topic involving writers, or segments of the careers of writers, that have been ignored by literary history. As Vivian Gornick argues in *The Romance of American Communism* (1977), "people have been writing about the Communists with an oppressive distance between themselves and their subject, a distance that often masquerades as objectivity but in fact conveys only an emotional and intellectual atmosphere of 'otherness'—as though something not quite recognizable, something vaguely nonhuman was being described" (18). The Canadian literary artists who wrote from a Communist perspective were indeed human—complete with the eccentricities, conventionalities, hypocrisies, and capacity for imagination and artistic expression that characterize the species.

In this study of the Canadian radical literary past I have for the most part taken a simple chronological approach. Since my main interest is in the achievements of writers connected or sympathetic to the Communist Party of Canada, I have surveyed the evolving theory and practice of these writers from the founding of the Party in 1921 to the last literary efforts of ageing members in the 1980s. While aware of the biases built into the whole idea of "periodization" in historical studies, I would maintain that a simple historical structure based on easily recognizable points of demarcation is the most efficient means of organizing a study devoted largely to previously neglected matters of fact and interpretation. I begin with a chapter on nineteenth-century antecedents, since so much progressive political and aesthetic theory comes out of the nineteenth century, and because twentieth-century Canadian Communist writers made a particular point of relating their work to the national literary tradition that developed in the 1800s. After the Russian Revolution and the establishment of the CPC in 1921, the subject divides with remarkable neatness into decades. In the late 1950s and early 1960s old-line Marxist Communism in Canada was upstaged by the emergence of the so-called "New Left," in which various strands of socialism were united with Canadian nationalism, Quebec separatism, feminism, and radical movements imported or adapted from the United States relating to the reaction against the Vietnam War and racial discrimination. Various creative artists were associated with these developments, including many young writers who were also influenced by postmodern literary theories. The literary New Left in Canada probably deserves a book-length treatment of its own, but since my main subject is the literary activity associated with the old Communist Party of Canada, I have confined myself to sketching briefly some post-1950s developments in order to demonstrate both the continuity and discontinuity of these developments with older forms of radicalism.

Throughout this book I have tried to avoid getting too deeply involved in the subtleties of Marxist and Marxist-Leninist theory and terminology. As I have discovered, it is extremely difficult to settle on definitive words and phrases to describe the partisan complexities of the Communist movement. In my title, for instance, I have followed the example of Margaret Fairley in referring to the "progressive" literary heritage. In *The Lyrical Left* (1986), a study of the "origins of cultural radicalism in America," Edward Abrahams opposes "progressive" to "radical," applying the words respectively to reformist and revolutionary movements. To most commentators sympathetic to the cause, Communist political ideology and activity are "progressive"; to commentators outside the movement the same ideology and activity are usually described as "radical," the word frequently carrying a pejorative connotation. Ambiguities emanate from the word "communism" itself, even from such apparent trivia, as Alan M. Wald points out, as the matter of spelling the word with an upper or lower case "c" (*Writing from the Left* 7). "Socialist" and "Marxist" can raise similar problems. As one gets deeper into the specialized terminology of Communist literary theory, the problems multiply in the direction of verbal chaos. "Socialist realism," "critical realism," and "proletarian" are only a few of the terms I have been obliged to struggle with, as I have discovered meaning shifting from one source to another. As Susan Suleiman illustrates in her study of the ideological novel, the use of such terms as "political novel," "roman à thèse," and even the familiar "realism" invokes so many questions that the literary critic might spend much energy on definition, revisions of definitions, and further explanations. In the end, the literary historian can only tread through the minefield of theory and jargon as carefully as possible, defining and invoking authority wherever it seems appropriate, while hoping that the specific expositions of the forms and themes of literary works will clarify meaning as a whole.

Ultimately, however, I am no more interested in reducing Marxist terminology and ideology to a single definitive meaning than in placing the work of Marxist creative writers in a fixed position in any literary canon. My main purposes are to present a historical narrative of the development of progressive literature in Canada, to call attention to writers and works that have been neglected and, where appropriate, to defend their achievements as aesthetically significant. I have attempted to make this work comparatively comprehensive, but I am well aware that I have passed over lightly or even failed to mention writers some readers will regard as important. My purpose has not been to analyze the work of every Canadian literary artist who has expressed radical socialist political opinions, but to give a clear and specific idea of the overall form and content of the progressive tradition in Canadian literature. More succinctly put, my purpose is to reveal that the life of "social struggle" has been a significant part of the Canadian literary heritage.

# 1

# The Progressive Heritage in Canadian Literature
## Beginnings to 1900

According to Margaret Fairley, the Canadian progressive literary tradition can be traced all the way back to seventeenth-century New France and the French colonial discovery of the egalitarian basis of aboriginal society. Her anthology, *Spirit of Canadian Democracy* (1945), begins with excerpts from the *Jesuit Relations* of 1635, in which Father Jean de Brébeuf expresses his admiration for the social unity, hospitality, and courtesy that prevail among the Hurons:

> We see shining among them some rather noble moral virtues. You note, in the first place, a great love and union, which they are careful to cultivate by means of their marriages, of their presents, of their feasts, and of their frequent visits....Their hospitality towards all sorts of strangers is remarkable....They never close the door upon a Stranger, and, once having received him into their houses, they share with him the best they have. (Fairley, *Spirit* 16)

Fairley was undoubtedly attracted by the suggestions of primitive communism in Brébeuf's picture of aboriginal society. But as a Marxist, Fairley would believe that the social and moral virtues of primitive societies represent ideals that were lost to European-based cultures with the advent of feudalism and industrialism. According to the anthropological basis of the Marxist conception of history, as expressed for instance in Frederick Engels's *The Origins of the Family, Private Property and the State* (1884), the social equality within tribal and clannish cultures was supplanted over the centuries by hierarchical societies dominated by patriarchal power and capitalistic greed. Fading vestiges of pre-historic innocence and virtue serve as glimpses of the classless society that Marxism represents as the ultimate ideal of human felicity. The history of post-tribal civilization is the history of the struggle of the oppressed classes to regain their lost heritage.

In Canada, this struggle accompanies the growth of European colonization and settlement, and crystallizes into a localized version of the conflict that had been raging for centuries in the Old World, between the entrenched privilege of feudalism and the emerging idea of democratic individualism. According to Fairley, the first important literary expression of the democratic struggle against feudalism appeared in the 1820s. Fairley's edition of the *Selected Writings of William Lyon Mackenzie* (1960) presents a broad representation of Mackenzie's journalism and essays from 1824, when he began publishing a newspaper, the *Colonial Advocate*, until the eve of the Upper Canada Rebellion of 1837. One of Fairley's main purposes was to establish Mackenzie's life and writings as comparable to the life and writings of a hero of US history who was idealized by American Communists, Thomas Paine. Fairley even indicates a direct influence: "In July and August 1837 Thomas Paine's *Common Sense* was reprinted [in Mackenzie's second paper, the *Constitution*] almost in full" (106). As the work of both Paine and Mackenzie demonstrate, in the eighteenth and early nineteenth centuries journalism was still to a great extent a literary art. Although much debased by a tendency to sensationalism and acrimony—as Mackenzie's writing often reveals—newspaper writing remained an important influence for creative writers and thinkers well into the twentieth century. Indeed, the art of journalism as a creative means of political persuasion became especially important to the Communist movement, in the writing of Marx himself and down through that of the Russian revolutionaries of 1917 and foreign supporters like the American John Reed.

In paying tribute to Mackenzie's abilities as a journalist, Fairley was setting herself against a widespread Canadian impression of him that had prevailed since the failure of his rebellion, and that had been recently reinforced by a new biography. William Kilbourn's *The Firebrand: William Lyon Mackenzie and the Rebellion in Upper Canada* (1956), like Fairley's anthology, locates the climax of its narrative in the events of 1837. But Kilbourn's ultimate point is that Mackenzie's character, actions, and literary efforts are anomalies in Canadian life. Mackenzie, says Kilbourn in his introduction, "represents a way we did not take. He is the sort of character we most emphatically did not become. Canadians are a people of the law rather than the prophets, and those few of them who are genuinely seized with the spirit [must] prepare to pay the penalty of ostracism or exile or madness." According to Kilbourn, Mackenzie belongs to "the crankier and shabbier ranks" of those whose lives were devoted to "the pursuit and direction of power"; people who include "Lenin…Sam Adams, and William Cobbett" (Intro. n. pag.). As far as his writing is concerned, Kilbourn continued, Mackenzie's style was "something of a cross between Old Farmer's Almanac and a threadbare Ciceronian rhetoric" (*The Firebrand* 33).

To Fairley, these remarks were intolerable. She saw no disparagement in assigning Mackenzie to a historical context that included Lenin, or the early nineteenth-century English journalist and traveller Cobbett, whose criticism of landowners and politicians was much admired by twentieth-century Marxists. Fairley could also not countenance the suggestion that the primary motive of revolutionaries like Lenin, Cobbett, and Mackenzie was merely the "pursuit and direction of power." Still less could she endure the accusation that Mackenzie was not a competent writer. But although her edition is, in part, a refutation of Kilbourn, Fairley makes no mention of *The Firebrand* beyond listing the book in a brief note on "further reading." For her main secondary source of information she went back to the first biography, Charles Lindsey's *The Life and Times of William Lyon Mackenzie* (1862). Unlike Kilbourn, Lindsey saw the rebel leader not as an atypical eccentric but as representative of democratic ideals prevalent among the Canadian middle class in the early nineteenth century, and as one of the creators of responsible government in Canada. Fairley likewise strove to present Mackenzie as a creator of the bourgeois revolution which, according to Marx, was a necessary prerequisite to the establishment of proletarian power. She carefully selected and organized her material, not only to reveal the author at his stylistic best but also to show how his thought and political career can be placed in relation to Marxist historical dialectic. She also emphasized a nationalist theme that is the direct opposite to Kilbourn's: far from expressing "a way we did not take," Mackenzie's commitment to political independence through revolution is offered as a quintessential expression of the Canadian character.

Beginning with a chapter entitled "The Canadian Scene," in which she reprints some of Mackenzie's published comments on the landscape and settlements of Upper Canada, she goes on to present his reflections on education, literature and journalism, and European and North American politics. Each of these topical sections is arranged internally in chronological order from 1824 to 1837, to create a multiple-strand narrative of his life and opinions that leads repeatedly toward what Fairley regards as the climactic moment of nineteenth-century Canadian political life. Fairley also emphasizes Mackenzie's "immense respect for factual evidence" (12), partly to counteract the impression of him as a "firebrand" whose commitment to armed rebellion was only the characteristic gesture of a violently emotional person. Her interest in Mackenzie's love of fact is also part of an attempt to see his involvement with the material world as comparable to the political and social realism of Marxism. But although Mackenzie's principal writings—his newspapers the *Colonial Advocate* (1824-34) and the *Constitution* (1834-37) and his *Sketches of Canada and the United States* (1833)—predate the *Communist Manifesto* by only some fifteen years, Fairley does not try to suggest that his language and thought are thoroughgoing and consistent prefigurations of Marxism. She is pleased to find in his work language that seems to anticipate Marxist terminology, but she also recognizes distinctions. She notes, for instance, that Mackenzie repeatedly labels the victims of economic exploitation as "the people," a term that by the 1940s had supplanted "the workers" in Communist rhetoric. But Fairley acknowledges that unlike Marxists, for whom the primary unit of social revolution remains the urban industrial proletariat, Mackenzie was a spokesman for farmers, and meant by "the people" the small freeholders of Upper Canada, sometimes including "the mechanics and apprentices living in the towns" (174).

Thus Mackenzie's concept of reform is much more closely related to that of Paine, and to Thomas Jefferson's vision of America as a nation of yeoman farmers. The Mackenzie who emerges from the *Selected Writings* is not a radical proletarian revolutionary but a nineteenth-century bourgeois in reaction against the lingering feudalism of British imperialism. But Fairley also emphasizes that Mackenzie did not simply try to replace feudal privilege with the power of industrial and finance capital. Mackenzie's role as a spokesman for the inarticulate farmers is enhanced by his commitment to education, based on his belief that an educated yeomanry is essential to the advent of responsible government. In "The Canadian Scene," Fairley reveals how Mackenzie was eager to show Canadians the political, social, and economic truth about their country, so that they would become more aware of injustice and the means of redress.

Like his precursor Paine, Mackenzie at first preferred the term "reform" over "revolution," but he ultimately came to accept the idea that tyrannical power could make revolution necessary. Like Marx, furthermore, Mackenzie saw the reform/revolutionary movement as a worldwide process—that is, within the limited global perspective of his day, he envisaged that it would encompass all the agriculturally based industrializing nations in North America and Europe. Hence he was at pains to learn as much as he could about analogous conditions abroad. Also like Marx, Mackenzie based his political ideals partly on his faith in the human capacity for mastery over Nature. Although his vision of society was essentially agrarian rather than industrial, he accepted the idea of a technology that would complement the aims of the Canadian agricultural society, especially by resisting economic domination from the United States. Fairley's edition includes several of Mackenzie's appeals for the development of domestic manufacturing to forestall the inundation of the Canadian market by British and American goods. Mackenzie was among the minority of Canadian observers of his day who promoted a St. Lawrence Seaway: "it would be the interest of both Canadas that the 38 miles of artificial navigation which are required in the valley of the St. Lawrence should be excavated, so that European ships might be able to reach the great lakes" (44).

Unlike Marx, Mackenzie does not direct his anger against the capitalists who would develop industry for narrow personal gain at the expense of the wider social good. Such capitalists in 1820s Canada were still not numerous enough to wield the kind of power their counterparts were beginning to exercise in Europe. Rather, he is mainly interested in revealing how the Canadian provinces lagged behind their republican neighbours in replacing feudalistic with liberal democratic institutions. In comparing the political condition of the Canadian provinces with that of the United States, he attacks the feudalistic oligarchy of crown-appointed bureaucrats and church officials, and their bourgeois allies. "Our neighbours beyond the Niagara river," he says ironically, "only require the presence of a *Strachan*, a *Maitland*, a *Colborne*, and a *Sherwood* [officials of the British colonial oligarchy, and their Canadian supporters]...to become as wise, as happy, and as contented, as the dutiful loyal subjects of March and Durham appear to be." "It is alleged too," he continues, "that the republicans are troubled with frequent elections, while it would seem as if our paternal government were about to save us the necessity of any further legislative labour, by itself assuming and exercising without *control* all the powers of the constitution, with (as some think) a few extra powers to boot" (151-52).

But he does not rely exclusively on irony or negative criticism. In spite of the political and economic corruption in British North America, he continues to express a belief in the possibilities of the New World as a source of relief for the problems of the Old. Like Jefferson, he believes in the capacity of the New World to alleviate the stifling concentrations of population that produce so many social evils in Europe. But he warns Canadian farmers of the dangers of becoming "slaves attached to the soil," like the serfs of Russia (183). The most effective means of averting this danger, he insists, is education.

His greatest hope for Canada is that it will be populated by a culturally literate people who will be able to apply their learning in the
arena of practical politics and take control of their own destiny.

In the section entitled "The Scene Abroad," Fairley demonstrates
the evolution of Mackenzie's conviction that Canadians could only
break the hold of European feudalism by means of armed revolt. This
section of the *Selected Writings* consists of letters he wrote back to the
assistant editor of his newspaper during his only return trip to
England and Scotland, which he made as an envoy of the Upper
Canada House of Assembly in 1832-33. The formal purpose of the
trip was to present a petition to King William IV through the Colonial
Secretary, urging reforms to the administrative system of British
North America. Arriving in England just as the First Reform Bill was
being debated, Mackenzie briefly had hopes that the incipient democratic changes happening in England would spread to Canada. In his
travels in England and Scotland, Mackenzie saw how industrial capitalism exploited a surplus of labour to drive down wages, to force
workers to compete with one another instead of forming alliances of
common interest, and to create a proletarian class of wage slaves.
"Labour is the true source of wealth," he writes in a succinct paraphrase of an essential idea of Adam Smith (215), but modern capitalism, like feudalism before it, sees wealth entirely in terms of narrowly centralized economic and political power. Urban Britain under
industrialism presented him with a concrete spectacle of economic
imbalance that contrasted to the abstract political reforms offered by
the parliamentary councils. In London he saw severe poverty, epitomized by the many child street peddlers. He also noted similar conditions in his native Scotland. "It is a melancholy fact, that in proportion as a nation becomes very rich and very full of people, with the
wealth produced by its industry placed in the hands of a few, the very
poor become more and more wretched" (170).

Even after seeing the results of the industrial revolution in Britain,
Mackenzie was still hopeful that the Crown would be receptive to the
idea of more autonomy for the Canadian provinces, especially after the
passage of the Reform Bill in 1832. "The dissolution of [the current
parliamentary session] is the beginning of a new era in the annals of
the British Empire," he wrote to the *Advocate* in November (312).

Shortly before meeting with the colonial secretary, Mackenzie received
further encouragement from the Irish nationalist Daniel O'Connell. "I
have heard Mr. O'Connell, the great Irish agitator and champion of
emancipation," he announced in a letter published 16 August 1832.
He especially admired O'Connell's use of oratory to arouse the people
of Ireland "to a sense of [their] wrongs....The misconduct of the different Irish administrations has added to his strength and power as a popular leader," Mackenzie continued, "and he *will* succeed in his object of
giving freedom and equality of rights to his countrymen" (157). "He
has also manifested the warmest attachment to the Canadas; and the
kind manner in which he spoke to me of our affairs...entitles him to
my lasting gratitude" (158). In London he also had a brief meeting
with William Cobbett, after which he reported to the *Advocate* that
"I believe his object is to increase the comforts and lessen the misery
of the great body of the people, but it is evident he is not very
scrupulous as to the means of bringing about this great good."
Among other things, Mackenzie continued, Cobbett in his journalism
was inclined to put forth "in a powerful strain of sarcasm or invec-
tive against political opponents, statements not always so correct as
they might be" (160-61).

Mackenzie was likewise not overly scrupulous in his attacks on the
Family Compact and the colonial government in Canada, especially
when it became increasingly evident after he had returned home that
his appeals to the British colonial secretary had fallen on deaf ears. In
spite of Lord Goderich's bland assurances of "his earnest desire to promote the happiness of Upper Canada" (324), nothing was done to end
the abuses of which Mackenzie complained. It was mainly this betrayal
by the representative of the king, Fairley's anthology suggests, that
turned Mackenzie anti-monarchist and pro-republican, anti-British
Empire and pro-United States. By 1837, he was prepared to agree with
Thomas Paine that the law of the land was superior to the arbitrary
dictates of a monarch, and that (in Paine's words) "a government of
our own is our natural right" (Paine 34).

But Fairley does not follow Mackenzie's career into the abortive
Canadian attempt to establish such a government by force.
Mackenzie's journalistic activities in Canada ceased in December
1837 with his active support of the uprising, the rout of his ragtag

army and his own flight to the United States. His editor might have continued the story by including some of his defiant proclamations from Navy Island in 1838 and excerpts from his journalism in the United States during his years of exile and in Canada after he was pardoned. Instead, she ends by quoting from one of the last issues of the *Constitution*, in November 1837, to show how almost to the last moment Mackenzie retained his preference for peaceful transition to popular government, and was forced into the uprising by the intransigence of the lieutenant governor, Sir Francis Bond Head.

> One course yet [Sir Francis] might take, and thereby avert much evil—he might dissolve the Assembly, call a free parliament...and simply tell the freeholders that if it should be their wish through their representatives he would agree to regulate our local affairs...by and with the advice of an executive council....Moderate men would see in this, the fulfilment of [Governor John Graves] Simcoe's promise to give us the British Constitution....Such a course all parties would advise, if they dared, but we have no hope of Sir Francis. He has roused the minds of the people in every district in the colony, and in two short years become more generally disliked than all the governors who were before him. (364)

This is not the voice of a half-mad "firebrand" obsessed with the pursuit of power. Mackenzie's tone of regret suggests the voice of a reasonable man who is being forced into extreme measures by an opponent who refuses to think or act reasonably.

When Mackenzie fled into exile, his place was filled almost immediately by a new arrival on the literary and journalistic scene, another immigrant from Scotland, Thomas MacQueen (1803-61). Also a journalist, MacQueen confined his newspaper activities to various small Upper Canada settlements, but his antagonism to class privilege and political corruption and his advocacy of universal education were as vigorous as Mackenzie's. Unlike Mackenzie, however, MacQueen was also a poet. According to Margaret Fairley, who chronicles his career in a 1955 article in the magazine *New Frontiers*, he was perhaps the first "socialist poet of Upper Canada." His socialism—or more accurately, his bourgeois humanitarianism—is expressed in such long poems as "The Exile" (1836) which attacks the glorification of war, and "The World" (1840), a similarly aggressive criticism of the British factory system, imperialism in India, and the hypocrisy of the established church. All these themes, and many others more specifically related to the Canadian scene, MacQueen developed at length in his journalism.

Although MacQueen certainly deserves to be ranked with Mackenzie as a Canadian reform journalist, his designation as a "Canadian" poet is open to quibble, since virtually his entire output of verse is included in three volumes published in Scotland, before he immigrated. But even if MacQueen is excluded from the nineteenth-century Canadian poetic tradition, the socialist or generally progressive element in this tradition is still abundant. As N. Brian Davis demonstrates in his anthology *The Poetry of the Canadian People 1720-1920* (1976), both the English and French national communities, as well as the native people of Canada, have rich lyric traditions celebrating the value of work and the struggle for survival against the forces of exploitation. Davis was especially interested in the folk tradition of poetry, and includes songs and translations collected by ethnographers and anthropologists, as well as verse from local newspapers, union periodicals, and self-published or ephemerally published volumes. The result is an impressive collection of verse written or popularized by ordinary working people, frequently complaining of the hardships of their lives, and supporting such causes as the 1837 rebellions, the Northwest rebellions, the "Nine-hour Movement" of the 1870s, and the Winnipeg General Strike. The book makes an effective case for Davis's contention that Canadian cultural historians have badly neglected the lyric folk tradition, especially those writings that express strong feelings of communal pride, defiance of arbitrary and exploitative authority, and rebellious or revolutionary political sentiments. Davis's research, with its use of sources unknown or unavailable to Fairley, provides a useful elaboration of the proletarian view of pre-1917 Canadian cultural history that Fairley presented in her *Spirit of Canadian Democracy*. In the long run, however, his emphasis on folk traditions represents an interest different from that of most Communist cultural historians who, although by no means indifferent to folk culture, sought to discover a politically sophisticated Canadian literary tradition which could be explicitly made to reflect a Marxist view of history.

The twentieth-century Communist view of nineteenth-century Canadian poetry is epitomized by a small anthology published by *New Frontiers* entitled *The Stone, the Axe, the Sword, and Other Canadian Poems* (1955), featuring work by Alexander McLachlan, Isabella Valancy Crawford, Archibald Lampman, and Peter McArthur. Although no editor is identified on the title page, the anthology was most likely prepared by Fairley, perhaps with the assistance of the *New Frontiers* associate editors. The book is made up mostly but not exclusively of poems dealing with the agrarian experience from the point of view of the Canadian settlers, their struggles against nature and political/economic corruption, and their belief in a new society based on social equality, in contrast to the rigid European class structures from which they had fled.

The poetry of Alexander McLachlan (1818-96) is in the tradition of Robert Burns, one of the principal literary heroes of English-speaking Marxists. Like Burns, McLachlan makes use of the ballad form, dialect, the experience of lower-class people, and egalitarian and revolutionary sentiments. Of McLachlan's poems included in the *New Frontiers* anthology, the dialect poem "The Cringer Rebuked," for instance, denounces a sycophant for doffing his hat, and asserts the equality of all people:

> It's time that potentates and kings,
> And men o' ev'ry station,
> Should learn that honor never springs
> Frae human degradation.

"Old England Is Eaten by Knaves," the refrain from McLachlan's long poem sequence *The Emigrant*, attacks the English oligarchy that drives the lower class out of their country to find an uncertain destiny in the New World. "Young Canada, or Jack's as Good's his Master" is a tribute to the spirit of equality in the new country, where "no one moils…that snobs may thrive."

"All too often McLachlan wrote doggerel," admits V.G. Hopwood in an article on "A Burns of the Backwoods" in *New Frontiers* (Fall 1952). But McLachlan's lapses of form and language are offset by "his vision of the realities of Canadian society." In Scotland, Hopwood points out, McLachlan had participated in Chartist activities, and his chartism "takes the form of sympathy with labour, and radical criticism of the politics and commercial piracy of the time" (32).

"The Sword," by Isabella Valancy Crawford (1850-87), appealed to the *New Frontiers* editors because of its pacifism, a doctrine particularly emphasized by the Communist Party in the mid-twentieth century. Crawford's allusive description of the forging of a sword is a symbolic representation of the coming into the world of war, genocide, and, significantly, misogyny:

> At the forging of the Sword
>   Kind mother Earth was rent
>   Like an Arab's dusky tent,
>   And, monster-like, she fed
> On her children, at the forging of the Sword.
>
> At the forging of the Sword
>   The maid and matron fled
>   And hid them with the dead;
>   Fierce prophets sang their doom,
> More deadly than the wounding of the Sword.

The final stanza is a vision of the Sword being reforged into an agricultural implement that will "learn to prune the laughing vine" when the world is finally ruled by "plough and hook" in a restored Eden or communistic Utopia. *The Stone, the Axe, the Sword* also includes three short excerpts from Crawford's long poem *Malcolm's Katie*. One is a song that a workman sings in apostrophe to his axe as he chops down a tree; the others feature images of nature—the wind and moon—allusively personified as native American Indians. Crawford's long and cryptic poem has yielded many kinds of critical interpretation, including a Marxist one. A commentary of the 1970s, for instance, calls attention to the poem's emphasis on the function of nature as the Canadian settlers' refuge from the industrialism that has driven them from Europe (Hughes and Sproxton 59-60). Obviously the *New Frontiers* editors were attracted by Crawford's idealization of labour, and by her identification of aboriginal people—like Fairley's, in the excerpt she chose for her anthology from the *Jesuit Relations*—with the lost Edenic ideal that inspires the Marxist struggle.

The editors of *The Stone, the Axe, the Sword* also acknowledged the work of the more conventionally descriptive Canadian landscape poets of the late nineteenth century. "Archibald Lampman is our best nature poet," Fairley observed in an article written in 1952 ("Our Cultural Heritage" 5), and she featured four of his poems in the *New Frontiers* anthology. Lampman was especially appealing to twentieth century Communists, for he was a formally committed socialist. In the Toronto *Globe* column "At the Mermaid Inn" to which he contributed in 1892-93, he criticized the prevailing money-grubbing capitalistic business ethic and exploitation of land, and expressed admiration for current New Zealand experiments in land redistribution and government ownership of essential industry. Several of his poems, most notably his fantasy "The Land of Pallas," reflect the influence of William Morris's Utopian socialist romance *News from Nowhere* (1890). Around 1895 Lampman wrote, but left unpublished, an untitled essay in which he expressed his belief in the historical inevitability of socialism.

Much critical opinion on Lampman has emphasized the supposed incongruities between his nature lyrics and his poems of social criticism. Lampman fled from an uncongenial urban milieu, this argument suggests, and produced his best poetry when he was able to forget this milieu by immersing himself in the restorative atmosphere of the rural woods and fields. Subsequent commentators have challenged this paradigm, and one of the first to do so was Margaret Fairley. Lampman's escape into the country, she argues, was only a preliminary stage in the expression of his ultimate desire: "he craved a human life which he could enjoy as he enjoyed the hills and rivers; he could not forget that he was a citizen" ("Our Cultural Heritage" 5). In the selections for *The Stone, the Axe, the Sword*, Fairley demonstrated the unity of Lampman's love of nature and his desire for a better society. The first of these selections, "April in the Hills," seems a typical celebration of the poet's enjoyment of nature, but the poem is also centrally concerned with the idea of liberation. "I break the spirit's cloudy bands," declares Lampman—that is, he breaks through the clouds that usually hang over the human spirit in modern society. In the countryside the poet becomes "a wanderer in enchanted lands" like the travellers in *News from Nowhere* and in "The Land of Pallas."

In the final stanza of "April in the Hills," the conventionalities of a spring lyric—"new birth," "wakening earth"—merge with the suggestions of a new historical era based on the shared perfectibility of human and natural elements.

The second of Fairley's selections, "Paternity," deals similarly with the vision of human perfectibility, but relates this vision to both the social and personal contexts. Beginning as a quiet celebration of the birth of the poet's son, the poem moves on to the theme of the unity of humanity in an ideal of love:

> For thy sake nobler visions are unfurled,
>     Vistas of tenderer humanity,
> And all the little children of this world
>     Are dearer now to me.

The sonnet "To a Millionaire" is one of several Lampman poems that focus on an explicit criticism of capitalism. Dominated by his solipsistic obsession with wealth and power, the millionaire is alienated from both nature and humanity, unable to see either the splendour of the external world or the human suffering caused by his own greed. By promoting a social system based on selfishness and exploitation, the millionaire has replaced the ideal harmony between nature and spirit with a perverted balance between the sufferings of the toiling masses and his "one grim misgotten pile" of money.

"The Railway Station," one of Lampman's few poems about the urban proletariat, extends the evil of industrial capitalism beyond the personal degeneracy of the profiteer toward the effect of this degeneracy on society. Like other nineteenth-century artistic critics of industrialism from Charles Dickens through Henry Thoreau and the American painter George Inness, Lampman uses the railway as a symbol of the new forces that destroy nature and oppress humanity. In Emersonian fashion Lampman emphasizes the origins of the poetic and moral consciousness in the visual faculties: the words "I see," or variants, govern most of the catalogue of images through which industrialism is portrayed. The poet tries to achieve sympathetic contact with the victims of industrialism, the "hurrying crowds" in the station, and especially with their "eyes that are dim with pain." But this attempt at unity fails, for the poet is "blinded" by the lights, steam, and noise. His eyes are as dim as those of the people he reaches out to, and he cannot imagine their "unknown thoughts" and "various agonies." As the editors of this anthology imply by including this poem, the expansion of the literary imagination to encompass the agonies of the proletariat is to be a primary project of Marxist Communist writers.

In spite of the idealization of nature that he frequently expresses in his poetry, Lampman saw socialism as Marx did, not as a dream arising out of a beneficent pastoral world but as the inevitable byproduct of urban industrial civilization. In Lampman's scheme of things, the capacity to enjoy nature unhindered would be one of the most important benefits of socialist society. On this point, his social ideas differ markedly from those of a younger writer who also idealizes nature, Peter McArthur (1866-1924). *The Stone, the Axe, the Sword* concludes with a poem much less familiar than the work of McLachlan, Crawford, or Lampman. Although written in the early twentieth century, McArthur's "The Stone" celebrates the nineteenth-century agrarian ideal. McArthur's poem consists of about one hundred lines of free verse written in the manner of the American poet, Walt Whitman. Celebrating "a man of heroic mould," "such a one as Walt Whitman would have gloried in," the poem is a fable based on the pioneer experience of land-clearing. In the poem, the local farmers are all intimidated by a huge stone, reportedly so heavy and so apparently fixed in the ground that they are afraid even to try to move it. When the "man of heroic mould" finally does try, the stone turns out to be light and small:

> For it was no boulder, deep-rooted, needing dynamite,
> But just a little stone about the size of a milk-pail.
> A child might have moved it, and yet it had bumped us
> For three generations because we lacked public spirit.

McArthur concludes with an apostrophe that would especially appeal to the Communist editors:

> Tremble, ye Oppressors! Quake, ye Financial Pirates!
> Your day is at hand, for there is a man loose in Canada!
> ...A man who moves stones from the paths of his fellows!
> And makes smooth the way of the Worker!

McArthur's "worker," like Mackenzie's "people," refers of course to the farmer, whose independence and strength derive from his commitment to economic self-sufficiency as a freeholding tiller of the soil.

As Stanley Ryerson has pointed out in his Marxist historical study of the years leading up to and immediately following Canadian Confederation, the industrialization and urbanization of Canada was a smaller version of the eighteenth- and nineteenth-century European experience. In the 1850s, the number of steam-driven sawmills in what was to become Ontario doubled; between 1851 and 1871, the limited-capacity, family-owned mill almost completely disappeared, replaced by large, usually American-owned operations, employing fewer and fewer "hands" as processes became more and more mechanized, and paying below-subsistence wages. Industrial-ization was especially accelerated by the railway boom beginning in the 1850s, which produced subsidiary industries to supply the needs of the new form of transport, as well as the needs of businesses and settlers as the railways opened up new territory (*Unequal Union* 258-60). This kind of economic growth brought with it much the same consequences, good and bad, as those that followed the industrialization of Europe: boom-and-bust economies; immense fortunes for a few; moderate but unstable prosperity for others; poverty, oppressive working conditions, and chronic cycles of unemployment for a majority of the population.

This growth also brought angry reactions, if not from the workers who found themselves exploited by industrialism, at least from people who believed it was their duty to speak up on behalf of the exploited workers. Just as Mackenzie had defended the yeoman farmer in the *Colonial Advocate*, a new generation of journalists emerged to fight for the rights of the urban proletariat. The *Ontario Workman*, established in 1872 as an independent newspaper but expressing the official views of the Toronto Trades Assembly and the Canadian Labour Union, was the first Canadian periodical to speak to and for this segment of the population. The purpose of the *Workman* was to rally urban workers toward a vigorous assertion of their rights and to educate them to understand the historical and ideological basis of these rights. At first, the writers and editors were uncertain as to the relationship of imaginative literature to this purpose. The paper regularly featured poems, short stories, and serialized novels, but most of this material exploited the form and subject matter of popular verse and romantic or adventure fiction, and was intended as diversion from the serious political content. Much of this escapist material, furthermore, was reprinted from the *American Workman*, the US publication on which the *Ontario Workman* was modeled. When the Canadian paper did finally publish a creative work on a working-class theme, it too was simply a reprint from the US paper. The serialized novel *The Other Side* (*OW*, 27 June 1872-17 February 1873), a response to the British novelist Charles Reade's anti-labour novel *Put Yourself in His Place* (1870), was written by an American and concerned characters and situations in the US. The Pennsylvania-born author, Martin A. Foran (1844-1921), a barrel-maker by trade, led a successful strike of coopers in Cleveland in 1870 and became the first president of the Coopers' International Union. In 1874 he qualified as a lawyer in Ohio, and in 1884 he was elected to the US Congress. In 1886 he brought out his novel in book form, as *The Other Side: A Social Study Based on Fact*, possibly to counteract the influence of the anti-union novel *The Breadwinners* (1884) by the American politician John Hay (Commons 75).

Foran's work was thus part of a proliferating international dialectic on the so-called "labour question," which was attracting journalists, social critics, and novelists. Aware that he was writing in a new literary mode, Foran included with the first instalment a brief introduction emphasizing the importance of encouraging the habit of reading among workers by taking advantage of their taste for popular fiction. Foran did not mean that fiction should be merely a form of idle amusement: he describes the purpose of his own novel as "didactic and defensory." Pointing out that the enemies of labour do not hesitate to use fiction for their purposes, Foran emphasizes the importance of hearing both sides of the argument, and "to throw what light we can on that side so carefully hidden."

In spite of the efforts of the *Workman* in propagating novels like Foran's, pro-labour fiction did not flourish in Canada in the late nineteenth century. Indeed, there was little to compare with the fiction of social and economic reform that was emerging in England and the United States of this time. There were no writers like Elizabeth Gaskell or Rebecca Harding Davis, for example, to expose the evils of the factory system; no Utopian novels like Edward Bellamy's *Looking Backward* (1888) to dramatize the possibilities of socialistic or other kinds of reform. The most promising attempt at a Canadian literary exposition of this type was a work of discursive prose rather than fiction, Phillips Thompson's *The Politics of Labor* (1887). Thompson (1843-1933), an acquaintance of Bellamy and admirer of his work, was born in England and brought to Canada as a boy, where he established himself as a journalist and advocate of socialism. In his *Political Experiences of Jimuel Briggs* (1873), Thompson used semifictional satire in the tradition of Thomas Chandler Haliburton's Sam Slick sketches, but for the more extensive and serious statement of his socialist position he preferred the straight plain prose of socio-economic criticism. Also, even though Thompson had spent only four years of his working life in the US, in *The Politics of Labor* he insisted on writing about US conditions and addressing a US audience. Like some other Canadian radical writers throughout the nineteenth and twentieth centuries, he evidently assumed that a serious attack on the modern industrial capitalist system must be addressed to the nation that was becoming the heart and centre of that system. Nevertheless, *The Politics of Labor* is of considerable relevance to the Canadian radical literary heritage. Besides being the most thorough Canadian critique of modern capitalism since the journalism and travel essays of William Lyon Mackenzie, it provides an appreciation of the urban proletariat comparable to Mackenzie's tribute to the rural freeholder. Unlike Mackenzie, Thompson is an ideologically committed socialist. Indeed, his book reveals a familiarity and sympathy—if not wholehearted agreement—with the writings of Karl Marx, among other socialist philosophers and political economists. Like Marx, Thompson warns that the struggle between labour and capital could lead to social catastrophe. Appealing to the historical consciousness of his American readers, he compares the battle for workers' rights to the anti-slavery conflict. Thompson does not, however, believe that a violent conclusion to the conflict between capitalists and wage slaves is inevitable. Rather, he places his faith in the potential of the American working class to gain political power through the gradual processes of education and organization.

Much of the book emphasizes the corruption and irresponsibility of capitalism, and traces these vices by implication to inherent qualities of human nature. By means of a desert island fable he demonstrates how human beings seem naturally inclined to unite only in the service of selfishness to create oligarchies of power in order to appropriate the labour of others. Although he describes the modern worker's struggle against monopoly power as a "war," he is confident that workers can eventually establish by peaceful means a collective system of production and distribution. Like many socialist reformers of his era, however, he is vague about how this change will occur. Thompson can only express his confidence in the intellectual capacities of the workers and the potential political strength of labour organizations.

Thompson also celebrates the labour movement in poetry, although his verse belongs to a primitive populist tradition rather than to the more bookish context of the work of Lampman or Crawford. Thompson's *Labor Reform Songster* (1892) is a pamphlet collection of doggerel adapted to various familiar musical settings of hymn tunes and political anthems. Most of the poems—written, with a few exceptions, by Thompson—rely on generalized allusions to capitalist exploitation, militant exhortations to revolutionary action, and repetitive refrains expressing the sufferings and hopes of workers. "In the Reign of Justice," for instance, set to the tune of "In the Sweet By and By," promises eventual compensation to downtrodden labour:

> There's a glorious future in store
> When the toil-worn shall rise from the dust,
> Then the poor shall be trampled no more
> And mankind to each other be just. (Thompson, *Songster* 13)

But Thompson's verse scarcely belongs to the category of proletarian "literature," since it is written to make unapologetic appeal to a virtually sub-literate audience. At an opposite extreme, at least one Canadian novelist in the 1890s attempted to adapt the problems of the modern industrial and commercial society to the conventions of the genteel novel. Agnes Maule Machar's *Roland Graeme: Knight* (1892) is an iconoclastic literary statement in its criticism of the insensitivity of the upper classes towards workers, and its idealization of the Knights of Labor trade union movement. Machar's vision of the social ideal is similar to that of William Morris, involving a village society in which the industrialists and employees work together for the mutual good. The workers as a class are presented as hard-working and decent; their leader, Roland Graeme, is the epitome of the spirit of social commitment. But Machar's ideal is not quite socialistic. As her many allusions and echoes drawn from Charles Dickens's *A Christmas Carol* suggest, she advocates the development not of an egalitarian social system, but of a charitable spirit among those set in the higher social strata, such as the employers, the professional class, and the clergy, who should devote themselves to social harmony through public benevolence that will improve the quality of life for all. Machar does believe in working-class organization, for Graeme is an advocate for the Knights of Labor; but the Knights represent a cautious approach to cooperation between employers and workers that is far from the class struggle that later unions and radical socialist parties engage in. Still, if *Roland Graeme: Knight* is not a proletarian or revolutionary novel, it expresses a sympathy for the working class and a belief in the possibility of progressive social change that point toward the Marxist and other anti-capitalist literary efforts to come.

# 2

# Antecedents and Alternatives to Bolshevism

B y the early twentieth century there were several anti-capitalist and/or pro-socialist periodicals in Canada, the most literarily significant of which was probably the *Western Clarion* (founded 1903) of Vancouver, which was the official newspaper of the Socialist Party of Canada from 1905 to 1920. Besides publishing translations and reprints from European and American literary sources, the *Clarion* in 1913 introduced the poems of Wilfred Gribble, a talented versifier whose poems satirizing capitalist corruption and advocating labour reform were collected in a slim volume entitled *Rhymes of Revolt.* A cut above the doggerel of Phillips Thompson, Gribble's poems tried to make both a didactic and a melodious appeal to the working-class reader. His "Makers of History," for instance, summarizes the chronicle of labour from the emergence of tribal societies to the rise of industrialism to demonstrate how the workers in their evolution from thralldom to knowledge are the real makers of history.

> It was the toil of countless slaves
>   Which built society;
> Not those who spoiled, but those who toiled
>   Made all real history. (Davis, *Poetry of the Canadian People*
> *1720-1920*, 186)

"The Call of the West" more specifically summarizes "the spread of the socialist movement in Canada," to convey impressions of the vigour and solidarity of the movement:

> From ocean unto ocean now
>   Our standard proudly floats,
> From Coast to Coast a swelling host
>   For revolution votes. (192)

The socialistic poetry of the *Western Clarion* was the most prominent Canadian version of a rapidly proliferating international trend. By the first decade of the twentieth century, imaginative literature criticizing industrial capitalism was common in Britain and the United States. First in novels, then in plays, George Bernard Shaw attacked the social and political institutions and customs of Britain from a Fabian socialist perspective. In the US, Upton Sinclair's novel *The Jungle* (1906) likewise dramatized the socialist conception of the conflict between capital and labour; in 1911, *The Masses* of New York began as a magazine of labour news and social criticism, and soon evolved into the most durable and influential American left-wing literary magazine. Anti-capitalist fiction also continued to appear in Canada in the first decade of the twentieth century. Between 1900 and 1914 novelists dealt with the so-called "labour question," some expressing a sympathetic socialist or Christian perspective, others expressing an angry antagonism to unions. But novels like A.R. Carman's *The Preparation of Ryerson Embury* (1900) and H.P. Blanchard's *After the Cataclysm* (1909) tended to be for the most part sentimental romances or pious Christian lessons addressed to a genteel bourgeois readership. *Aleta Day* (1919), the only novel of Francis Marion Beynon (1884-1951; a woman, in spite of the male spelling of her given names) is a somewhat angrier and more subversive exposition of the author's feminist, pacifist, and socialist opinions. Set in Manitoba, the novel provides an impressive panorama of the turmoil of radical ideology and political activism in the years preceding the First World War. Beynon's main message is pacificism, which takes precedence over political or socio-economic analysis, but much of the book is concerned with condemning the widespread poverty and social inequality in Canada.

Another popular form of anti-capitalist fiction in the early twentieth century was the male-oriented novel and story of heroic action. Promoted in Britain by Rudyard Kipling, in the US by Jack London and in Canada by "Ralph Connor" (Charles W. Gordon), this kind of writing might seem to be the antithesis of pro-labour or socialistic fiction, for it exalts a rugged individualism consistent with the rapacious social Darwinist conception of economic rivalry. In its most humanistic versions, however, strenuous-life fiction tempers its social Darwinism with ostensibly gentler and more rational values. Ralph Connor's farmers, loggers, and Presbyterian ministers restrain their brawling conquest of the eastern Ontario and northwestern frontiers with Christian piety. British decency makes Kipling's imperial soldiers and adventurers more like missionaries than conquistadors; Jack London invokes socialism to offset the rapacious individualism that can degrade men to the level of beasts. In the first two decades of the twentieth century, three notable Canadian writers emerged in the Connor-Kipling-London tradition to expound fictional critiques of modern capitalism. Colin McKay (1876-1929) wrote of the fishermen of the Atlantic Coast; Bertrand Sinclair (1878-1972) dealt with cowpunchers and fishermen in British Columbia; Douglas Durkin (1884-1968) depicted farmers, adventurers, and financiers in Manitoba. None of these three were members of a socialist party or any other partisan political movement, although all three shared vigorous anti-capitalist opinions, and were concerned with the search for remedial human values in a ruthless naturalistic world.

Colin McKay's contribution to the progressive literary heritage consists mainly of short stories. Published in Canadian and American magazines and newspapers between 1899 and 1913, his stories remained uncollected until an edited selection finally appeared in 1993 as *Windjammers and Bluenose Sailors*. Born and raised in Nova Scotia, McKay came to know the marine labourer's life at first hand, through his service at all levels from seaman to master in the merchant marine and government coastal patrol in the last decades of the era of sailing ships. Also a working journalist, he alternated his sea experience with spells in newspaper offices. As his modern editor points out, most of his stories are written as realistic alternatives to the romanticization of the age of sail in turn-of-the-century popular fiction depicting the frequent tragedies and occasional triumphs experienced by men working in the harsh world of the sea (Ian McKay 22-27). But nature alone does not threaten the sailor in his tales. Indeed, McKay frequently demonstrates that the physical and intellectual capacities of the typical sailor are more than equal to the forces of nature; the sailor's real life-and-death struggle is against the incompetence, cruelty, and greed of other men—especially those placed in authority by corporate shipping interests whose only concerns are with profits.

McKay's fiction, therefore, is essentially about the struggle between workers and capitalists or the representatives of capitalism. It is not exactly socialistic or Marxist in implication, however, for McKay does not idealize the sailors as a collective class. His favourite type of plot involves the unexpected emergence of a working-class champion who takes control in a crisis and almost single-handedly achieves redress for the grievances of his otherwise impotent and long-suffering shipmates. In "The Spread Eagle" (first published 1902), for instance, the captain and mate of a notorious hell-ship keep the crew subjugated by physical brutality, until their cruelty provokes the rebellion of the second mate. Using his ingenuity as well as his physical strength, the mate contrives a situation where the two senior officers impose well-deserved physical punishment upon each other. In "The Mate from Maine" (1903), an unprepossessing-looking new mate turns out to be an experienced sailor who saves the storm-tossed ship from its captain's cowardice and incompetence. In a similar story, "The Galoot" (1905), an apparent misfit reveals himself to be a skilled mariner who takes authority from the cowardly captain and saves the ship. By way of variation, the captain in "Coming on the Coast" (1903) is a decent and competent leader, but when he is injured during a storm the mate takes over to rally the crew and bring the ship safely to harbour. McKay's stories, in short, are most frequently melodramas of heroic individualism. As parables of rebellion or revolution, they are more like wish-fulfilment fantasies than blueprints for social action, since they often focus on the virtually single-handed assertion of retributive justice by a hero who emerges unexpectedly from obscurity. Nevertheless, McKay portrays the perilous working experiences of sailors and the social conflict that aggravates their peril with a realism of detail that prefigures later proletarian novels.

The realistic portrayal of physical danger and social conflict is a primary element in Bertrand Sinclair's novels of fishermen, cowpunchers, and loggers in British Columbia. Sinclair's name is identified, when it is remembered at all, with the novel of frontier adventure rather than the novel of political radicalism. But like Jack London, who directly influenced him, Sinclair frequently used fiction to dramatize the search for meaning and value in a world where both nature and human beings seem to be governed by a ruthless struggle for survival. Born in Edinburgh, Scotland, Sinclair came to the western United States with his parents in 1889. Raised in Montana, he dropped out of school to become a cowpuncher while still in his teens. After selling his first magazine article in 1902, he settled in Santa Cruz, California, to devote himself to a full-time writing career. Inspired by London's success with Canadian settings and themes, Sinclair wrote *Raw Gold* (1908), a historical novel about the advent of the Northwest Mounted Police into the Cypress Hills in the 1870s. His second novel, *The Land of Frozen Suns* (1910), is indebted to London's *The Sea Wolf* (1904), with a comparable plot of a young American man who is rescued from a river accident, then carried northward against his will. Like London's naive protagonist, Sinclair's hero comes to maturity in a series of episodic adventures. In 1912 Sinclair moved to British Columbia, first to Vancouver, and subsequently to the coastal village of Pender Harbour, where he lived until his death (biographical details from various documents in Sinclair Papers).

Unlike McKay, who excluded women entirely from his Atlantic stories, Sinclair was interested in applying his concepts of individualism and social organization to both sexes. His typical male hero, the rugged pioneer who would forge a new society out of the wilderness, is sometimes paired with a female counterpart, the independent "new woman" of the twentieth century. Sinclair's *North of Fifty-three* (1914) criticizes decadent urban society and idealizes the wilderness life with a story of a young woman who is ostracized from the city by the machinations of a lecherous business man, and rescued to a new life by a rugged but genteel frontiersman who instils in her his love of the northern forests. *Big Timber* (1916) is a more sophisticated critique of modern industrialized society and a more elaborate development of the theme of the liberated woman. The heroine of this novel is likewise introduced to wilderness life, but makes a disastrous marriage with a power-obsessed lumber entrepreneur, and finally finds liberation and self-fulfilment in a career as a singer. *Big Timber*, like all of Sinclair's novels, achieved at the time of publication only a transient popularity among readers of western adventure stories. But many years later it drew the admiration of the feminist/socialist Dorothy Livesay, who approved both the critique of capitalism and the theme of a woman's artistic self-discovery (autobiographical fragment, n.d., Livesay Papers).

Sinclair never entirely freed himself from his dependence on the melodramatic plot artifices of popular adventure fiction, but his novels often feature a knowledgeable basis in socio-economic fact. *Big Timber* presents a detailed exposition of the power struggles within the British Columbia logging industry in the early twentieth century. An even more thorough realism underlies his novelistic treatment of the coastal fisheries. *Poor Man's Rock* (1920) attacks post-World War I corporate greed and corruption, and idealizes the returned veteran who devotes himself to asserting economic and social justice within the capitalist system. Set on and around "Squitty Island," a barely fictionalized version of Lasquiti, one of the so-called "Gulf Islands" in the Strait of Georgia, the novel contrasts the exploitative practices of the large fishing, packing, and shipping operations with the lives of the small-boat fishermen who cluster around "Poor Man's Rock," a place inaccessible to the larger trolling vessels. The hero, Jack MacRae, is positioned between the two economic extremes, as the impoverished scion of a once-wealthy island family, who sets up a small wholesale packing and shipping business. Unlike the larger corporate members of the Packers' Association which combine to fix the prices paid to fishermen, MacRae builds up his business by remaining independent and offering a fair return to his suppliers.

Sinclair's economic ideals are simply stated in a conversation between MacRae and a cannery operator who argues that "to buy as cheaply as you can and sell for as high as you can…is a fundamental of business." MacRae grants this principle, but argues that "you will get farther with a salmon fisherman, or any other man whose labor you must depend on, if you accept the principle that he is entitled to make a dollar as well as yourself" (109). Sinclair relates MacRae's notion of capitalistic fair dealing to the context of modern socio-economic change. The returned soldiers like MacRae "conceived the idea that they were coming back to a better world," but "found living costly, good jobs not so plentiful, masters as exacting as they had been before.…Big Business throve, even while it howled to high heaven about ruinous, confiscatory taxation." Meanwhile, "labor organizations were strengthened…by thousands of their own members returned, all semi-articulate, all more or less belligerent" (218). Sinclair's protagonist perceives that "the world…was suffering from the grab-instinct functioning without control. He had a theory that society would have to modify that grab-instinct by legislation and custom before the world was rid of a lot of its present ills" (237). In the meantime, MacRae does his bit to bring about this modification of society by applying his ingenuity and commercial morality to his battle with the monopolistic corporations. So *Poor Man's Rock* becomes a story of virtuous individualism within capitalism, rather than a defense of labour organizations or socialist movements. Indeed, Sinclair further dilutes his theme of the triumph of virtuous individualism by relating it, as Colin McKay frequently does, to a theme of personal retribution: MacRae is motivated not simply by a desire to see abstract justice prevail, but also by a determination to ruin the man who had years earlier ruined his father. Sinclair's social thesis is further complicated by a racist motif that reflects the "yellow peril" fears of early-twentieth-century white North Americans, especially on the Pacific coast. The novel denounces the increasing presence of Japanese fishermen, who allegedly band together to undercut not only the fishermen of European descent but even the packing corporations who encouraged the importation of non-European labour in the first place. The whole situation "would never have happened," MacRae complains, "if this had been kept a white man's country, and the white fisherman had got a square deal" (109).

Sinclair tries to develop a more consistent critique of the vices of capitalism in *The Inverted Pyramid* (1924). The social and economic pressures on modern humanity alluded to in the title image are illustrated by the wealthy Norquay family, timber operators in the Gulf Islands, who are divided between their sense of a traditional commitment to the land as the descendants of early settlers and their recognition of modern economic imperatives. The division is dramatized in the conflict between two brothers, one of whom pursues the ruthless accumulation of money and power, while the other goes off to fight in the First World War. Influenced by a Marxist friend as well as by his war experiences, Rod Norquay concludes that the reality behind the "war to end war" was simply "loot" (191). His disillusionment is aggravated by the suicide of his brother, who has been appropriating the company's profits, but Rod resolves to take over the operation and clear its debts. While rival corporations take advantage of the post-war labour surplus to cut wages and degrade working conditions, Norquay tries to treat his employees fairly, but finds it almost impossible to compete. He finally achieves his two aims of clearing the company debt and retaining the family home, but at the cost of over-cutting the islands where he holds the timber rights. The novel thus ends ambivalently, with the author offering only a vaguely ameliorative view of human history, and wistfully advocating a social doctrine of benevolent authoritarianism:

> Until Utopia comes in the millennial dawn men must exist under
> a social and industrial system that is not the creation of a class or
> a period, but is the slow growth of centuries. Under it the strong,
> the acquisitive, the self-disciplined, the men of force and char-
> acter somehow get to the top. But having got to the top, being
> secure in their power, if they were wise they neither despised nor
> trampled on those at the bottom. (282)

Sinclair more explicitly expounded the problem of moral responsibility within the capitalist system in a letter to California novelist Stewart E. White in 1923. Commenting on a recent book advocating a cooperative system between capital and labour, Sinclair points out that such systems are always foiled by economic imperatives. Workers and employers may agree to work together for their mutual advantage, Sinclair argues, but sooner or later overproduction will reduce profit and necessitate layoffs if the producer is to stay in business. As far as Sinclair can see, industrial capitalism is by its very nature unable to create durable prosperity. The economic riddle of material prosperity, furthermore, is a reflection of the "riddle of the universe," a phrase that Sinclair uses in a letter of 6 November 1924 to describe the theme of *The Inverted Pyramid* (Sinclair Papers). "If I were so constituted that I had to have a religion," Sinclair wrote to an admirer in 1921, "I think I should bow down to worship before Herbert Spencer's special god, the unknowable." This concern with the antinomies of intellectual inquiry perhaps accounts for Sinclair's turning away from novels of ideas and back to uncomplicated tales of adventure like *Wild West* (1926) and *Gunpowder Lightning* (1930), before giving up fiction altogether to spend the last three decades of his long life as a part-time commercial fisherman.

Douglas Durkin seems to have been similarly troubled by the contradictions inherent in modern industrial society, although he tried to come to a positive resolution in his fictional critique of capitalism, *The Magpie* (1923). Born in Northern Ontario, Durkin moved to Manitoba with his parents around the turn of the century. After earning a BA from the University of Manitoba, he married and taught school for a few years, but abandoned both marriage and schoolteaching in favour of novel writing. His early novels, *The Heart of Cherry McBain* (1919) and *The Lobstick Trail* (1921) were, like Sinclair's early and late works, tales of frontier adventure and romance that scarcely reflect his growing concern for modern socioeconomic problems. *The Magpie*, like *Poor Man's Rock* and *The Inverted Pyramid*, deals with a young veteran's struggles against capitalist corruption amid post-World War I economic inequities and social unrest. Besides using the Great War as the epitome of modern historical crisis as so many early-twentieth-century novelists do, Durkin gives his novel a regional context that further emphasizes the sinister aims and methods of entrenched capitalist power in the world of historical actuality. Set in Winnipeg, the novel opens in July 1919, just weeks after the General Strike has been ruthlessly suppressed by the army and police. Durkin's hero Craig Forrester, a trader on the Winnipeg Grain Exchange, is caught between his commitment to the capitalist system and his disillusionment with that system. Having returned from the war with high expectations for a new era of prosperity and social justice, he is disappointed to find the financiers and wealthy families vigorously reestablishing the social and economic hierarchies of the pre-war years. Slow and reluctant to express his feelings (as his nickname, "The Magpie," ironically asserts), Forrester recognizes the truth bitterly voiced by a former comrade-in-arms from the war: "We've spent four years of the best part of our lives fighting for the big fellows, and we'll spend the rest of our days working for them just the same as we did before the war" (12).

This sense of hopelessness is shared by the revolutionary socialist leader Amer, who is ultimately silenced and driven into exile by his capitalist enemies, led by the smugly autocratic Blount. Blount, as Forrester recognizes, represents "little more than a fatuous defense of an arrogant feudalism" (206). Most of the characters in the novel typify one consequence or another of the depredations of capitalism. Gilbert Nason is a well-meaning but ineffectual employer who is forced to subordinate his humanistic inclinations to business practicalities; his son Dick takes refuge from reality in a dilettantish aestheticism; Claude Charnley, another trader on the grain exchange, typifies the thoroughly cynical and amoral acquisitive instincts of the business world. Like Sinclair, Durkin also regards gender issues as an important part of the modern socio-economic dilemma. The main plot strand of *The Magpie* concerns Craig Forrester's ill-considered marriage to Marion Nason, whose political opinions consist of an insistence that social problems are best left to the people who hold socio-economic power. She is contrasted to Jeannette Bowden, a mournful but resolute war widow who has joined Amer in the socialist cause. Marion is also contrasted to Martha Lane, an artist who is associated with true ideals of beauty and spiritual contentment. Even though Durkin's characters are rather one-sided abstractions, *The Magpie* is a strong exposition of the nature and consequences of early-twentieth-century Canadian socio-economic problems. Like Sinclair, Durkin is unable to find clear solutions to the dilemmas created by capitalism; any available recourse is likely to be personal and domestic rather public and political. At the end of *The Magpie* Forrester and Martha Lane withdraw from urban society altogether, to start a new life on the Lane family farm.

The ideology expressed in this fiction conforms to what Georg Lukács called "romantic anti-capitalism," a historical antagonism to industrial capitalism and its social and cultural consequences that can be traced back to the Romantic movement of the early nineteenth century. This antagonism reflects a hostility toward machine production and the divisions of labour it creates; toward the growth of cities and the decline of rural communities; and toward a general spread of rationalism, impersonalization, and dehumanization. As Lukács further suggests, this kind of fiction lacks the commitment to proletarian revolution that was to evolve in later novels through the influence of Marx, and tends toward pessimistic conclusions, or falls back on a faith in individual heroic action and on an idealized nostalgic pre-industrial pastoral vision of the world (Lukács, *Essays on Realism* 4).

A few years before Durkin wrote *The Magpie*, Peter McArthur applied romantic anti-capitalism more extensively to the pastoral ideal in his *In Pastures Green* (1915), a collection of newspaper pieces based on the author's experiences farming in western Ontario. Unlike Durkin, who presents agrarianism as a vague remedial sequel to the urban industrial society's oppression of virtuous idealists, McArthur develops a detailed exposition of farming as a valid alternative to industrialism. Originally published in the Toronto *Globe* and the *Farmer's Advocate*, these prose sketches with a few interpolated poems were dated successively from January to December as if recording the author's observations and experiences over a year. As this journal structure suggests, and as McArthur acknowledges several times in his book, much of the writing in *In Pastures Green* is inspired by Henry Thoreau's *Walden* (1855). McArthur had presumably picked up his enthusiasm for Thoreau, Walt Whitman, and other American writers during the years between 1890 and 1909 that he spent as a journalist and magazine writer in the United States. Like Thoreau, McArthur presents a series of discursive reflections on various moral, political, and metaphysical subjects against the backgrounds of his routine of daily labour and the seasonal cycle of nature. McArthur's book is more whimsical and less infused with transcendental symbolism than Thoreau's prose or Whitman's poetry, but he shares with both writers the inclination to contrast his rural experience to the political and economic evils of urban North

America. In its criticism of these evils, *In Pastures Green* is also reminiscent of Thoreau's essay "Civil Disobedience" (or "Resistance to Civil Government," as it was editorially retitled in the late twentieth century). Like Thoreau's, McArthur's political thought might be described as "anarchistic," with its emphasis on self-sufficiency and its deep distrust of government.

*In Pastures Green* is also in the tradition of the journalism of William Lyon Mackenzie. Although much lighter and more facetious in his approach than Mackenzie, McArthur is concerned with attacking the agricultural policies of the Canadian government and bureaucracy, on behalf of small landowners like himself. McArthur's political position, like Mackenzie's, could also be described as "conservative" in the sense that he seeks to conserve a traditional way of life against the depredations of modern industrialism and the uncritical belief in technological progress. Convinced that with all its hardships farming is the most appropriate national vocation for Canadians, McArthur advocates a "back to the land" movement to stem the migration of younger people to the cities and factory work. As a convinced individualist, he rejects the idea of the nationalization of land, or any other form of government-sponsored collectivization. Nevertheless, there are many elements of his contrast between the rural ideal and urban life that would appeal to Marxist Communists. Such elements include his repeated attacks on the ruthless international economic rivalry that has led to the arms race and crushing national debts, and his attacks on modern corporations with their sacrifice of the human factor to an efficiency whose only aim is the accumulation of profits. "In the factories work has none of the charm it had for the old-time artisan who performed every operation himself. It is simply machine-driven drudgery, and the man who thinks that kind of work preferable to work on a farm deserves no better employment" (95). McArthur likewise condemns the farm machinery manufacturers who sell substandard equipment "to save the wages of mechanics in assembling their implements" (191). To be fair, he acknowledges that farmers can be avaricious, citing the local tradition of the old farmer who made a fortune during the Crimean War and subsequently yearned for "another war with Roosha, so the price of wheat would go up" (207). In the matter of war profiteering, however, McArthur mainly singles out the financial institutions and governments who pursue the arms race to the brink of national bankruptcy. The essays in *In Pastures Green* appeared in newspaper form in 1913, and the preface to the book was written shortly after the outbreak of the First World War; in this atmosphere of international crisis, McArthur writes that "the next great European war will be fought by soldiers who have nothing left to fight for but a national debt" (19).

The attacks on corporate greed and irresponsible government make up a relatively small part of *In Pastures Green,* whose main focus is on the celebration of nature and the rural life. But these attacks were prominent enough to disconcert readers who preferred McArthur in his idyllic and comic moods. Even the most perceptive commentator on his work has emphasized the rural humorist over the social critic, and has tried to dismiss McArthur's attacks on big business by the non sequitur that McArthur became a business executive himself (Lucas 686). *In Pastures Green* has even been bowdlerized by an editor who did not like McArthur's anti-establishment political and economic ideas. In a 1948 edition, K.M. Wells removed the author's anti-war comments and much of his political and economic criticism, to try to turn the book into a pleasantly innocuous pastoral idyll. As V.G. Hopwood wrote in *New Frontiers,* the result was simply to trivialize McArthur's thought (Hopwood, "The Sage of Ekfrid," 43).

Another attack on urban-centred financial and political power, also written just before the outbreak of the First World War, was Stephen Leacock's *Arcadian Adventures with the Idle Rich* (1914). Like McArthur, Leacock was essentially a political and economic conservative. If his own childhood on a farm bred in him doubts about the virtues of rural life, he still preferred the unsophisticated streets of a small town to the sinister corridors of money power in the city. The smaller centre is not free of stupidity and greed, Leacock acknowledges in his *Sunshine Sketches of a Little Town* (1912). The politicians and electors of his Mariposa are not above taking an occasional bribe or payoff; the local barber might dabble in questionable mining stock in hopes of making a quick killing. But the perpetrators of these amateurish deals ultimately retain an air of countrified innocence. The financial ghouls eyeing their prey from the deep chairs of the Mausoleum Club in *Arcadian Adventures,* on the other hand, are the representatives of a thoroughly decadent urban civilization. Significantly, while the little town of Mariposa is located in Ontario, Canada, *Arcadian Adventures* is set in a US city—unnamed, but probably Chicago, where Leacock studied for his PhD in politics and economics. The stories of financial wheeling and dealing are also in part inspired by the ideas of one of Leacock's University of Chicago professors, Thorstein Veblen, a vigorous critic of classical laissez-faire economics and an advocate of government economic intervention.

Like Veblen, Leacock stops short of any sympathy with socialist theory. Leacock's main complaint against socialism was that it offered oversimplified and visionary solutions to problems which, as he suggested in his 1920 essay *The Unsolved Riddle of Social Justice*, elude all practical and theoretical attempts at resolution. But his criticisms of laissez-faire capitalism were much angrier than his objections to socialism. In the opening paragraphs of "A Little Dinner with Mr. Lucullus Fyshe," the first story in *Arcadian Adventures*, the overfed denizens of Plutoria Avenue are oblivious to the working-class slums only a few blocks away. Interred in the plushly appointed "caverns" of the Mausoleum Club, they come alive only to hatch schemes against each other, or to set financial traps for the occasional intruder into their den, such as a visiting English aristocrat. The clumsy stalking of the Duke of Dulham for what turns out to be his illusory wealth constitutes a parable of the continuing conflict between the rising capitalist bourgeoisie and the fading feudal aristocracy—a conflict that seems to come straight out of the Marxist conception of history. Leacock's plutocrats even seem to be aware of Marx when they occasionally express a hypocritical sympathy with the working class, and claim to recognize the inevitability of proletarian revolution. But they envisage the coming revolution as aimed not against themselves but against "the British aristocracy" with their "feudal estates." When the denizens of the club are inconvenienced by a waiters' strike, furthermore, their real attitude to the workers becomes vociferously evident. Leacock's second story, "The Wizard of Finance," continues the satire against the urban bourgeoisie and the idealization of rural life. A farmer who has become rich by the discovery of gold on his property gives up his uncomfortable life as a city millionaire to return eagerly to his farm when the gold turns out to be the product of a swindle.

The final story in the book, "The Great Fight for Clean Government," attacks both the commercial and political worlds by exposing the self-seeking motives underlying a municipal reform movement that "cleans up" the council by returning the same old gang of business-men to power.

Even though Leacock ultimately rejected socialistic solutions to economic evils, his caricatures of predatory American capitalists and bureaucrats and his sympathy for the working-class poor would be of interest to Canadian Marxists. But another attack on the capitalist oligarchy, published like *Arcadian Adventures* just months before the outbreak of the First World War, appealed even more strongly to Communist readers and writers. Gustavus Myers's *A History of Canadian Wealth* (1914) is not really a literary work in the usually accepted senses of the term—even less so than Thompson's *Politics of Labor*. Still less does it qualify as "romantic anti-capitalism," for Myers's book is intensely realistic. Far from sharing Leacock's nostalgia for the past, Myers condemns the Canadian past vigorously. Strictly speaking, furthermore, *A History of Canadian Wealth* is not even a Canadian book, for Myers is the inverse of Thompson, an American who writes about Canada. But its subject matter as well as its influence in Canada justify its treatment here. Myers (1872-1942) was a native and lifelong resident of the United States, a newspaper and magazine feature writer, and what was once called a muckraker but perhaps would now be called an investigative reporter. Engaging in comprehensive economic and political archival research that would do credit to a modern-day social scientist, Myers produced, among other works, *The History of Tammany Hall* (1901) and *History of the Great American Fortunes* (1909-10), before embarking on his study of the origins and development of Canadian industrial capitalism.

*A History of Canadian Wealth*, the first volume of a projected two-volume study left unfinished as a result of dislocations arising from the 1914-18 war, examines especially the fur trade and the railway business. The pervasive revelation of both his Canadian and American histories is that the great capitalist fortunes were not based on thrift and superior intelligence as the American myth of success would have it, but on dishonesty. Again and again, through an abundant accumulation of detail, Myers demonstrates the chicanery of mercantile interests in the degradation of native people, the murderous feuds between rival fur companies, the suborning of public officials, the misappropriation of public money and land, the use of substandard material in railway building—a prodigious chronicle of criminal activity on the part of the pioneers of capitalist entrepreneurship and "free" enterprise. The remarkable feature of Myers's book is its reliance on documented fact. Drawing on Canadian official sources such as Royal Commission reports, court and parliamentary records, and government Blue Books, the author established virtually fool-proof support for his accusations. "So scrupulous was his research-ing of the facts that throughout his long career...he never had to face a suit for libel," noted Stanley Ryerson in his introduction to a 1972 reprint of Myers's book (xiii). Even a hostile *New York Times* reviewer grudgingly acknowledged that "his facts are not denied" (cited in *A History*, ed. Ryerson, 339). But Myers was so obsessed with the accumulation of fact that he had little time either for theory or for thematic synthesis. His book is an overwhelming accumulation of raw data which achieves a vast inorganic impression of corrup-tion, but offers little in the way of either historical analysis or possi-ble solutions, and still less of general insights into the motives and meanings of human greed.

Whereas Marxists—as Ryerson repeatedly emphasized—were essentially humanistic in their conception of history, Myers insisted that most historians mistakenly tried "to present personalities" rather than "sharply contesting economic forces" as "the determiners of events" (xxxv). Whereas Marxism is essentially optimistic in its belief in the ultimate triumph of social justice, Myers's voluminous empha-sis on the moral evil and material success of capitalism leaves a strongly pessimistic impression. But his emphasis on fact also rein-forces the reality of the socio-economic conditions that Marxism is opposed to. Just as Margaret Fairley used William Lyon Mackenzie's "immense respect for factual evidence" to present a revisionist view of the significance of political corruption and the impulse to revolu-tion in Canadian history, Communist writers used Myers's penchant for economic fact to rewrite the myths of success. Even with its lack of theory or sense of unified purpose or social relevance, *A History of Canadian Wealth* was of considerable interest to the socialist movement in Canada. Soon after its publication by the socialist co-operative publishers, Charles H. Kerr of Chicago, the book was advertised and sold by the *Western Clarion*, the weekly organ of the Socialist Party of Canada. The weekly *Worker*, the official newspaper established in 1922 by the Communist Party of Canada, included it in the list of publications it offered for sale by mail order. Numerous Canadian Communist writers, from the 1920s through the 1970s, used it as source material for both historical and fictional representations of the Canadian past.

Myers was what would now be called a private scholar, one who conducts research apart from any university. Throughout the nineteenth and early twentieth centuries, anti-capitalist literary activity in Canada was largely conducted outside the universities. Leacock wrote *Arcadian Adventures* while he was a McGill professor, and the book is based on his academic grounding in political economy and his familiarity with the work of Thorstein Veblen, but *Arcadian Adventures* was written as extra-curricular activity and aimed at a non-academic readership. The reluctance of most university scholars to make direct attacks on capitalism probably reflects the political timidity of the Canadian academic community in the early twentieth century. There were a few exceptions to the dearth of radicalism in Canadian universities, however. One of the earliest and most significant of these exceptions emerged in 1917, when a new literary magazine appeared on the campus of the University of Toronto. Created by Barker Fairley, a professor of German, and Sam Hooke, a professor of English, the *Rebel* featured a mixture of writing by undergraduates, faculty, and notable persons from outside the university. Aimed primarily at an undergraduate readership, many of the articles dealt with such matters as the quality of lectures and the effects of the war on the university, although there was a significant share of writing of wider interest, such as comments on contemporary Canadian painting and critical studies of classic literary works. The *Rebel* was by no means an innovative publication, for it was modeled on the little magazines that had flourished in the US and Britain in the 1890s to promote the aestheticism and decadence inspired by Walter Pater and Oscar Wilde. The editors were also aware of the emerging generation of little magazines concerned with socialist politics and modernist aesthetics, beginning with the *Masses* (New York) in 1911 and *Poetry* (Chicago) in 1912.

In the history of Canadian culture, the *Rebel* is significant on at least two counts. It was the direct predecessor of the *Canadian Forum*, which became the principal medium for democratic socialist opinion in Canada. Secondly, the associates of the *Rebel* included two people whose influence and achievements were especially important in shaping the progressive cultural heritage in Canada. Ironically, one of these people contributed only a few book reviews and two articles to the *Rebel*, while the other never wrote for the periodical at all, although he had considerable influence on the literary and political activity to which the *Rebel* was devoted. The non-contributing patron of the *Rebel* was a University of Toronto professor of mathematics named A.T. DeLury; the occasional contributor was Margaret Fairley, the wife of one of the founding editors. In 1951, Fairley wrote DeLury's obituary for the Communist weekly *Canadian Tribune*. "I first knew DeLury," she wrote,

> on the committee of the Open Forums which used to meet on Sunday afternoons, and I can remember the respect we all had for his understanding of the Russian Revolution and its meaning for Canadians. There was always a warmth in the policies of DeLury and always a sense of the many-sided human issues involved. For him the march of events was moral and artistic, as well as economic and political, and I think he will be remembered especially for this rich, balanced approach, which helped us who were far behind him in understanding. ("Prof. A.T. DeLury")

Alfred Tennyson DeLury was born in the village of Manilla, Ontario, northeast of Toronto, in 1864. Like his near contemporary, Stephen Leacock, as well as other scholars of their generation who were to contribute to high academic standards in Canada's universities in the early twentieth century, DeLury began as a rural schoolteacher. Also like Leacock, and in fact preceding him by only a year, he obtained a BA from the University of Toronto in 1890. After pursuing graduate studies in the US and France, he was appointed lecturer in mathematics at the University of Toronto. He became a full professor in 1908, head of the mathematics department in 1919, and

Dean of Arts in 1922. But although he was recognized as a brilliant mathematician and teacher, his interests ranged far beyond his specialization. The offspring of Irish immigrants, he took a particular interest in Irish culture, and in many visits to the country of his ancestors he got to know some of the notable figures of the cultural revival, including William Butler Yeats and his painter brother, Jack Yeats, as well as the poet George Russell ("AE"). But he also brought back from Europe—certainly from Ireland, and probably also from England—an interest in the problems of poverty and class conflict. In 1901, according to the surviving records he kept of his book purchases, he acquired copies of *The Condition of the Working Class in England* (1845) by Frederick Engels, and *The Evolution of Property from Savagery to Civilization* (1890) by Karl Marx's son-in-law, Paul Lafargue. Subsequent book acquisitions included Ferdinand Lasalle's *The Workingman's Programme* (1899) and Stephen Graham's *Russia in 1916* (1917). In the first two decades of the twentieth century he delivered occasional public lectures based on his political reading and thinking, as attested by surviving notes for a lecture on "The Failure of Democracy" (apparently delivered 1908) and a paper on "Socialism" read to the Faculty Club (possibly some time before 1916). His notes for the latter paper indicate that he was going to talk about the ideas of various significant figures in the history of socialism, including Pierre-Joseph Proudhon, Lasalle, Engels, and Marx (biographical information based on DeLury Papers).

As Sam Hooke indicated in a poem about him in the *Rebel* of February 1919, and as Margaret Fairley asserted in her obituary of him, DeLury took a special interest in the Russian revolution, and continued to express pro-USSR sympathies into the 1920s, 1930s and 1940s. During the Second World War, while in his late seventies, he was chairman of a local Society for the Study of Russia. De Lury seems never to have become directly involved with any socialistic political party, including the Communist Party of Canada, but his academic presentations on the history of European socialism and on the development of the USSR influenced a generation of younger leftists. Unfortunately, the full significance of DeLury's contribution to the progressive cultural movement can only be inferred, for he was careful not to provoke the antagonists of Bolshevism who formed a majority of the academic community in Toronto. However, the surviving evidence confirms that he was a leader in the pro-Marxist, pro-USSR intellectual currents operating among Canadian academic intellectuals even earlier than 1917.

These currents are more explicitly embodied in the life and career of Margaret Fairley (1885-1968). Although she did not join the Communist Party of Canada until 1936, Fairley personifies the best elements in Canadian progressive thought that emerged in the post-Russian Revolutionary period. A cultural nationalist, she strove to relate her intense loyalty to Canada to her understanding of Marxist internationalism. Her attempts to come to grips with these and other questions of importance to her, furthermore, were grounded in her early and continuing academic abilities. Born Margaret Adele Keeling in Bradford, Yorkshire, she was the youngest daughter among the nine children of Henrietta (Gedge) and William H. Keeling, headmaster of Bradford Grammar School. Receiving her early schooling at home and at the Bradford Girls' Grammar School founded by her father, Margaret Keeling absorbed much of the social gospel type of Christianity espoused by her father and other Church of England clergy in the northern industrial cities. In 1904 she was sent up to Oxford, where she enrolled as a scholar in one of the new women's colleges, St. Hugh's (founded 1886), and in 1907 took a first in the school of English Language and Literature. Following the standard vocational expectations for academically inclined women of the time, she spent a year at St. Mary's College, Paddington, to obtain a teaching certificate. After a brief stint of teaching in inner-city London, she was called back to Oxford in 1908 to take up a position as English tutor and librarian at the newest women's college, St. Hilda's (founded 1893). In addition to her tutorial and library work, Keeling committed herself to scholarly research and writing. Attracted to the revolutionary aesthetics and ideologies of the English Romantic poets, she edited for Oxford's Clarendon Press a volume of selections by Samuel Taylor Coleridge, *Poems of Nature and Romance 1794-1807* (1910), and an annotated *Rime of the Ancient Mariner* (1912). The literature of the nineteenth century, she declared in her introduction to the earlier volume, constituted a reaction "against such sides of eighteenth-century life and thought as had been unadventurous and complaisant" (30). Unlike his predecessors and most of his contemporaries, Coleridge looked beyond the narrow cultural and political boundaries of England. In order to understand his poetry "the main principles of the French Revolution must be kept in sight, for it is on the theoretic side that he comes closely in touch with it" (32). Keeling goes on to identify the important eighteenth-century influences on both the revolution and Coleridge's poetry as the international romanticism of Jean-Jacques Rousseau, William Godwin, and Thomas Paine.

It is tempting to find here a prefiguration of Fairley's later interest in the Russian Revolution and the internationalist ideologies of Marxism-Leninism. If A.T. DeLury encouraged her to understand the Russian situation, her early scholarly activity inspired her interest in the interaction between political revolution and literary art. If Coleridge's ideas appealed to her developing political sympathies, furthermore, the painstaking work of preparing the Coleridge texts obviously appealed to her academic tastes. The two Coleridge volumes marked, in fact, the beginning of a scholarly career that was to climax in Canada with *The Selected Writings of William Lyon Mackenzie*—appropriately published by the Canadian branch of the publisher that had brought out her Coleridge work in England fifty years earlier.

Keeling's acknowledgements in *Poems of Nature* include an expression of gratitude to the eminent Helen Darbishire of Somerville College. In an alternative world Keeling might have followed Darbishire's example and become one of the pioneering women literary scholars who emerged from Oxford and Cambridge in the early twentieth century. But Keeling was not happy with British academia. Oxford did not grant degrees to women until 1920, and the segregation and enforced celibacy of the women's colleges offered limited opportunities for professional advancement or personal fulfilment. Perhaps further inspired by her studies of the Romantic poets, Keeling had developed a fondness for travel, particularly to remote, exotic places. During one long vacation she went out to Egypt to keep house for one of her brothers, who was in the Foreign Service there. During another break, she took an excursion to Canada, riding the Canadian Pacific transcontinental railway across the country. Back in Oxford in 1912, she met H.M. Tory, the president of the new University of

Alberta (established 1908), who offered her a teaching position and an appointment as Dean of Women. Since she could not have an Oxford degree, Tory offered to confer on her his university's own BA. As an instructor in English at the University of Alberta Keeling developed her interest in Canadian literary history, especially under the encouragement and tutelage of the head of her department, E.K. Broadus. Keeling's career at the University of Alberta was, however, very brief. In Edmonton she met a twenty-five-year-old instructor in German, also a native of Yorkshire, Barker Fairley, and in 1913 Keeling and Fairley were married. In accordance with standard academic regulations of the time, the new faculty wife had to give up her teaching position. By the same set of social assumptions underlying such regulations, her husband's academic career took precedence over hers, although this precedence was reinforced by the strength of Barker Fairley's doctorate. In 1915 Barker Fairley accepted an appointment to the Department of German at the University of Toronto (biographical information on Keeling/Fairley from Schabas; Kimmel, "Spirit"; and the archives of St. Hugh's and St. Hilda's Colleges, Oxford).

In Toronto, the Fairleys were absorbed into the active and stimulating cultural life that gave rise to the *Rebel* and the *Canadian Forum*. Margaret Fairley contributed to both magazines, beginning in the second issue (March 1917) of the *Rebel* with a brief critical commentary on Romain Rolland's immense roman-fleuve, *Jean-Christophe* (ten vols., 1905-12). Fairley's early Canadian writing both prefigures and contrasts her later work as a Communist critic and editor. Just as she saw Coleridge's poetry in terms of the cultural implications of the French Revolution, she emphasizes Rolland's use of European social and political upheavals of the late nineteenth and early twentieth centuries. But she is not ready to conceive these decades in terms of Marxist or any other ideology. In fact, she eagerly approves Jean-Christophe's rejection of ideology. "In these days of rebellion," she writes, "it is good to be reminded that life cannot be confined within the bounds of a theory or of a formula, political, moral or religious" (8).

The opening words of this sentence presumably refer to the Russian Revolution. In March 1917, as Fairley's article went to press, a provisional government had been established in Russia; on 15 March, the czar abdicated. Although A.T. DeLury was probably urging his Toronto colleagues to consider the implications of these events, Fairley was not ready to think of Rolland's novel primarily in terms of its relevance to a new revolutionary age. She was more interested in how the German Jean-Christophe finds a sense of intellectual fulfilment and unity in France, thus prophetically undercutting one of the primary nationalistic antagonisms of the First World War. All of Fairley's early writing for the *Rebel* and the *Canadian Forum* reflects her democratic socialist political philosophy, interacting with pacifism and a moderate feminism. She believed that both ideology and public policy should always be flexible, and subordinate to humanistic notions of fairness, generosity, and social justice. Commenting in the *Rebel* of October 1918 on a new "Women's Party" organized in Toronto the previous month, she acknowledges that "suffragists," including herself, have been "insisting for years that we wish to be treated as human beings rather than as mere women"; but she objects to the pro-war and anti-labour implications of the new party's platform. Contrasting this platform to the Fourteen Point peace proposals of US President Woodrow Wilson, she objects to the WP's support for the continuation of present political alliances and the punitive economic subjugation of Germany. The WP, she acknowledges, is "moderately progressive" in matters that involve the welfare of women and children, but she condemns the Party's opposition to "all social and industrial unrest" which the Party claims is provoked by "enemy propaganda." "I will throw in my lot with the best wherever I may find it," she concludes, "and will remember that I am just as likely to find it among men as among women" (27-29). Fairley repeats her criticism of modern women in the only published poem of her writing career, "A Woman's Confession," which appeared in the *Canadian Forum* of August 1921. Although the clumsy iambics and prosaic diction justify Fairley's decision not to pursue the writing of verse, the poem succinctly expresses her iconoclastic view of both women and the Great War. Women, she admits in the poem, are equally to blame with men for the carnage of the war and the injustice of the peace. Like those who established the Women's Party, many women were militantly pro-war, cheering men on to their deaths while denouncing talk of negotiated peace:

We failed, as men have failed,
No longer can we claim a purer heart;
In the great game of war we played our part,
Full with the tide we sailed. (333)

Fairley's other contributions to the *Forum* in the 1920s are articles that reveal her growing interest in feminism and literary modernism, particularly as conveyed in the writings of such British authors as H.G. Wells, George Bernard Shaw, and Virginia Woolf. "Creative Evolution" (January 1922) extols the spirit of spontaneity and individualism advocated by Wells and Shaw as the primary virtues of the new "religion" that should evolve from the decayed Puritanism of Christianity. "These Prejudices: Supermen" (May 1925) warns of the dangers of a Utopianism that degenerates into irresponsible romanticism, denying the imperatives of real life. "Virginia Woolf" (March 1930) is a sensitive appreciation of Woolf's insight into female psychology, especially the psychology of the woman artist. But Fairley's work did not appear very often in the *Forum* during the 1920s, for between 1915 and 1926 she gave birth to five children. Maternity brought her both the obvious burden of domestic duties (which she gently lamented in a *Forum* article of November 1921, "Domestic Discontent"), and a measure of tragedy. One of her children died in infancy and another was stricken with an undiagnosed chronic illness, possibly cystic fibrosis, that culminated in his death in his early twenties. In spite of these pressures, however, she kept up with her reading, writing, and political/cultural contacts, studying socialism and the new USSR with DeLury and others, reading widely in European social theory and modern literature.

So by the time that the USSR was moving toward the consolidation of Bolshevik power, first under Lenin and more brutally under Stalin, Canada had an anti-capitalist intellectual and literary tradition that was at least receptive if not committed to Russian Communism. This tradition was manifest in a variety of literary forms, from the masculine novel of northern adventure through comic and satirical prose sketches to academic critical and literary essays, reflecting the dissatisfaction of many Canadian writers and thinkers with the political and economic circumstances in which they lived.

# 3

# The 1920s
## Communists and Fellow Travellers

W hile some of the journalists and intellectuals associated with the *Rebel* and the *Canadian Forum* moved slowly and tentatively toward Marxist-Leninist Communism in the 1920s, other individuals and groups were moving quickly and decisively. In the spring of 1922, while the *Forum* entered its second year as a broadly non-partisan socialist culture magazine, a twice-monthly (later, weekly) newspaper entitled the *Worker* appeared in Toronto, proclaiming itself the "official organ of the Workers Party of Canada." As eventually became evident, the Workers Party was the legal front for the clandestine Communist Party of Canada. The founders of the CPC had followed the examples of their colleagues in the US and some European countries, where government and police repression forced Communists to operate underground. When the Communist International (Comintern) decided in 1924 that conditions in Canada did not justify this cumbersome two-level system, the Workers Party was eliminated and the *Worker* began to identify itself as the "official organ of the Communist Party of Canada" (See Angus 87-102).

Like most of the pro-labour and socialist newspapers that preceded it in Canada, the *Worker* at first devoted comparatively little attention to literary culture. Historical accounts differ on the number and identities of the people who attended the secret founding meeting of the CPC in a barn on the outskirts of Guelph, Ontario, on 28 and 29 May 1921, but it seems clear that the delegates had little interest in discussing literary and artistic subjects. Indeed, in the early years the main priority of the members was probably the Party's bare survival. The little band of would-be revolutionaries had to struggle against both the hostility of domestic authorities and Soviet Russian officialdom's ignorance and indifference towards Canada to establish a self-sustaining affiliate of the Communist International. The membership of the early Party, furthermore, was dominated by workers rather than intellectuals. Perhaps the only intellectual among them was the first editor of the *Worker*, Maurice Spector. Born in Ukraine in 1898 and brought to Canada as a child, educated in law at the University of Toronto, Spector was a brilliant political theorist and a zealous activist. At university he had served on the editorial board of the student newspaper, the *Varsity*, and had almost been expelled in 1918 for writing and publishing a letter criticizing the pro-war sentiment on campus (Angus 15, 77). His expert knowledge of political history and theory, and especially of Marxism and the Bolshevik revolution, got him elected chairman of the CPC (not the top post, but an influential position in the governing circle) and appointed editor of the *Worker*.

Although the *Worker*'s main commitments were to the reporting and interpretation of political news and the dissemination of ideology, the new editor was prepared to acknowledge the promotion of literary culture as part of the paper's responsibilities. In this policy he was following an example being established in the Soviet Union, where the Communist Party was giving the arts a high priority. In 1917, even before the October Revolution, the Bolsheviks had established a Proletarian Cultural and Educational Organization ("Proletcult"). These preparations led to the First All-Russian Conference of the Proletcult in 1920, and to the creation of the All-Russian Association of Proletarian Writers (VAPP) in the same year. Russian writers and artists flocked eagerly to the new political cause. Even in the unsettled years of the civil war, the Proletcult and VAPP were able to publish and circulate somewhere around twenty literary periodicals (Brown, *The Proletarian Episode* 7, 9). Contrary to anti-Communist opinion that persisted throughout the twentieth century, this activity was not sub-jugated to a dogmatic party line dictated by culturally ignorant bureaucrats. On the contrary, the new generation of post-revolution-ary writers, left alone for the most part to manage their own affairs, soon fell to arguing among themselves about aesthetic theory and practice, just as their counterparts in capitalist societies perennially do. In 1925 the Central Committee of the Communist Party of the Soviet Union tried to cut off such debate by establishing a fixed policy on pro-letarian literature, but the writers in the VAPP and rival organizations quickly lapsed back into their contentious habits (See Foley 77-78 and Murphy 26). Although the Proletcult had theoretically been estab-lished as a means of bringing to the working masses a cultural tradi-tion that would be politically beneficial to them, there was little agree-ment about exactly what this tradition should consist of. Serious differences of opinion also arose concerning the relationship between post-revolutionary art and pre-revolutionary cultural traditions. Many writers, furthermore—enough, in fact, to form an influential break-away group in 1919—insisted in defiance of Proletcult assumptions that the real business of writers should not be mass education but the creation of durable works of art (Brown 10). Leon Trotsky, in a series of essays written for *Pravda* and later collected as *Literature and Revolution* (1924), challenged the idea that a distinctive proletarian culture was possible at all.

Details of this cultural foment did not immediately reach the Canadian Communists. Although Canadian socialist and labour newspapers had been publishing translated excerpts from major European revolutionary books and periodicals since the 1860s, most of this writing concerned political and economic theory and, after 1917, political events in Russia. Nor was there in Canada, as there had been in Russia, a great rush of creative writers to the cause, or a proliferation of left-wing literary magazines. The sole outlet for the few radical poets who emerged in the 1920s remained their partisan newspapers. The *Worker* published a translation of one of Trotsky's articles on "Literature and Revolution" in 1925 and a translation of a Russian short story in 1926, but a comprehensive representation of the cultural situation in the USSR was not available to Canadian Communists until the 1930s, with the appearance of multilingual editions of the Moscow-based periodical, *International Literature*. In this respect, the Canadian situation was not a great deal different from that in the US: according to James F. Murphy, "a review of the *Daily Worker* [of New York] in 1924 and 1925 reveals how far removed American communists were from the discussions over proletarian culture taking place in the Soviet Union" (58).

Canadian Communist writers in the 1920s, as their publications in the *Worker* revealed, continued like their radical predecessors to owe more to nineteenth- and early-twentieth-century British, Canadian, and US traditions than to the Russian Revolution and its aesthetic reverberations. Early issues included as fillers the same sort of doggerel poems about worker defiance and capitalist degeneration as had appeared thirty years earlier in Phillips Thompson's *Labor Reform Songster*. Indeed, the 13 April 1922 issue of the *Worker* included a "Notes and Comment" column written by Thompson himself. Eighty years old and blind, Thompson was unable to continue the column, but the appearance of the feisty old socialist in the *Worker* reveals the dependence of the Canadian Bolsheviks on an indigenous socialist past. But the few creative writers who appeared in the early issues of the *Worker* inclined, consciously or otherwise, to the Russian Proletcult ideal of using art to educate the masses. This is the obvious aim of a one-act play entitled "The Very Idea!," published in the *Worker* of 2 October 1922, and signed with what was probably a pseudonym, "K.C. Jones." A parodic drawing-room comedy, the skit features upper-class Englishwomen drinking tea and complaining of how labour unrest is interfering with their convenience and comfort. A prefiguration of the caricature techniques of the agitprop drama in the 1930s—the influential Canadian play *Eight Men Speak* (1933) would open with a similar scene—"The Very Idea!" attempted to convey in colloquial language and a simplified literary form the Communist perceptions of the inequalities of life under capitalism.

In its issue of 4 July 1923 the *Worker* introduced a writer who was to become even more successful and popular in introducing Proletcult literary ideals to Canada. "Awake!," a poem consisting of six quatrains of iambic tetrameter, at first glance appears to be a conventional critique of social injustice and a call to action in the tradition of the work of Alexander McLachlan, Phillips Thompson, and Wilfred Gribble. But in spite of the author's evident indifference to the modernist forms and language that were revolutionizing anglophone poetry in the 1920s, "Awake!" is not doggerel. An appeal to the workers to reclaim the heritage stolen from them by capitalism, the poem devotes most of its attention to reminding the proletariat of its latent strength.

> You hacked in halves a hemisphere
> To bring two alien oceans near
> And striding across a continent
> You made earth blossom wherever you went.
>
> And plunged your hands in pockets of Earth
> To toss its coin like a spendthrift forth;
> And rising above the flight of birds
> You smoked the sky with your chosen words.

The poem conveys an image of the working class as a personalized, folkloric figure, a god-like colossus, or perhaps a more indigenously North American Paul Bunyan or Johnny Appleseed. In the second stanza, the colossus is a benevolent thief, extracting the earth's bounty not in order to horde it but to distribute it lavishly for the benefit of all. Thus the proletarian creative act is opposed to the selfish capitalistic theft of the world's wealth, alluded to in subsequent stanzas. The second stanza also associates the working class with the Judeo-Christian conception of divine creativity: like the god whose utterance is the initial creative act, the workers' munificent labours are the "chosen words" that transcend and subdue nature. More precisely, the mystical words of the workers "smoke the sky," a reinforcement of their validity in the North American context by identifying them with aboriginal smoke signals. In subsequent stanzas, this transcendent vision is contrasted to the historical reality of the world of modern capitalism. The poet addresses the worker as a "Blind and broken and shackled slave," "Spinner of all, but naked yet," and "Homeless in cities, built by your hands." The deity-prisoner paradox resolves in the Marxist appeal for worker unity to achieve the triumph brought closer by the success of the Russian revolution:

But now deliverance comes at last,
The world is locked in the struggle vast:
Rise to your Russian comrades' call,
Masters are nothing! Men are all! (*Joe Wallace Poems* 93)

Joseph Sylvester ("Joe") Wallace (1890-1975)—the author of "Awake!"—was to be the most successful, durable, and prolific of the writers associated with the Communist Party of Canada. A member of the Party until his death, Wallace was to be published, translated, widely read and critically acclaimed in the USSR and China, although his readership in his native country was almost entirely limited to members and sympathizers of the Party. Like many members of the Canadian Communist literary community, Wallace was bourgeois in family background, with infusions of working-class influences. Of Irish descent, he was raised in the Roman Catholic Church, a lifelong loyalty which he integrated with his political radicalism in his poetry as well as in his life. Born in Toronto, he was the fourth of seven children of Thomas Wallace, a travelling salesman, and Mary (Polly) Redmond. When his mother died in childbirth in 1897, the father moved his family to Nova Scotia, where they lived for varying periods in Truro, North Sydney, and Halifax. In 1897 Thomas Wallace remarried, to a woman who turned out to be negligent and abusive toward the children. When Joe ran away from home at the age of eleven, his father deferred to community notions about problem children and had his son committed for a year to a reformatory, St. Patrick's Catholic Home for Boys. Although late-twentieth-century society has concluded that such institutions are as likely to contribute to delinquency as to correct it, Wallace claimed that he profited from the time at St. Patrick's. "I got to know boys who were mainly from the slums. They were in there for arson, for theft...and all kinds of petty crimes; but to me...they were just like other boys, good ones, practically no vicious ones and ones with all kinds of promise" (Safarik and Livesay 35).

Young Joe also showed considerable promise, especially in academic and creative ways. After coming out of the reformatory he moved to North Sydney with his family, where he completed elementary and high school. Early in elementary school his love of poetry had been inspired by hearing a teacher read Longfellow's "Hiawatha."

Soon he was trying his hand at writing his own poetry. Later, as a student at St. Francis-Xavier University, he cultivated his talent by writing poems for the student literary journal, the *Xaverian* ("A Tribute from His Old School" 9). But immature behaviour resulted in his expulsion. With this dubious university record Wallace's prospects were not good, but his older brother Frank finally found him a job as salesman for the American mail-order International Correspondence Schools. At first he was "too lazy and too timid to make any kind of a real success of it," Wallace claimed, but he soon settled down to the work (Safarik and Livesay 36). By 1911, ICS had appointed him Halifax district manager. For a time Wallace's life moved in a conventional middle-class direction. In 1915 he married Theresa Dorothy ("Dot") Granville, with whom he had four children. Excluded from military service by recurrent illness, he continued to work for the correspondence school until 1916, when his brother took him into his new business, the Wallace Advertising Service. Since his university days, Joe had enjoyed public speaking and debate, and now as a member of the Young Men's Liberal Club of Nova Scotia he began to make a name for himself locally as a political orator. His efforts in this respect were so successful that he was brought to the attention of Wilfrid Laurier (Griffin, "J.S. [Joe] Wallace").

But his political interests were shifting. His reading included books on social and political reform, such as Henry George's *Progress and Poverty* (1879), which helped him clarify his inclinations toward cooperative solutions to economic problems. In 1914 he had begun writing articles for the *Canadian Railroad Employees' Monthly*, a union publication that originated in Halifax in that year and soon became "one of the most influential Canadian labour journals," with an international circulation (Elliott 224). By 1919 his interest in radical politics had been further inspired by the Russian Revolution. In 1920 he resigned from the Liberals to join the Halifax Labour Party, which subsequently affiliated with a province-wide organization, then with the national Canadian Labour Party. Wallace retained his position in the family advertising business, but also took on the editorship of the weekly socialist newspaper, the *Citizen*. In 1922, the Canadian Labour Party affiliated with the newly formed Workers Party of Canada. Wallace's career as a Communist writer now began in earnest, when

he resigned from the *Citizen* to become a regular contributor of
poems, news items, and editorials to the *Worker*. Keeping his new
political affiliation secret from his business associates, Wallace held on
to his advertising job until 1933, and through the 1920s and early
1930s was an important financial supporter of the Communist Party
(Wallace, letter to Annie Buller, n.d. [1927?], CPC Papers, PAO).

Wallace did not devote himself wholeheartedly to poetry until the
early 1940s, and published his first book of poems in 1943, when he
was over fifty. In the early years of his career as a literary radical, he
served primarily as a journalist. The *Worker* valued him as their Nova
Scotia correspondent, especially through the bitter and violent conflict between the Cape Breton coal miners and the British Empire Steel
Corporation (BESCO) that erupted in 1921 and ended in 1926 with
BESCO's financial collapse. Wallace's lively colloquial reports from
Cape Breton, a notable relief from the often stiff and jargony
reportage of most radical journalists, included an exposé of the slave-
like working conditions in BESCO mines (22 August 1923), and a jail-
cell interview with the Communist union leader J.B. McLachlan,
arrested on a trumped-up charge of sedition (14 November 1923).
From 1925 to 1929 Wallace contributed to the paper a weekly column, "Between the Lines," consisting of editorial comment on current
events. But he also found time to turn out an occasional poem, often
based on his reporting assignments, or on recent news items from
elsewhere. "Better That!" (*Worker* 9 February 1924) is a dramatic
monologue representing McLachlan defiantly proclaiming from
courtroom and jail cell his willingness to sacrifice personal dignity,
freedom, and family relationships for the cause of relieving the suffering of workers. The second of the poem's three stanzas obviously
invokes Wallace's jail-cell interview with McLachlan:

> The prison bars
> May sear my soul
> Like irons hot in
> The heat of hell:
> But better that
> Than men dig coal
> For a cutthroat crew
> And not rebel. (*JW Poems* 15)

His "Lenin Lies Asleep in Moscow" (26 September 1924), tries through a combination of conventional elegiac diction and vigorous rhythm to suggest the vitality and durability of the new society of the USSR which, in spite of the death of its leader, persists as inevitably as the cycles of nature and human labour:

> Lenin lies asleep in Moscow;
> Lenin lies asleep in a deep, a dreamless sleep,
> While the harvest-heavy rains
> Flush with wheat the Volga plains,
> And the sickle sings of life. (*JW Poems* 96)

Another of Wallace's *Worker* poems, "Probably Six" (3 March 1928), takes its title from an insensitive newspaper report of the number of men killed in a recent mining accident in Northern Ontario. Pretending to understand the phrase as the name of one of the victims, Wallace restores individuality to the men by imagining the last heroic actions of "Probably Six," warning his comrades before succumbing to smoke and gas inhalation. In his conclusion, Wallace ridicules the newspaper's inhuman statement that the accident did not seriously affect the performance of the mining company shares on the Stock Exchange:

> So Probably Six drank lots of grief
> Through the cheesecloth folds of his handkerchief.
> . . . . . . . . . . . . . . . . . . . . . . . . . . .
> While the Stock Exchange had a cheerful day,
> —More gold to mine and less men to pay. (*JW Poems* 18)

Wallace's poems were the only distinguished literary contributions to the *Worker* until 1926, when from February through most of 1927 the literary content of the paper increased substantially. At first, most of the new items were reprints of works by American and European radical authors, but this second-hand material was an effective way of demonstrating to *Worker* readers how artistic expression was an important element in the international Communist movement, and of encouraging would-be *Worker* contributors to try their hands at creative writing. The reprinted fiction included an excerpt from the American Fannie Hurst's 1923 novel *Lummox*, a short story and a one-act play by another prominent American Communist writer,

Michael Gold, and a story translated from the Russian of A. Serafimovich, a contemporary of Maxim Gorky. In the summer of 1926, two original Canadian short stories appeared, signed with the Celtic pseudonym "Cathal Boru." "I Am a Success" (in two parts, 24 and 31 July) portrays a young Canadian who swallows the modern American Horatio Alger gospel. "Fired with enthusiasm," he takes a course with the International Correspondence Schools, works as a low-paid machinist for the American-owned International Harvester Company of Hamilton, Ontario, then bounces from one job to another, suffering layoffs, wage reductions, and other forms of exploitation. Injured and hospitalized, he encounters an unsympathetic, pro-employer compensation board. In a closing comment on the downward spiral of his fortunes, with laconic irony he begins to "question the motivation of his dear friends the employing class."

There is a remote possibility that "Cathal Boru" was Joe Wallace. The Celtic pseudonym could be a reflection of Wallace's strong sense of pride in his Irish descent; the allusion to the International Correspondence Schools is a reminder that Wallace worked for ICS after leaving St. Francis-Xavier; and finally, the irony in the story is consistent with the prevalent tone in some of Wallace's poetry. But these are, of course, very slight items of evidence. The second story by Cathal Boru, "The Life of Pat Quinn," published 26 August, is a different kind of narrative, a straightforward tale of a British immigrant who comes to Canada in 1901, settles in Toronto, serves in the First World War, and works toward a career in provincial politics. The purpose here seems to be simply to demonstrate the clichéd, futile life of a middle-class person under capitalism.

Whoever Cathal Boru was, the appearance of these stories in the *Worker* can be traced not only to the increasing emergence of Party members with literary ambitions, but also to the editorial efforts of one such member in particular. In 1922 the Party organized a Young Workers League, renamed the Young Communist League in 1924, in which year the YCL established its own newspaper, the monthly *Young Worker*. In May 1926 the editorship was taken over by the twenty-one-year-old secretary of the YCL, Oscar Ryan. Ryan (1904-88) was born in Montreal, the son of Sara (Rein) and Adolph Weinstein. Raised and educated primarily in Montreal, he was able to complete only a high-school education, which he supplemented with wide reading, especially in political theory, history, and literature. By the time he had finished high school, he had two complementary ambitions: to work for radical social change, and to be a creative writer. In the early 1920s he moved to Toronto, where he joined the YCL, rising quickly to the positions of League secretary and editor of the *Young Worker*. Like Joe Wallace, Ryan found that his journalistic obligations left him little time to pursue his literary ambitions, but he combined these two interests by using his editorial position to encourage creative writing among Party members. It was probably he who urged Maurice Spector to increase the literary content of the *Worker*. Ryan also opened the pages of the *Young Worker* to the creative efforts of members of the YCL (biographical details from Adams, "Oscar Ryan").

Most of the original works in the *Young Worker* of 1926-27 are short stories. None of the authors of these stories evidently pursued their literary careers very far, although this inference is rendered doubly speculative by the probability that many of the names are pseudonyms. All the stories are politically oriented, involving the struggles of workers to survive in a corrupt, bellicose capitalist system. Jim Sparks's "Paper, Sir" (June 1926) enforces a straightforward and simple political lesson. The discouragement of a poverty-stricken paper boy turns to optimism when he becomes politically aware and joins the Young Communist League. But most of the short stories concentrate on the tragedy and misery of poverty and the futility of resistance to capitalism. In A. Hall's "Company D" (August 1926) a politically conscious mine worker-turned-soldier preaches revolution to other soldiers, but when he persuades a group of them to join their "fellow workers" in the enemy lines, they are killed by their own artillery. The same author's "In the Mine" (November 1926) briefly recounts the death of an agitator in a mining accident, and the gratification of the bosses at the death. In Martin Moriarity's "Mother" (August 1927), a son tries to escape poverty by joining the army, to the great grief of his mother. Even a comic story is bitterly ironic: in K.C. Jones's "Red and White" (May-June 1929), a worker loses his job and faces starvation just after his doctor has advised him to change his diet.

As these stories indicate, the conventions of proletarian fiction were still not fixed in the 1920s. In general, writers of short stories tended to emphasize the destructive effects of capitalism rather than the positive possibilities of Marxism. As the work of Joe Wallace suggests, writers seemed to find poetry more suitable than fiction to the expression of the positive aspects of the revolutionary struggle. The defiant and visionary qualities of revolutionary action are central to the poetry of Oscar Ryan, who contributed several of his own poems to the *Worker* while serving as editor of the *Young Worker*. His poems are always very political in content, but their form and diction suggest that, unlike Wallace, he had been reading with appreciation the work of the so-called Imagists, who were emphasizing conciseness and direct sensuous appeal over commentary and elaborate figurative language. Ryan's brief "Prelude to Insurrection"(*Worker* 2 October 1926) incorporates these features into a suggestive invocation of a workers' demonstration:

> Songs
> And the stamp of feet
> Come sweeping down the factory street,
>
> And workers
> Bearing banners high
> Surge forward
> On a threatening cry.

He was also trying his hand at longer, more discursive poems that achieve proletarian art through the strength and vividness of the colloquial idioms and revolutionary attitudes of workers. His "To an Ivory Tower Intellectual" (*Worker* 1 January 1927) expresses in five free-verse stanzas the workers' antagonism to the academic writer who fastidiously condemns the workers for rebelling against the society that oppresses them. In the end, however, the workers will not need to "speak ugly" or "draw blood" in their conflict with the intellectuals, as they have to do in their violent struggle with capitalist employers and their "scabs."

> With the Revolution
> we will stick a pin into you
> . . . . . . . . . . . . .
> You will simply blow up
> Like a kid's balloon.

Over the course of a long career as a Communist writer, editor, and activist, Ryan was to work in many literary forms, including drama, fiction, biography, book and theatre reviewing, and the essay. It is regrettable that he published only a few scattered poems, mostly in his early years, for he was one of the few Canadian writers to emerge in the 1920s interested in adapting modernist poetic techniques to a revolutionary political purpose. But as "To an Ivory Tower Intellectual" suggests, he was inclined to associate poetry with an effete academic intellectualism. The masses, he decided, were to be more effectively reached through fiction and drama than through poetry, with its burden of association with bourgeois aestheticism.

•  •  •  •  •

Ryan's encouragement of original creative writing among Party members attracted one especially promising author of fiction and drama. Although the published literary works of Trevor Maguire consisted of only one short story, one play, and one novel, he deserves to be recognized as an important literary innovator in the early Canadian Communist movement. Like many Canadian Communists of that era, he has left a very fragmented and sometimes unverifiable biographical record. In fact, one of the main sources of information about him is Oscar Ryan's reminiscent autobiographical novel, *Soon To Be Born* (1980), which includes brief sketches of several real-life Communists. Canadian census records confirm Ryan's statement that Maguire was a native of Carleton Place, Ontario. Born 22 June 1887, he was the seventh of nine children of Thomas C. Maguire, a harnessmaker, and his wife Mary. Although no details survive of Trevor Maguire's early life and education, it is likely that he was apprenticed to his father's trade. According to an article in the *Worker* of 13 May 1922, Maguire joined the original Fifth Infantry battalion of the first Canadian contingent to be sent to France in 1915; in May of that year he received a severe arm wound in the Battle of Festubert, was awarded the Distinguished Conduct Medal and invalided back to Canada. In Canada, according to Ryan, Maguire was put to work with a Win-the-War recruiting team (*Soon To Be Born* 232). But his battle experience, plus the grim business of persuading youngsters to share the horrors he had undergone, worked on his political sensibilities.

After his discharge, he joined the Socialist Party of Canada. According to William Rodney, Maguire was present at the founding meeting of the CPC at Guelph and served on the credentials committee. Maguire was also a founding member of the Workers' Party and was appointed assistant secretary, as well as business manager of the Party's newspaper, the *Worker* (Rodney 37, 51).

Maguire thus began his Communist career as a loyal and tireless Party worker, participating in a "harvester trek" to proselytize among wheatfield labourers in Saskatchewan, serving as liaison to the striking Cape Breton coal miners, escorting a Comintern agent from the US into Canada, and delivering speeches at worker rallies and Party demonstrations (McEwen 55; Rodney 54, 67). In 1922 he became the first member of the CPC to be charged with sedition, after he made a speech in a May Day demonstration at Queen's Park in Toronto. In spite of the vigorous efforts of a defense committee organized by the Party, Maguire was convicted and sentenced to six months in jail. In later years, Party members would accumulate police records boldly and bear them proudly, but in these early years Maguire's isolated conviction would make him known to police and vulnerable to harassment. Perhaps for this reason, he appears not to have resumed his job with the *Worker*. Soon after his release he apparently moved to Vancouver. Nothing further appears by or about Maguire in the Party press until 1927, when the *Worker* featured a short story credited to him, in its issue of 12 February.

"Over the Top," as the title suggests, is based on Maguire's experience in the war. Like most other stories in the *Worker* and the *Young Worker*, it emphasizes the suffering of the victims of capitalism. Beginning in documentary fashion, the story describes the typical routine of trench warfare on the Western Front, then focuses on a Corporal Rigby, who suffers a nervous collapse and refuses to join the attack. After the battle he is arrested, court-martialled, and executed. If it had been written a few years later, "Over the Top" would appear only as a competent but derivative contribution to the rapidly proliferating fiction of anti-war realism. But Maguire's story was published two years before the most famous and influential of anti-war novels inspired by the 1914-1918 conflict, Erich Maria Remarque's *All Quiet on the Western Front* (1929). "Over the Top" also precedes the first novel of this type to deal with the Canadian war experience, Charles Yale Harrison's *Generals Die in Bed* (1930). Maguire may have read such early anti-war fiction as Henri Barbusse's novel *Le Feu* (available in English translation in 1917), and may have been familiar with the work of Siegfried Sassoon, Wilfred Owen, and other British war poets. But "Over the Top" most likely derives primarily from the author's impressions and experiences, rather than from his reading.

This generalization also applies to Maguire's most ambitious literary effort, the novel *O Canada!: A Tale of Canadian Workers' [sic] Life*, which began weekly serialization in the *Worker* of 19 February 1927. The novel develops what was to become a popular theme of proletarian fiction: the experience of the immigrant who comes to North America with high hopes, and encounters exploitation in underpaid and tedious or backbreaking jobs, interspersed with periods of unemployment. This kind of novel was not new in the 1920s: its prototype in twentieth-century literature was Upton Sinclair's fictionalized exposé of working conditions in the Chicago meat-packing industry, *The Jungle* (1906). *The Jungle* and other early muckraking novels did not at first inspire a substantial anti-capitalist literary tradition; not until after the stock market crash of 1929 did writers turn in great numbers to this kind of fiction. But as Ronald Liversedge observed in his *Recollections of the On to Ottawa Trek*, "the great economic depression of the thirties did not start on that memorable day in November, 1929" (3). For thousands of workers in North America in the early twentieth century, the problems of inadequate wages and unemployment were perennial facts of life. Canada's economy had been especially unstable since 1914. Eager to wrest quick profits from uncertain markets, and supported by government anti-labour policies, employers forced workers to compete for below-subsistence wages, refused to recognize unions, and denied their employees even the most basic measures of job security.

These are some of the prevalent impressions of Canadian society conveyed in Maguire's *O Canada!* The novel opens in the first decade of the century, in England, where George Hawtrey, youngest son of a Methodist parson, decides to immigrate to Canada. In Toronto, he finds employment as a junior clerk in a bank. Transferred to Winnipeg, he is speedily disillusioned by his boring, low-paying job, the economic domination of the country by the United States, the lack of culture in Canada, and Canadian antipathy to English immigrants. Transferred to a small town in Saskatchewan, he is at first fascinated by life on the western frontier, but from conversations with a homesteader and a rancher he learns of the terrible struggles of the settlers for economic survival. With the outbreak of the First World War, Hawtrey enlists and suffers the horrors of trench warfare, but manages to survive with a respectable service record. After the armistice Canada shows no particular favour to its veterans; in fact, the country is in a recession, and Hawtrey joins "the army of the unemployed," roaming across the country, forced to accept temporary and low-paid jobs. In Northern Ontario he finds seasonal work with a farmer, who bitterly describes the same sort of heartbreaking struggle that Hawtrey heard from the Saskatchewan farmer before the war. On a railway construction gang, Hawtrey encounters slave-driving bosses and exhausting physical labour; joining the harvester trek to the wheatfields, he discovers that there are too many workers and too few jobs. Along the way he encounters other victims of the capitalist system, including many disillusioned immigrants like himself, and a native Indian, ruined by alcohol and chronic unemployment.

As a fictional chronicle of the experiences of the immigrant and the veteran of the Great War, *O Canada!* can be usefully compared with two other Canadian novels that also appeared in 1927. Frederick Philip Grove's *A Search for America* is a chronicle of the disillusionment of the European newcomer who arrives with extravagant hopes of establishing himself in a bourgeois social environment, and in the unfamiliar and unstable North American economy rapidly falls to the level of migrant labourer and tramp. But Grove's novel, although critical of many aspects of North American capitalism, is far from being shaped by sympathy with an exploited working class. *A Search for America* is ultimately interested in the themes of self-discovery and the search for national identity, as Grove makes explicit in his conclusion, when he explains how his protagonist's "view of life" changes from a European "historical" view to an American "ethical" one (382). Grove's understanding of the American ethos is inspired, furthermore, not by Marxism or by any other political economic theory, but by the nineteenth- and early-twentieth-century transcendental idealism of Ralph Waldo Emerson and John Burroughs. Hubert Evans's *The New Front Line,* dealing with the post-war problems of a Canadian veteran, is much closer to Marxism in its criticism of modern capitalist political economy. Evans's protagonist, Hugh Henderson, is repelled by post-war Canadian urban society, which seems to be rigidly divided between "the people who made things and the people who sold them," and is based on the artificial creation of markets for surplus luxury goods. "Sometimes it seemed that the less useful work a person did the more money he made" (109-10). *The New Front Line,* like Douglas Durkin's *The Magpie,* contrasts the modern urban commercial ethic with a humanistic agrarian ideal. But the novel does not go on to advocate a militant revolutionary response. Evans's character, like Durkin's, escapes from the urban commercial world into the pastoral serenity of farming.

For Maguire, the farmer's life is merely another form of drudgery enforced by the capitalist economy. Surprisingly, however, *O Canada!* does not resolve toward Marxist solutions to the problems of the war veterans, itinerant workers, and farmers, even though the novel conforms in structure and theme to a pattern characteristic of the Marxist proletarian novel. As Barbara Foley has pointed out, the proletarian novel is often "redundant," not in a sense implying structural faults, but in the sense that patterns of repetition "enable a writer to convey the meaning [i.e., the intended political lesson] in an unambiguous way." In the typical proletarian novel, the protagonist is exposed repeatedly to experiences that contribute to his political education, and either does or does not achieve the desired level of political awareness, "for reasons that are made clear to the reader" (Foley 267-68). The main character of Maguire's novel, in spite of his numbingly redundant exposure to the injustices of the capitalist system, fails to achieve political awareness, for reasons that are by no means clear.

According to the formula established in Sinclair's *The Jungle* and to be developed in the fiction of the 1930s, Hawtrey's story might have climaxed with the main character finally resolving to work for reform or revolution, through a socialist or Communist organization. This sort of conclusion must surely have occurred to Maguire, who had experienced such a political awakening himself. With the weekly instalment of 16 July 1927, however, the serialization of *O Canada!* abruptly stopped, leaving the protagonist in one of a long succession of dead-end jobs, with no relief of his situation or change of his political consciousness in sight. In the 27 August issue of the *Worker*, the narrative just as suddenly resumed, to be brought to a conclusion a week later. This conclusion, incongruously, reverses the one that Grove uses in *A Search for America*. Grove's protagonist in the end chooses Canada over the failed dream of the US. In the final chapters of Maguire's novel, Hawtrey is persuaded by one of his fellow workers to migrate to the United States. "Supposing he went to the United States," the narrative ruminates, "would it be just another case of far off pastures looking green? Maybe, but it could not be any worse than the life he was living, and there was a possibility that fortune might again smile on him." As a believer in scientific socialism, Maguire could scarcely be unconscious of the connotations of such words as "possibility" and "fortune" in this inconclusive vision of his worker-hero's future. Far from offering solutions to the problems of the worker in a capitalist society, Maguire depicts only an escapist dream.

The conclusion of *O Canada!* is so abrupt, arbitrary, and mechanically introduced that it invites speculation about the possible influence of external circumstances. It may be that Maguire aborted the novel because of his health: when Oscar Ryan met him in Vancouver in 1928, he looked "frail and [seemed] to be ailing—his heart, I'm told" (*Soon To Be Born* 232). This might account for the month-long hiatus in the serialization, followed by a hastily written conclusion. It is also worth noting that by the late summer of 1927 the literary initiative introduced in the *Worker* the previous year had disappeared and the paper was no longer running any creative writing apart from Maguire's novel. It may be that the editor Maurice Spector insisted that Maguire bring his serial to an early end, to make room for hard political news and editorial commentary. By 1927 the source material for news stories and editorials included internecine Party conflict. In the USSR the death of Lenin in January 1924 intensified the ideological struggle between Leon Trotsky and a faction increasingly dominated by Joseph Stalin. As a foreign observer of the thirteenth conference of the Communist Party of the Soviet Union in Moscow in early 1924, Spector decided that the Stalin faction represented an aberration that could not really threaten the Marxist-Leninist orthodoxy of Trotsky's position. By the summer of 1927, however, the Stalinists had control of the Comintern, and at the fifth congress of the Comintern held in June, one of the Canadian representatives was Tim Buck. Thereafter, the clash between the Trotskyist Spector and the Stalinist Buck rapidly came to a head; by November 1928, Spector had been expelled from the Party (See Angus, chapter 10).

So *O Canada!* may have been a casualty of the priorities established by the Party and its newspaper at a time of bureaucratic and political turmoil. There is no evidence, however, that Maguire's novel was cancelled because he was directly involved in the Stalinist-Trotskyist conflict. In fact, the three noteworthy literary contributors to the *Worker*, Maguire, Ryan, and Wallace, all silently moved with the prevailing Stalinist tide and remained with the Party for years. Although Maguire seems to have written no more fiction, he was contributing political commentary to the Party newspaper in Vancouver, the *People's Advocate*, as late as 1938. Of course, the conclusion of *O Canada!* need not be related to external circumstances; it can be read as deliberately ironic, with the protagonist George Hawtrey persisting blindly in his pursuit of the elusive American dream. Much of the Communist-inspired fiction published in the 1920s tended to be heavily ironic, even pessimistic, as Maguire's "Over the Top" and other short stories in the *Worker* and *Young Worker* indicate. A full-blown fiction intended mainly to expound principles of Marxist-Leninist theory would not be developed until the 1930s, although writers like Maguire were working in directions that anticipate the socialist realism of the next decade. Even if the ending is regarded as weak or inappropriate, Maguire's novel is still, like his anti-war short story, an innovative venture into the fiction of social criticism.

The third of Maguire's only published works, a one-act play entitled *Unemployment* (1928), is equally innovative. Set in "the kitchen of a poverty stricken working-class home" (Wright and Endres 5), the play relentlessly chronicles the emotional tensions of an unemployed labourer, his wife, and their seventeen-year-old daughter. Almost the entire dialogue of the play consists of the angry outbursts against each other with which these people try to relieve their fear and resentment as they face hunger and the disintegration of the family. Escapist dreams such as the one that concludes *O Canada!* do not relieve the sordid, claustrophobic atmosphere. At the end of the play the capitalist economic system that has lured them into this trap proceeds on its exploitative course when the finance company repossesses most of their shabby furniture. Significantly, however, there is no mention of the threat of eviction. Maguire has a concluding image more forceful and desolate than the spectacle of homelessness to express the alienation of the characters. Although the daughter flees the tenement in desperation, her parting words implying that she will turn to prostitution to survive, the husband and wife remain in the barren rooms, raging against their misery and against each other, like prisoners in a cell.

In 1928 such naturalistic dialogue and action and expressionistic use of setting were still rare in the English-language theatre. In the United States, Eugene O'Neill and the Provincetown Players had been experimenting in this direction since before the First World War, but in English Canada the professional theatre was dominated by touring light entertainment. The closest Canadian parallel to *Unemployment* was probably Merrill Denison's realistic drama of rural poverty, *Marsh Hay*, published in *The Unheroic North: Four Canadian Plays* (1923), but not produced until fifty years later. Maguire may well have read *The Unheroic North*; superficial similarities between his play and *Marsh Hay* include claustrophobic interior settings, bitter and pointless bickering among family members, and the main characters' elusive search for economic survival. Denison's play takes place on a farm as opposed to Maguire's urban setting, but the rural scenes in *O Canada!* indicate that Maguire would have agreed with Denison's ironic exposé of the kind of pastoral ideal envisaged in the novels of Durkin and Evans. There is no record that Maguire's play was ever produced, but the Party found it important enough to give it prominent circulation in its theoretical journal, the *Canadian Labor Monthly*. The *Monthly* was the outlet for official policy statements, commentaries on Marxist-Leninist theory, and interpretation of current political developments. Established 1928 and edited by the ubiquitous Maurice Spector until his expulsion from the Party later that year, the *Monthly* did not publish literary work, but made a unique exception for Maguire's play. The suggestion that *Unemployment* should be considered a valuable theoretical statement was perhaps the most significant official Party acknowledgement to date of the importance of literary art to the revolutionary cause.

• • • • •

Marxist-inspired Canadian literary activity was not restricted in the 1920s to members of the Communist Party. The term "fellow traveller" has so often been misused by the opponents of Communism, especially in the US, that it is useful to recall that one of its earliest applications was by Leon Trotsky in his *Pravda* articles published as *Literature and Revolution*. In Trotsky's meaning, the term is not a general designation for Communist sympathizers, but a specific label for creative writers who, though supporters of the revolution, were not members of the Party. Applied to Canada in the 1920s, the term might thus be appropriate to some of the members of the *Rebel/Canadian Forum* circle. It is also appropriate to at least three other writers who emerged at this time in different parts of Canada. Although Dawn Fraser, A.M. Stephen, and Charles Yale Harrison refrained from joining the Communist Party, all three were socialists inspired by Marxism and/or the Russian revolution. All three also saw military service in the First World War, which especially influenced their hostility toward capitalism and their determination to work for social change.

Oswald Vincent ("Dawn") Fraser (1888-1968), like Joe Wallace, was a poetic chronicler of the Cape Breton labour disputes of the 1920s. Lacking Wallace's education and more sophisticated grasp of poetic form, Fraser wrote folk ballads and popular verse in the songster tradition of Phillips Thompson. Born in Cumberland County, Nova Scotia, Fraser spent his early life in that area and in Cape Breton and New England. Enlisting in the Canadian army in the First World War, he was sent to Siberia in 1918 with the allied expeditionary force supporting the White Russian government against the Bolsheviks. Settling in Glace Bay on Cape Breton after the war, Fraser self-published his first book, *Songs of Siberia* (1919?), a collection of poems in the manner of Rudyard Kipling and Robert Service, depicting the tedium and meaninglessness of army life and expressing his pacifism. Thereafter his prodigious output appeared regularly in local newspapers, especially the *Maritime Labor Herald* of Glace Bay, and in several self-published volumes, most notably the 1926 *Echoes from Labor's War* (see Frank and MacGillivray x-xx).

Fraser's poetic defense of the coal miners and their union leaders in their struggles against the British Empire Steel Corporation relies on straightforward, unambiguous statement, occasionally tinged with irony and sarcasm, but uncomplicated by ambiguity of tone or complexity of idea. Described in this way, Fraser's writing scarcely seems to qualify as poetry at all; it might as well be called commentary or description that happens to be couched in rhythm and rhyme. But like all good folk art, Fraser's work has the potential strength of direct contact with human emotion: many of his lines are as difficult to ignore or to forget as the face-to-face speech of an angry person. Recounting the true story of a Cape Breton worker who starved to death when the mines closed down, he turns the sentimental ballad-like beginning of his story into an accusation:

> His name was Eddie Crimmins
> And he came from Port aux Basques,
> Besides a chance to live and work
> He had nothing much to ask;
> No, not a dream he ever had
> That he might work and save—
> Was quite content to live and die
> And be a working slave.
> And yet, he starved, he starved, I tell you,
> Back in nineteen twenty-four,
> And before he died he suffered
> As many have before.
> When the mines closed down that winter
> He had nothing left to eat,
> And he starved, he starved, I tell you,
> On your dirty, damned street. (Fraser, *Echoes* 3)

Fraser has little time or patience for explanation, analysis, theory, or even argument. He does not seek a sociological or political answer to the question of how and why a worker could starve to death in urban Canada in 1924; nor does he even direct the blame more specifically than to "you," which seems to implicate all readers, until the pronoun is identified in the closing lines of the poem with an impersonal, monolithic "Capital." This is not poetry that tries to convey either argument or sentiment beyond its own unanswerable, all-consuming anger.

In "The Case of Jim McLachlan," a long poem about the Communist union leader imprisoned for sedition, Fraser makes more of an attempt at defending an ideological position. But the defense is expressed as a mock ballad ("Listen, my children and you shall know") deliberately couched in simplified language as if capitalist injustice needs to be spelled out to the naive understanding of children living in a post-revolutionary world. "The Hair-Breadth Escape of Red Malcolm Bruce" is a sarcastic comment on a much-publicized incident in 1923 when a warrant was issued in Cape Breton for a Communist Party leader from Toronto, and the local police were unable to find him, even though "this man so hunted down/Was hanging 'round about the town/From Thursday night 'til some time Monday" (Fraser 34). Fraser's verse is strengthened not only by the emphasis on narrative, but also by the vivid impression that his narratives are true: Fraser convinces the reader that people starve on the streets of Cape Breton mining towns, and that the policemen and judges who persecute Communists and union leaders are inept clowns. His poetry might thus be regarded as a remarkable combination of polemical speech, primitive folk art and populist journalism. As such, it could be dismissed as inadequate to the intellectual demands of the relatively complex political-economic ideology it is supposedly intended to convey. But this objection is cancelled by the fact that Fraser never did become a doctrinaire Marxist Communist: leaving the ideologies and partisan politics to others, he specializes in asserting what appear to him to be the simple and observable truths of social justice.

In many ways, A.M. Stephen (1882-1942) is as remote from Fraser in his attitude to poetic form and theme as he was in terms of geography. Born in Bruce County, Ontario, Alexander Maitland Stephen lived most of his adult life in British Columbia. Sent as a young man to article in his uncle's law firm in Victoria, BC, Stephen restlessly shifted to schoolteaching, followed by stints of prospecting and ranch labour. Breaking with his family, he went to Chicago, where he studied architecture and engineering, then married before settling in Calgary in 1914. Several months after war broke out he went to England for further architectural study, and joined the Royal Fusiliers of the British army. Severely wounded in his right arm in May 1916, he was invalided back to Canada, returning briefly to Calgary before moving to Vancouver (biographical details from the Stephen Papers, UBC).

After the war Stephen turned to the writing of poetry, inspired in part by his varied travel and experience, but more profoundly by his eclectic reading. The most important influences on him at this time were texts of the theosophical movement, the essays of Ralph Waldo Emerson, and the poetry of Walt Whitman and Bliss Carman. In an article entitled "The Great War and After" in the *Western Women's Weekly* of September 1919, Stephen reveals his current intellectual perspective. Expounding an Emersonian view of history governed by the law of compensation, he attributes much of the world's trouble to the "sex problem"—meaning both the subjugation of women and the suppression of sexual instincts. Expressing his faith in a "new age" that will bring "a higher and nobler ideal of life," Stephen also sees hope for "a new movement towards unity among nations," based especially on the "working class movement." "Everywhere," Stephen concludes, "we see a sharp demarcation between the hosts of Labour and Capital." But "the solution of the labour problem…will not be brought about by the substitution of Socialism….There must be a spiritual basis to the new civilization or it is doomed to as complete failure as the one now passing" (clipping, Stephen Papers). By the late 1920s, however, Stephen had developed more confidence in the possibilities of socialism, and although he rejected the Stalinist policies of the Communist Party, he began to study Marxist theory. His first two books, *The Rosary of Pan* (1923), and *The Land of Singing Waters* (1927), reflected little of his ultimate political position: still much influenced by Whitman and Carman, he concentrated on nature lyrics that emphasize musical quality and express a gentle mysticism. Although his early poetry was extremely well received, he may have been discouraged by the small financial return, so he tried his hand at a novel, *The Kingdom of the Sun* (1927), a historical romance about the voyages of Sir Francis Drake, which mingles swashbuckling adventure with theosophist ideas. Encouraged by the success of this work, he produced a second novel in 1929. *The Gleaming Archway* is his first literary exploitation of the capital-labour conflict. Set in

Vancouver and regions north of the city around the time of "Bloody Sunday" in Czarist Russia in 1905, the novel explores through a rather melodramatic plot various kinds of socialist, anti-socialist, and revolutionary attitudes and actions. As the allusion to Tennyson's "Ulysses" in Stephen's title suggests, the novel dramatizes the infinite possibilities of experience that open out to the protagonist, Craig Maitland. Unlike Tennyson's aging Ulysses, Maitland is on the threshold of adult life, although he has already become disillusioned with the frenetic pace of modern urban society.

Travelling northward in search of respite, Maitland discovers among backwoods settlers and loggers the representatives of a remarkable spectrum of political ideology, including a revolutionary socialist, a Russian anti-Czarist refugee, a Marxist newspaper editor, and an anti-socialist British remittance man. Maitland regards himself a moderate socialist who believes "in evolution but not in revolution" (43). The novel expresses sympathy with the Russian victims of "Bloody Sunday," but Stephen associates direct revolutionary action with animalistic primitivism. The principal advocate of revolution in the novel, significantly named "Powers," is a brutish and duplicitous man who seems to Maitland "in essence, the terrific strength of stubborn earth, dark and passionate, which had always opposed the upward flight of the spirit" (191). In contrast to Powers is a moderate reformer who incorporates both the intellectualism of William Morris's socialism and a compassionate emotional commitment to the cause of working people. In the novel's climax, these two kinds of impulse clash, when a strike provoked by the Industrial Workers of the World (IWW) reveals to Maitland both the impressive force of mass action and the dangers of revolution. In the end, the novel suggests that the problems of modern society will only be resolved in the reconciliation of these two tendencies. But Stephen's main character seems to reject both in favour of more individualistic alternatives. With startling incongruity he seems to turn away entirely from the real world of action toward the realm of fantasy and vision, as for a time he seriously considers joining an expedition in search of the lost continent Atlantis. Finally, however, he retreats into a romantic resolution, and the novel ends with his prospective marriage.

*The Gleaming Archway* was perhaps too melodramatic in its dramatizations and too subtle in its exposition of ideas to please either the critics or the reading public, although it received polite reviews. William Arthur Deacon in the Toronto *Globe* liked Stephen's romantic plot, but refused to believe that anyone could make a successful novel out of socialist ideology; Lionel Stevenson in the *Canadian Bookman* recognized *The Gleaming Archway* as probably the first Canadian novel to focus on "the social problems of current civilization" (scrapbook clippings, Stephen Papers). The main problem with it is that Stephen in 1929 was too uncertain about such problems. The novel deals far too much with unclearly stated and unresolved dialectics, and in the end the problems are simply abandoned in favour of a conventional romantic dénouement.

A far more effective anti-capitalist novel is *Generals Die in Bed* (1930), by Charles Yale Harrison (1898-1954). Born in Philadelphia, Harrison lived most of his life in the United States, and is a Canadian by a certain extension of the term. A school dropout and would-be journalist, Harrison came north in 1914 to work for the *Montreal Star*. On the outbreak of war he joined the Royal Montreal Regiment, and served in France until he was severely wounded in the Battle of Amiens in August 1918. Invalided back to Canada, he worked in Montreal briefly, but soon returned to the US, where he worked as a journalist and publicist until 1926, when he joined the staff of the left-wing literary magazine, the *New Masses*. Harrison never joined either the Canadian or American Communist parties, but he was one of the founding members of the John Reed Club, established in 1929 by the *New Masses* and designed to enlist writers to the Communist cause by giving them opportunities to associate with like-minded creative people and to pursue their literary interests. Expelled from the Club in 1933 for expressing pro-Trotsky sentiments, Harrison went on to write proletarian novels in the 1930s, but made no further significant use of his Canadian army experience. Excerpts from *Generals Die in Bed* appeared in the *New Masses* in 1929, and the novel was published in England in 1930, followed quickly by an American edition, then by several European translations (Nielsen, n. pag.).

*Generals Die in Bed*, like Maguire's *O Canada!*, is a bleakly ironic and repetitive demonstration of how the proletariat is oppressed by the powers in control of the capitalist system. Unlike Maguire's work, it is primarily a novel of action rather than exposition, written in spare understated language modeled on the stylistics that Sherwood Anderson and Ernest Hemingway were developing in the 1920s. But the author subtly weaves his political ideas into the fabric of his narrative. The opening chapter makes clear that the young working-class Canadians who enlist at the outbreak of war are incited by their own innocent bravado and the enthusiasm of male camaraderie, by an artificially created militarism of marching bands and fireworks displays, and—as other critics of the war, including Margaret Fairley, were to suggest—by the provocations of women. In the opening sentence, Harrison also emphasizes the simple capitalistic motive of financial greed. Beginning with a scene of overexcited, newly enlisted soldiers in their barracks, he announces that "it is after midnight on payday" (3). Having made the initial act of surrender to the war machine, the soldiers become passive objects, easily manipulated. "We are taken from the trenches" (36); an officer orders "that we must shave every day" (37); "they take everything from us" (49). Soldiers, the unnamed young narrator realizes, are conditioned to face death, to accept the irrationalities of war, to suppress their instincts and behave according to the war's artificial sense of order. "It would be better, it seems, to dash into No Man's Land and chance death....But we are disciplined....We must carry on, carry on" (55-56). This commitment to automatic behaviour is virtually independent of the soldiers' knowledge. They know, or soon learn, that underlying the war are the cynical motives and manipulations of capitalism. While billeted in the town of Béthune, the narrator learns from a Frenchman that the area is free from artillery damage because the local mines are owned by German corporations. The soldiers, while out of the line on rest, speculate among themselves about the financial side of the war: "I'll bet somebody is making a profit on those shells whether they are fired at the Germans or whether they just blow up" (216). In spite of these intimations about the economic significance of the war, the soldiers continue to do their duty, killing enemy soldiers and trying to avoid death themselves. As Harrison demonstrates in an effectively dramatized episode based on a real incident, the Canadians come closest to revolutionary action in the spring of 1918, in the days before the bloody battle of Amiens, when a battalion of weary and hungry soldiers riot in the evacuated town of Arras. But the looting and drunkenness are merely self-indulgent and ideologically empty gestures of anger and frustration, not genuine acts of rebellion. After blowing off steam, the soldiers readily submit to regimental discipline, and march off to fight and die.

Harrison's novel concludes, like Durkin's *The Magpie*, Maguire's *O Canada!*, and Stephen's *The Gleaming Archway*, with a withdrawal from the immense political and economic questions of the struggle against capitalism. Wounded in the Battle of Amiens, the narrator is invalided out of the war, relieved to be alive and finished with it, although with the irrationalities and contradictions of his experience still unresolved. On the hospital train an encounter with an arrogant captured German officer dilutes his discovery in the trenches of the humanity of his supposed enemies; he also hears rumours that his own army has been guilty of atrocities. In the final sentence he is passive, unthinking, now more than ever a mere object, to be transported home by hospital ship: "I am carried up the gangplank" (269).

Like other anti-capitalist fiction of the 1920s, Harrison's novel avoids any suggestion of solutions to the problems it explores. The cynicism and intellectual limitations of the characters make the possibility of solutions all the more remote. Much of the Marxist-inspired Canadian literary activity in the 1920s emphasizes the virtually irremediable evil of capitalist society, and the bleak prospects for a successful revolutionary struggle. Only the poets are inclined to be more optimistic: Joe Wallace's work usually pays lyrical tribute to the revolutionary strength of the masses and their leaders, and Dawn Fraser alternates his angry attacks on capitalism with expressions of admiration for the heroes of labour conflict.

# 4

# The 1930s

## Socialist and Other Realisms

I n the summer of 1931 a small group of writers and graphic artists in Toronto formed the Progressive Arts Club. Not officially sponsored by the CPC and not restricted to Party members, the PAC attracted a variety of artists and would-be artists, mostly younger members of the Party and people recently provoked by the Depression to an interest in left-wing politics. Founding members and early supporters included Oscar Ryan; actress Toby Gordon; cartoonist and painter Avrom Yanovsky; journalist Edward Cecil-Smith (later commander of the Mackenzie-Papineau Battalion in Spain); and several other would-be poets, playwrights, fiction writers, and graphic artists, including a recent graduate from the University of Toronto, Dorothy Livesay. One year after its formation the PAC began publishing a culture periodical entitled, in imitation of the most prominent US left-wing publication, *Masses*. Each issue consisting of ten or twelve unnumbered pages, the magazine was intended as a monthly, but ultimately appeared only about six times a year. The derivative title, sparse contents, and homemade appearance, however, were offset by the contributors' enthusiasm for experiment and controversy. The unsigned editorial entitled "Our Credentials" in the first (April 1932) issue, written according to his own later claim by Oscar Ryan (T.G. Ryan 27), attempted to set forth the periodical's aesthetic and political commitments. Beginning with an account of the origins of the PAC and *Masses*, Ryan proclaims the club's intention "to provide the basis for the development of a militant working class art and literature" in opposition to the work of complacent bourgeois artists "with their puerile ignorance of and contempt for social questions." As in his poetry in the *Worker*, Ryan takes a low-brow position against elitist art that tries to isolate itself from politics, emphasizing the PAC as "a movement of workers" that "addresses itself to the workers, to the poor farmers, to the jobless man in the bread-line." Art, Ryan declares categorically, "is propaganda, or more precisely, a vehicle of propaganda....Art is the product of the current (and previous) social and economic conditions."

The emergence of *Masses* with its militant proclamation of a new propagandistic art was in part traceable to recent developments in the Soviet Union. After the collapse of capitalist financial markets in 1929, Russian political and cultural leaders increased their attempts to influence thought and action outside their country. In his speech to the Sixteenth Congress of the Communist Party of the Soviet Union in June 1930, Josef Stalin gloated that the economic crisis in the West was a sign of the approaching end of capitalism. Overproduction and consequent unemployment were regular features of capitalist economies, but the vast scale of the current depression suggested that a final collapse was at hand. In accordance with the principles of Marxism-Leninism, it was incumbent upon world Communism to incite workers in capitalist countries to actions that would hasten the collapse and the establishment of the proletarian dictatorship (Stalin 12:242 ff.). This process was to include culture workers. The International Bureau of Revolutionary Literature in Moscow invited the Communist parties in various countries to send delegates to a conference of writers at Kharkov in Ukraine set for 6-15 November 1930. At Kharkov, the International Union of Revolutionary Writers (IURW) was founded; a periodical, *Literature of World Revolution* (retitled in 1932 *International Literature*) was established in editions of several languages for the dissemination of cultural news and Marxist-Leninist critical theory; delegates were exhorted to urge colleagues in their home countries on to greater activity in the cause of socialism; and dialectical materialism was elevated to the status of an artistic credo. National groups responded enthusiastically to the initiatives of Kharkov. As the subsequent debates in various literary journals indicated, the problems of applying dialectical materialism to literary art elicited the involvement of Party members and fellow travellers in Europe, North America, and elsewhere.

But writers wanted further clarification of what seemed a vague bureaucratic directive rather than a literary manifesto. Clarification was soon forthcoming, at a 1932 Conference of the Organizational Committee of the All-Russian Union of Soviet Writers. The committee secretary, V.I. Kirpotin, in a report published the following year in *International Literature,* proclaimed the new literary credo of "socialist realism." "By socialist realism," declared Kirpotin,

> We mean the reflection in art of the external world...in all its essential circumstances and with the aid of essential and typical characterization. We mean the faithful description of life in all its aspects, with the victorious principle of the forces of the socialist revolution....We set socialist realism against idealism, subjectivism, the literature of illusion in any form whatever, as an untrue and distorted reflection of reality. (qtd. in Murphy 100)

The "literature of illusion" was attacked by socialist realist theorists under many names, including "bourgeois realism," "social realism," "critical realism," and "naturalism." These labels usually denoted representational art forms that had historical value as sources for basic realist techniques but which were inadequate to the new age because they reflected bourgeois capitalist assumptions, or they consisted of exclusively negative social criticism and failed to extol the "victorious principle of the forces of the socialist revolution."

At first the Kharkov conference provoked little reaction in Canada. Although the CPC regularly sent delegations to the political congresses of the Comintern and the CPSU, it sent no one to Kharkov, nor did the *Worker* report on the meetings there. In spite of urging from Moscow, the Canadian party remained lethargic in the matter of promoting culture among its members. Writers within the Canadian party had nothing like the official recognition and influence enjoyed by members of Party-affiliated organizations in the United States, such as the League of American Writers (est. 1935). This situation was no doubt a reflection of the cultural indifference of the majority of CPC members as well as Party leaders. Also, the CPC in 1930 was still dealing with the international reverberations of the Stalin-Trotsky conflict in the USSR and with the aftermath of power struggles within its own leadership circles in Canada. The RCMP and municipal police forces continued to put pressure on Communist groups, banning their meetings and arresting their speakers and leaders. Membership in the Canadian party, far from growing with the advent of the Depression, declined between 1928 and 1931 (Avakumovic 65), a problem that left little time for official promotion of such frills as creative writing. Both the *Worker* and the *Young Worker* continued to publish a few poems and short stories, many of them reprints from foreign sources. In 1930 the two Party newspapers were supplemented by the *Canadian Labor Defender*, a monthly periodical published by the Canadian Labor Defense League, an organization established to deal with the legal and financial problems of the growing number of Party members indicted under Section 98 of the Criminal Code. The *Defender* occasionally published poems by Joe Wallace and others, and a few short stories.

The 1931 emergence of *Masses*, a magazine devoted almost exclusively to creative writing and aesthetic criticism and theory, was the most encouraging sign of the growing commitment to imaginative activity among CPC members and sympathizers. Although the Canadians still lacked detailed familiarity with the cultural debates taking place in the Soviet Union, the *Masses* editorials and articles indicated their eagerness to catch up with the subject, and especially to apply the debates on the social and political functions of literature to their own national conditions. The Canadian version of these debates began with a reply to Ryan's proclamation that all art is propaganda. The article "In Defense of Pure Art" under the signature "T. Richardson" in the fourth (July/August 1932) issue of *Masses*, agrees with Ryan that art can serve the cause of socialism by exposing "the decay and rot of official culture." But Richardson is not pre-pared to accept Ryan's limitations on artistic method. Challenging the contention that all art is propaganda, Richardson points out that the recent proclamation of socialist realism in the USSR elicited objec-tions from some Russian writers who insisted on preserving their freedom to use any artistic means to achieve a diversity of aesthetic and political ends. The effectiveness of the artist's use of technique, not the subject matter of the work, is the main factor governing the value of a work of art. "Propaganda is not art"; a literary work's social message, if it happens to have one, does not create its artistic merit. It is true, on the other hand, that "art can be propaganda," although the propaganda function is not obligatory. The freedom of the artist takes precedence over every other consideration. "The artist is the friend of socialism," says Richardson, "but he must be free to create."

In the same issue of *Masses*, E. Cecil-Smith replied to Richardson with an article entitled "What Is Pure Art?" There can be no art inde-pendent of society, Cecil-Smith insists. Subject matter, not technique, is the essence of art, and the subject matter of art is always relevant to the well-being of people in society. Artists who claim to be creating "pure" art divorced from social questions are merely expressing the ideology of the capitalist ruling class which seeks to keep the masses compliant. Artists who alternatively claim to be merely expressing their own inner selves are anarchists. With this editorial pronounce-ment Cecil-Smith appeared to conclude the debate. Almost two years later, however, in "Propaganda and Art"(January 1934), he revived the argument, in terms suggesting that in the meantime he had been studying the theoretical articles in *International Literature* and other source material coming out of the Soviet Union. Commenting on a recent debate on propaganda and art in the University of Toronto stu-dent newspaper, the *Varsity*, he invokes N. Bukharin's approval of art that deals with the feelings of humans considered as social beings. He also cites V. Lunacharsky's denunciation of a "critical realism" or "naturalism" that claims to provide an honest reflection of society, but reveals the distortions of a bourgeois perspective. The critical realist, says Lunacharsky, may believe that bourgeois society is degen-erate, but implicitly represents this degeneracy as an inevitable state of things that art can reflect but not influence. In effect, such realism approves bourgeois society as the highest form to which history can aspire, and rejects the more optimistic socialist assumption that human beings can improve the world. Like Marx himself, who proclaimed that "philosophers have so far only interpreted the world in various ways; the point, however, is to *change* it," socialist realists commit themselves to a dynamic view of history. Unlike the bourgeois realist, who sees society as a stasis, the socialist realist artist recognizes the contradictions that are constantly disturbing the equilibrium of society, and recognizes the forces that will reestablish this equilibrium on a new and higher basis.

Cecil-Smith's argument is, on the whole, a moderate interpretation of the socialist realist position. In the course of developing this argument, however, he became embroiled in further ambiguities that prompted new opposition. Remembering the earlier controversy with Richardson, Cecil-Smith insists that the socialist realist's critique of society is not "propaganda," but "simply the telling of the whole truth." The "whole truth," however, is not to be limited too rigidly to the Marxist-Leninist ideological position. Cecil-Smith chastises a *Young Worker* columnist for writing that "proletarian art...must be judged entirely on the basis of whether or not it expresses the program and fighting policy of the class struggle." This, says Cecil-Smith, is a "leftist" position, which detaches proletarian art from other aesthetic traditions, reduces it to the narrowly defined subject of political conflict, and ignores questions of technique. Proletarian art, like the bourgeois art it is destined to replace, consists of both subject and form. "If we believe that we are the ones who must carry on the development of art from the point where the bourgeoisie have left off, we must at least see to it that we have the technical ability to accomplish our tasks."

The next issue (March/April 1934) of *Masses* carried a response to Cecil-Smith from a recent recruit to the Party. Twenty-three-year-old Stanley Bréhaut Ryerson (1911-98) was the sort of young intellectual that the Party wanted but had trouble recruiting and keeping. Like Maurice Spector, he was a brilliant graduate of the University of Toronto. In contrast to Spector's working-class immigrant background, however, Ryerson's origins were solidly Canadian bourgeois. Son of a professor of medicine and great-grandson of the Methodist preacher and educator Egerton Ryerson, he was descended on his mother's side from a seventeenth-century settler of New France. While majoring in modern languages and literatures at Toronto, he spent the academic year 1931-32 on exchange at the Sorbonne, where from his observations in Paris and travels in Spain he learned of radical political responses to working-class poverty and capitalist tyranny. On his return to Toronto he joined the Young Communist League and began writing for *Masses* (Kealey, "Stanley Bréhaut Ryerson").

In "Out of the Frying Pan..." Ryerson insists that in denigrating the supremacy of subject matter Cecil-Smith is reconstituting proletarian art as merely one stage on a continuum that includes both proletarian and bourgeois art. But proletarian art is not simply a preferable alternative to bourgeois art. It is the uniquely valid art form that is to replace all others, and it is to achieve this by establishing that art is essentially an expression of the class struggle. "Proletarian art and poetry must be judged from a proletarian standpoint—i.e., a Marxist one; they must be judged entirely as an expression—from the technical and political viewpoints—of the proletarian class struggle for the socialist revolution." Furthermore, says Ryerson, in denying that proletarian art is "propaganda," Cecil-Smith has accepted the bourgeois definition of propaganda, i.e., "the spreading of subversive, untrue ideas." Artists of the established classes in capitalist society either unconsciously ignore class as an aesthetic factor, or arrogantly assume that the values of their own class represent universal and objective truth. "The bourgeoisie, in its fight for its existence, must inevitably try to pass as 'universally human' and 'objectively true' all that represents its reactionary class interests; and hence, furiously repudiates the suggestion that it is merely 'propaganda' that it is spreading."

In his reply, Cecil-Smith grants Ryerson's objection to his definition of propaganda, but persists in his own objection to Ryerson's reductive argument that proletarian art must deal only with the class struggle. Cecil-Smith ends by calling for more discussion of the questions raised. There was to be no more such discussion in *Masses*, for the periodical folded with the March/April 1934 issue. But throughout its three-year life the search for appropriate literary expression was being carried out on another level, in the creative contributions published in the magazine. In its literary application, the term "socialist realism," like "realism" in general, usually referred to fiction, and in the Canadian Communist literary community "fiction" usually meant short stories rather than novels. Even in Canadian society at large, especially during the Depression, the small national market seldom made the publication of novels profitable, except in the case of formula fiction of adventure or sentiment. Canadian Communist writers, shunned by commercial publishers and limited to a small readership, were especially at a disadvantage. Discouraged from writing novels, they turned to short stories, which they could at least place in Party publications. This genre, thus emphasized by default, turned out to be especially adaptable to the aims of socialist realism. A short story is usually better suited to political didacticism than a novel for at least one obvious reason. A novel with a narrow theme or ideological focus, as Maguire's *O Canada!* demonstrates, is liable to lapse into repetition, as the author merely makes the same basic point by means of a series of parallel characters or narrative situations. This repetition can have value as a means of emphasis and verisimilitude, but it almost inevitably courts reader tedium. The short story, on the other hand, can limit details of plot and characterization to emphasize the social message, making up in clarity and emphasis what it loses in subtlety.

The short story also adapted well to politically radical literary purposes because the novel tended to retain a historical identification with bourgeois individualism. The novel's association with individual character development certainly implies a conflict with the collective purposes of Communism. The short story is much less bound to the idea of extensive character revelation and more easily exploits the climactic incident, the surprise revelation, or the concluding moral. But the short stories published in *Masses* reveal as much uncertainty and disagreement among Communist creative writers as among the critics and theorizers about what socialist realism should achieve and how it should achieve its ends. Lunacharsky's insistence that the new literature of the proletariat should deal with the "victorious principle of the forces of the socialist revolution" proved difficult to reconcile with the tendency to associate literary realism with the sordid and oppressive aspects of human experience. According to the tenets of socialist realism, to write only about the suffering of poverty-stricken workers provided an incomplete view of reality; yet even converts to

Marxist-Leninist historical optimism found it hard to break away from dominant realist literary models.

The first short story in *Masses*, published in the second (June 1932) issue, illustrates the difficulties. Written by "M. Granite"–possibly a pseudonym for Oscar Ryan, who also wrote as "Martin Stone"–"Fellow Workers" describes a demonstration of the unemployed, and focuses on one demonstrator, who is arrested, beaten, and at the end of the story, thrown in jail. The author's basic method is documentary—much of the narrative reads almost like a news story—with impressionistic glimpses of the appearance and feelings of the participants. In its narrow and literal focus on the class struggle, the story certainly satisfies Stanley Ryerson's leftist definition of proletarian art. In fact, the story comes close in conception and narrative method to a theory of fiction advocated in Russia by the "Left Front of Art" (LEF), in opposition to the socialist realism of the IURW. According to the LEF formulation, creative literature was to be "totally rational and concentrate on facts. The writer was to be seen as an artisan" (Murphy 32). At the extremity of this position, fiction was to be virtually indistinguishable from reportage, avoiding explicit commentary and allowing the unadorned facts to speak for themselves.

But few Canadian writers were prepared to go as far as the LEF position. Most preferred the prevailing tendency within both bourgeois and socialist realism to use literary technique to express or imply a moral. Most of the *Masses* short-story writers, however, remained dubious of the current Russian socialist realist idea that the moral should somehow relate to the ultimate victory of the socialist revolution. A. Poole's story "Fish" (*Masses* July/August 1932) tells of how a young man imprisoned under the capitalist system evolves from a naive new arrival to an embittered convict. Poole ventures somewhat further towards a socialist message than the author of "Fellow Workers" does, when he explains that his title refers both to the idea of innocence ("fresh fish") and to victimization, and suggests possible moral connotations by means of two rhetorical questions: "Are these men fish because they got caught in a vain attempt to become rich? Or are these the fish, the ones outside who toil and slave and die without knowing they have been fish since their birth?" But the message here is entirely negative, emphasizing only the illusions of young workers under capitalism, and making no suggestions about how to escape these illusions. The title of George Winslade's "Rainbow Chasing" (July/August 1932), similarly emphasizes the illusions experienced under capitalism. An unemployed merchant seaman signs on a freighter sailing from British Columbia to California, where he is discharged because of a dock strike and soon finds himself in much the same circumstances as he was at the beginning of the story. A similar circularity emerges in Robert Hall's "Breadline" (December 1932), featuring an unemployed man waiting in a breadline who is caught trying to steal extra bread for his wife and children. The magistrate arbitrarily gives him a harsh sentence merely to balance the lenient penalties he has handed out earlier in the day. Even more pointedly than the sailor in "Rainbow Chasing," the young man in Hall's story ends where he began, for at the conclusion he has served his sentence and is back waiting in the breadline.

Images of circularity and entrapment pervade the stories in *Masses*, as they pervade most of the fiction dealing with the problems of the Depression. "Freedom of Contract" (March/April 1933) by Frank Love (writing as "H. Francis") uses an ironic title to emphasize the deterministic universe to which the Depression unemployed have been consigned. A young man is sent to a "pogey house," 1930s Canadian slang for an unemployed workers' shelter. The narrator offers a tentative comment on the significance of this situation: "Ollie had thought that it was work he wanted, but now he had discovered that what he really wanted was the right to participate in useful production for himself and his family." But the worker's desires are defeated by a combination of fortuitous and determined circumstances: he gets into a fight with a spy for the Relief administrators, and is sentenced to thirty days in jail. Faced with the insuperable weight of such circumstances, the worker can only take refuge in bravado: "'Aw what the hell do I care,' he said truculently. 'They got lights on in jail, anyway.'"

Other stories in *Masses* likewise emphasize images of entrapment and futility, but offer more explicit critiques of the capitalist social system or more explicit appeals for class unity. In Dan Faro's "Colonist Freight" (November 1932), a trainload of recent immigrants is being carried west, the people jammed into overloaded passenger cars and provided with rotten food. Instead of directing their resentment against the system that debases them, however, they vent their frustration in ethnic rivalries among themselves. Although the implication is only vaguely related to the immediate situation, the story implies the need for unity in the class struggle. In Robert Hall's "King and Country" (September 1933), the narrator makes explicit the need for class consciousness among the exploited proletariat, and suggests that such consciousness does eventually emerge from bitter experience. Recalling the boredom and horror of life in the trenches in the First World War, the narrator remembers one of his comrades saying, "I hate to think of my getting killed for nothing." "Suppose at that time I had been class conscious," the narrator comments, "I might have pointed out that Bill was not dying for nothing....The money barons who really know what war is all about, know as I do, that Bill and many others die to enrich a few." As his words emphasize, the narrator was not class conscious at the time, but has since come to recognize the profiteering economic facts underlying the war.

As these examples suggest, most of the *Masses* short story writers avoided the heavily didactic, explicitly pro-Communist formulas expounded by commentators like Cecil-Smith and Ryerson. Their ideas on how to write fiction are much less readily traceable to Russian theorists like Kirpotin and Lunacharsky than to the contemporary realism of such popular authors as Ernest Hemingway, Sherwood Anderson, and Somerset Maugham or, closer to home, some of the contributors to the *Canadian Forum*. The *Forum* throughout the 1930s was probably the most influential outlet for short stories in Canada. In politics, it was still basically the social democratic successor to the *Rebel*, an ideological position continued into the Depression by J. Francis White (1885-1955?), editor of the magazine from 1927 to 1934. Like Peter McArthur, White was a farmer, businessman, and journalist. Like most of the *Forum* staff a moderate socialist in politics, White served as business manager of the magazine before his appointment as editor. In 1932 he made a five-week tour of the USSR, out of which he produced a series of articles entitled "Russian Highlights," published in the *Forum* in 1932-33, paying tribute to Soviet progress in technology, social institutions, and gen-

eral quality of life. In 1934 he left the *Forum* to set up a small publishing company specializing in non-fiction books by Communist
writers and about the Canadian and international Communist movements. Under White's editorship the *Canadian Forum* became distinguished for its fiction. For 1931-32, the editor of the US annual *Best
Short Stories* ranked the *Forum* third on the list of "American" periodicals publishing short fiction ("Short Stories" 5). In spite of the leftist political leanings of White and others on the editorial board, however, most of the *Forum* stories in the early 1930s tended to
emphasize personal relationships—romantic love, parent-children
conflicts, coming-of-age experiences—rather than political or socio-
economic conflict. In the absence of a strong national tradition of
realistic political fiction, English-Canadian bourgeois writers
remained unattracted by themes of working-class poverty and the
economic struggle for survival, even when this struggle was going on
outside their windows—perhaps even when they found themselves
personally immersed in it.

One of the few contributors of socially realistic fiction to the *Forum*
in the 1930s was Mary Quayle Innis (1879-1972). The US-born and
-educated wife of Canadian left-liberal economist Harold Innis, M.Q.
Innis began early in the 1930s to write short stories using a Depression
background. The main thrust of most of this fiction, however, is feminist rather than socialist. Like Margaret Fairley, Innis was interested in
exposing the forms of oppression imposed upon women, especially
their entrapment within domesticity; also like Fairley, she laments the
occasional failure of women to think and act responsibly as members
of society. In "The Party" (June 1931), a socially competitive woman
learns at the end of her pretentious social gathering that her husband
has lost his job. But Innis's story has more to do with the psychology of
gender relations, the breakdown of communication between a man
and a woman, than with the economic situation. The point of the story
is the woman's foolish vanity, and her insensitivity to the husband's
emotional crisis. In Marxist terms, the wife with her determination to
show her neighbours how well off she is lacks a sense of class solidarity. But Innis is more concerned with her denial of reality, her desire to
"have the kind of [household furnishings] you saw in the movies," than
with the implied political lesson. Innis's "Holiday" (January 1932)

focuses more explicitly on the class conflict and the sufferings of the poor, but also highlights women's biological and social entrapment. A poverty-stricken young woman wanders with her infant through the aisles of a busy department store, immersing herself in the dazzling array of material goods. The clerks and shoppers see the woman as a negligent mother rather than as a frustrated victim of capitalism. The woman herself is constantly on two levels of awareness, the pathetic escapism of her "holiday" intermingled with her physical consciousness of the inescapable burden of the child. Trapped both biologically and economically, the woman seeks respite in a materialism that for her can only be an unattainable dream.

Other *Forum* stories use the Depression as a backdrop against which to explore themes that relate more to questions of individual human character than to the problems of society. In A.G. Cowan's "Hangover" (February 1933), the main character loses his white-collar job because of his self-indulgent insistence on marrying a young working-class woman. The author implicitly criticizes the capitalist system that imposes its authority over the personal lives of workers, but devotes particular attention to the man's self-pity and retreat into alcoholism. By highlighting the worker's personal weaknesses, the story comes close to a "blame-the-victim" kind of reasoning. The story does carry the political implication that any attempt at unity between the petite bourgeoisie and the working class—even one motivated by love rather than politics—is bound to be foiled by the capitalist establishment. But the conclusion, as in so many of the stories in the *Forum*, is clearly negative, suggesting the futility of resistance. Frederick Philip Grove's "Riders" (February 1934) similarly inclines toward a sense of futility, reflecting a substantial development from the transcendental idealism of the author's *A Search for America*. Grove himself lived on the margin during the Depression, trying to support his family by subsistence farming, writing, and occasional editorial work, and "Riders" probably recreates something of his own anxieties. The story dramatizes an encounter between an insurance salesman eking out a living in a small Ontario town and an unemployed hitchhiker (a former teacher, like Grove himself) who turns out to be a boyhood friend of the salesman. The story emphasizes the two closely related worlds of unemployed and marginally employed, as if the two men with their shared boyhood are alternate versions of one life, distinguished only by accidental circumstances. The driver of the car has barely "succeeded in keeping the wolf from the door," while his passenger is "a member of the huge army of workless men who were tramping the roads" (177). As the title implies, both driver and passenger become "riders," carried by circumstances on aimless and meaningless journeys.

As the preceding examples suggest, there is not a great deal of difference between the artistic strategies of the realist short-story writers in *Masses* and those in the *Canadian Forum*. In spite of all the theorizing about "socialist realism" and the necessity of incorporating "the class struggle" or "the victorious principles of the forces of the socialist revolution," the fiction written by Communists often relies on the ironies of character or circumstance, just as fiction written by bourgeois realists do. Some Communist writers tried to allude to points of Party dogma in their stories, but by the end of the brief life span of *Masses* they had still not become adept at incorporating their political theory into realist fictional idioms. An upsurge in both quality and quantity of Canadian socialist realist fiction only emerged after 1935, when the CPC began to move towards unity with liberal and social democratic political and economic reformist ideals. In the early 1930s the CPC was following Stalin's "class-against-class" line, which represented Communism as the authentic and exclusive grassroots movement to unite the workers in their struggle. This struggle was not only against blatantly capitalistic forces, but also against the allegedly false friends of the working class, especially the social democrats, who were to be regarded as "social fascists." In 1932 *Masses* began publishing a series of unsigned articles attacking the *Canadian Forum* and its authors. According to this series, "class enemies" writing for the *Forum* included University of Toronto literature professor E.K. Brown, liberal historian F.H. Underhill, classics scholar and poet L.A. Mackay, and other eminent Canadian intellectuals. Tentative approval was extended only to the editor J. Francis White, by then on his way to becoming a Communist, who "seems sometimes to accept the scientific socialist position."

But soon after the demise of *Masses*, the CPC followed the shift of line from Moscow, replacing the "class-against-class" concept with the united or popular front, according to which Communists were expected to make common cause with social democrats and liberals against the increasing threat of genuine fascism, blatant in Germany, Italy, and Japan and insidious in other capitalist countries. The change in ideology, combined with a deepening of Depression problems, contributed to an increase in the fortunes of the Canadian Communist movement, and a proliferation of its publishing activity. The *Young Worker* was replaced in 1936 by *Advance*, a cross between magazine and newspaper, with a prominent cultural element. In 1936 the Toronto *Worker* was replaced by a larger newspaper, the *Daily Clarion* which, in size and format and even in some of its contents (comics pages, sports sections), attempted to compete with the bourgeois papers. In British Columbia, several new radical newspapers appeared in the late 1930s, including the *B.C. Lumber Worker* (established 1934), western organ of the Communist-dominated Lumber Workers International Union; the *B.C. Workers News* (1935), succeeded in 1937 by the *People's Advocate,* and the *Fisherman* (1937), mouthpiece for the Communist-dominated fishermen's union. Most of these publications regularly printed short stories, poetry, and book reviews. The *B.C. Lumber Worker* tried to bring socialist realism to its working-class readership by including reprints of stories by well-known international Communist writers, including Michael Gold of the US, Geoffrey Trease of Britain and Henri Barbusse of France. It also included original stories, presumably by local writers, although most of them were unsigned. This policy of withholding the names of indigenous authors seemed to imply that original domestic writing was inferior to foreign reprints. But the *Lumber Worker* at least introduced into Canadian Communist creative literature an element of regionalism. Like their counterparts in the non-Communist western Canadian literary community, BC writers and editors wanted to challenge central and eastern Canada's domination of literary production. An emphasis on distinctive regional qualities in their subject matter and technique could have been seen from the perspective of Marxist ideology as a sectarian deviation from the ideals of internationalism and class unity. But perhaps because Party bureaucrats and the majority of the rank and file paid little attention to literary activity, no such objections ever materialized, and from the late 1930s onward regionalism became an increasingly visible element in Canadian Communist writing.

In terms of the overall development of a left-wing literary tradition in Canada, the important new publication of the late 1930s was the Toronto-based cultural magazine *New Frontier*. Although the magazine was only slightly more long-lived than *Masses*, lasting through seventeen issues from April 1936 to October 1937, it was extremely influential both in exploring the possibilities of social and socialist realism and in integrating Communist writing with the mainstream of Canadian culture. Its editorial collective and regular contributors included Communists and fellow travellers such as Margaret Gould, William Lawson, Dorothy Livesay, and J.F. White, as well as social democrats and liberals like Leo Kennedy, Graham Spry, Leon Edel, and Mary Quayle Innis. Some of the short stories published in *New Frontier* are quite specific in their Marxist-Leninist orientation, but most are like the *Canadian Forum* realist fiction in their tendency to use the social crisis as a backdrop for exploring a variety of psychological and moral issues. Notable *New Frontier* story writers include Innis, Thomas Murtha, Ted Allan, Dorothy Livesay, and Dyson Carter.

Innis's story "Staver" (April 1936), like her *Forum* story "The Party," explores the interaction between the social crisis and the moral limitations of a bourgeois woman. A prosperous but restless middle-aged housewife becomes obsessed with helping the unemployed man who comes repeatedly to her house looking for odd jobs, but her socially constructed inhibitions prevent her from establishing a comfortable relationship with him. When he finally stops coming and she learns that he has improved his economic situation without her help, she is left with an ambivalent sense of both relief and loss. Thomas Murtha's "Sharp Awakening" (May 1936), by contrast, is a story of a man's potentially successful emergence from the inhibitions of bourgeois life. A male high-school teacher, oppressed by a sense of the meaninglessness of his life and work, achieves a moment of mystical awakening as he hears the honking of Canada geese overhead in the autumn dusk. The last words of the story seem to metaphorically invoke Marxist ideals of class solidarity and commitment, though they are expressed in religious language: "He said prayerfully, 'My God, keep me thinking of the workers, of the strong fliers.' He was awake, standing straight and restless, ready to do things."

A more fully developed socialist realism is evident in "East Nine" (June 1936) by "Jack Parr," a pseudonym for a young Winnipeg Communist named Dyson Carter. Carter's story involves a factory repairman who is fatally injured when his boss ignores safety rules to speed up production and fill a much-needed contract. The capitalist is not a tyrant, but a sympathetic employer with a genuine concern for his workers; a factory shutdown, however, would bring disaster to himself through lost profits and to his workers through lost wages. The great evil is identified not as a person, but as the dehumanizing processes of industrial capitalism that engulf worker and employer alike. Carter ends his story with a prophecy of the workers' revolutionary control over the forces of history, pronounced chorically by the other injured workers in "East Nine," the hospital ward for industrial accident cases: "Fellow man, worker, comrade, farewell....We of East Nine who struggle and have yet to die, salute you. No volley will be fired. Some other dawn-time guns will greet your memory." The conclusion to Carter's story reflects a recurrent problem of socialist realist fiction which, as E. Cecil-Smith indicates in one of his *Masses* articles, was supposedly defined by Frederick Engels. In a letter written in 1888 to young British would-be writer Margaret Harkness, Engels emphasized the importance of the realistic literary treatment of the working-class struggle for emancipation, but apparently went on to warn against blatant authorial intrusion and manipulation of the narrative for the purpose of making a political point. Engels's exact words in the letter have been disputed, but according to the 1974 edition of *Marx and Engels on Literature and Art* prepared by Lee Baxandall and Stefan Morawski, he wrote, "The more the opinions of the author remain hidden, the better for the work of art" (116). His words are usually taken as a warning not only against the heavy-handed assertion of a concluding moral in fiction, but also against any kind of authorial intrusion that prevents the narrative from speaking for itself.

Carter was the most frequent contributor of fiction to *New Frontier*, with a total of four stories published over its seventeen issues. In most of this fiction he was reluctant to let his narratives speak for themselves. His didactic purpose is especially overt in his second *New Frontier* story, "Rush This One, Muxer!" (September 1936). The narrator, the operator of a "Multiplex" (a brand of teletypewriter), emphasizes his commitment to both conscientious job performance and collective organization, contrasting himself to a co-worker who is careless and inaccurate and thinks the union is a waste of time. The narrator even gives a capsule version of Marxist political economics, alluding in his colloquial fashion to the discrepancy between wages and profits: "hundreds of dollars business and just four bucks for us. Tell me, did you ever hear of surplus value?" The story ends, rather melodramatically, with the coming of the revolution: "Someone shoves a message in my face. Hey, you, rush this one, Muxer! PEOPLES FRONT GOVERNMENT TAKES OVER ALL COMMUNICATIONS" (18). Carter is a bit more subtle in two stories that return to one of his favourite subjects, industrial accidents and work-related illness. "The Boss the Mockingbird" (February 1937) dramatizes the effects of a serious accident on the worker-victim, emphasizing his embittered state of mind and the emerging tensions in his relationship with his wife. In "Exit R.N." (October 1937), several young nurses have been exposed to a potentially fatal disease while caring for working-class patients. Carter includes allusions to the aloof and unsympathetic attitude of the nursing supervisor and to the contrast between the wards for the working class and those for wealthy patients. The story thus illustrates the class struggle and the exploitation of workers, but the emphasis is on dramatization, not on exposition of the Marxist ideology involved.

As an alternative to Carter's rather didactic socialist realism, *New Frontier* also includes at least one specimen inspired by the LEF "literature of fact." Ted Allan (1916-95) the subsequent co-biographer of Norman Bethune and author of several novels, short stories, and plays, contributed to *New Frontier* his first published literary work, "Guilty! Mr. Croll: A Story of Hawkesbury" (January 1937). The "story" is actually a news report using a blend of fiction and journalism to expose the social injustice perpetrated on the people of the town of Hawkesbury in eastern Ontario by the provincial Liberal government represented by David Croll, Minister of Welfare. Allan charges that Croll ordered thirty-five local workers to northern Ontario work camps because town officials refused to break up organizations of the unemployed and maintain a quiescent surplus of labour for the local pulp and paper companies. Around the same time that the men were exiled, three Hawkesbury children died of starvation. On the day that Allan visited the bereaved families, Croll was in Hollywood, consulting with a movie studio about the making of a film on the Dionne quintuplets. Allan combines accusation and plausible descriptive details, including a contrast between the rosy faces of the quintuplets (familiar from magazine photos and newsreels throughout the late 1930s) and the emaciated faces of the victims of starvation, to transform the news item into a condemnation of government and capitalist persecution of workers and their families.

After *New Frontier* folded in 1937, the main outlet for radical literary works became the *Daily Clarion*. Unlike *New Frontier*, the *Clarion*, as an official CPC publication, relied largely on Party members for submissions, and many of the short-story contributions reflect advances toward the rigorous application of the formulas of socialist realism. Florence L. McPherson's "The River" (18 March 1938) dramatizes the endurance and solidarity of homesteaders threatened by spring floods, then compares the floodwaters to the internal and external forces propelling the working class toward revolutionary action. "The struggle of the folks down here to live decently, and not be swept under by the tide of rising prices and increased rents, reminded Marie of the little houses at the time of one of those spring floods. They too had been buffeted around a lot before they had finally built a foundation of joint action....Eventually the collective force of people like herself would rise up against the profiteers, just as the river keeps rising."

Harold Griffin's "Indian Strike" (17 May 1939) is one of the few early-twentieth-century Canadian works of fiction written in a realistic literary idiom to present a sympathetic treatment of native people. Griffin (1912-98), a Communist poet and journalist on the staff of the *B.C. Fisherman*, anticipated the work of his friend and *Fisherman* colleague Hubert Evans, whose novel *Mist on the River* (1954) bears some similarity of setting and situation to Griffin's story. Griffin presents his narrative through the eyes of an emissary who is sent by cannery authorities to persuade the native workers not to go on strike, and ends up joining them. Basically a conversion narrative, the story takes on added irony when Griffin makes the emissary a

Roman Catholic missionary, who is drawn away from his conservative social function and united simultaneously with the aboriginal cause of the native people and the modern cause of the working class.

John Weir's "The Grouser" (25 February 1939) is one of the few fictional treatments of the Spanish Civil War by a Canadian Communist writer. Narrated by an anonymous soldier in the Mackenzie-Papineau Battalion, "The Grouser" tells of a perpetual complainer who denies being "one of those political comrades," but who willingly sacrifices his life for what he recognizes as a "good cause." The story seems to contradict the Communist orthodoxy that emphasizes the importance of class consciousness to revolutionary action, but Weir's purpose is obviously to demonstrate the effectiveness of the united front, which can elicit support for the cause even from people who believe they have no political commitment.

As the 1930s drew to a close, Communist writers were becoming more conscious of war, impending and actual, as hostilities erupted in Spain, Ethiopia, and Asia. Norman Bethune (1890-1939) is usually regarded as a great humanitarian, not as a literary figure, although an edition of his selected writings published in 1998 may provoke a reconsideration of his achievements as an author. In "The Dud" (*Daily Clarion* 8 July 1939), his only work of fiction published during his lifetime, the evils of imperialist warfare are dramatized in the narrative of an old peasant who finds an unexploded artillery shell in his field in Japanese-occupied China. These evils are further epitomized by the weeds in his scant field. "His life seemed to him to be just one great never-ending struggle with his enemy—weeds," and China itself is "one big fertile acre of earth" overrun with weeds (Bethune 319). In an attempt to connect his struggle to the larger political and military conflict unfolding around him, the old peasant sets out to carry the shell back to the Chinese partisans who fired it so that it will not be wasted. Wandering through a land in the grip of a murderous enemy, the old man fulfills his self-imposed mission through an innocent belief in the cause to which he has committed himself. Although the partisans at first laugh at the old man, they recognize how important his mission is to him, and restore his dignity by praising him. Through his quixotic exploit, the old man reveals a vital force opposing the weed-like processes of war. The shell he has carried so far and so faithfully turns out to be a useless dud, and the whole journey, to a cynical mind, is meaningless. But the old man is allowed to believe that he has "done something to clear the field of China (324)." In Marxist-Leninist theory, each worker and peasant has a role to play, no matter how small or apparently insignificant, in the revolutionary drama. Bethune suggests that in this drama the ability to believe in the relevance of one's actions to the larger cause is more important than the intrinsic significance of the actions themselves.

But the most distinguished writer of socialist realist short stories in the 1930s was Dorothy Livesay (1909-96). Livesay has told the story of her literary career as a Communist in the 1930s in her anthology/memoir *Right Hand Left Hand* (1977). With this book she not only compelled a reassessment of her life and literary career by emphasizing her commitment to Communism, she also demonstrated her talents as a short-story writer, and revealed more effectively than any other Canadian writer in the 1930s the possibilities of socialist realism. In youth, Livesay was attracted to the writing of short stories as much as of poetry. Her manuscript papers in the University of Manitoba library reveal the care she devoted to both genres in her literary apprenticeship. Her earliest extant stories, written when she was in her twenties, are mostly about the developing female psyche and its obsession with emotional and social crises, but they reveal a preoccupation with public feminist issues that merges later with her Communist political concerns. In her first published story, "Beach Sunday" (*Canadian Forum* January 1931), for instance, the tensions between a young woman and a young man include a conflict between the man's gender-stereotyped romantic dreams and the woman's incipient desire for freedom.

Livesay joined the Progressive Arts Club in 1932 and the Young Communist League in 1933, became a full-fledged member of the CPC in 1934, and remained in the Party through the 1930s (diary notes on the thirties, written 1973-74, Livesay Papers). She retained a lifelong receptivity to Marxist and other socialist ideas and, as her *Right Hand Left Hand* indicates, regretted none of her activities as a Communist. In the end, however, she came to feel that the Party did not adequately respect and support creative writers, or use their talents appropriately. "I share the view of Lenin and Trotsky," she declared in an interview in 1969; the artist is not a political animal and cannot be handled as such" (quoted in Charles Boylan, "The Social and Lyric Voices of Dorothy Livesay," MA thesis, UBC, 1969; excerpt in Livesay Papers, Box 1). But in the early 1930s she was trying to learn to be a political poet and fiction writer. "I struggled to understand socialist realism in literature," Livesay reminisced, "and great discussions took place at the PAC" (diary notes, Livesay Papers). As a neophyte, Livesay perhaps felt unqualified to join in the published debates on literary theory in *Masses*, although she contributed reviews and poems to the magazine. Meanwhile, she experimented on her own with socialist realist themes and techniques, writing drafts and fragments of stories. Her published work and unpublished manuscripts include only ten finished socialist realist stories, four of which were published in the 1930s, although Livesay herself thought well enough of three others to include them in *Right Hand Left Hand*.

Her early attempts at socialist realism include two undated manuscripts, neither of which was ever published. "No Sale," like her *Forum* story "Beach Sunday," involves a young woman who is becoming restless and dissatisfied in a relationship with a conventional young man. The man believes in the capitalist myth of success, even in the midst of the Depression; the woman is the daughter of a striking worker. Her rejection of the man is not merely an expression of her personal independence but a recognition of her duty to a larger political cause. "No Address," written from a first-person male point of view in a colloquial idiom imitative of Hemingway, involves an unsuccessful quest that climaxes in an experience of political revitalization. A political activist looks vainly for his secret Party contact, to fulfill some unspecified duty. The details of the external action are deliberately left vague, to concentrate on the narrator's thoughts and feelings. As the conclusion emphasizes, the story is a lesson in political dedication and perseverance. Although discouraged by his failure and tempted to give up altogether, perhaps to go "hiking up to the mountains, out of this goddam town," the narrator reflects that "Mike would say: It can't be done. We've got to stick it." To emphasize the lesson of submission to Party authority, the narrative ends with the repeated words followed by an ellipsis: "Mike would say...".

Her early efforts also include a venture into reportage fiction like Ryan's "Fellow Workers" and Allan's "Guilty! Mr. Croll." "Zynchuk's Funeral" (written 1933-34, but published for the first time in *Right Hand Left Hand*) is a story of political illumination, based on an actual incident. In the story, the narrator goes out of "idle curiosity" to watch the funeral procession of a worker shot by a policeman while resisting an eviction order. The procession turns into a people's protest march. As the march degenerates into a riot when police armed with truncheons move in, the narrator both psychologically and physically loses her detachment from the protesters: "We were fighting not to run, to carry on, to wave the banner, hurl the slogan, raise the coffin shoulder-high on our long, burdened arms." Full commitment comes when the narrator is knocked down, injured, and seeks help from a pharmacist, who turns her away from his store. "I saw the man...sheltering the door against us," the narrator concludes. "And I came to my senses" (*RHLH* 87).

Livesay's first published socialist realist story, "Six Years," appeared in *New Frontier* (April 1936) under the pseudonym "Katherine Bligh." Like most of her Communist-inspired stories, the climactic focus of "Six Years" is an experience of political enlightenment, concerned with the principles of working-class solidarity and collective action, and the folly of bourgeois individualism. The attempt of a socially ambitious wife to remain aloof from her working-class neighbours breaks down under the weight of economic circumstances. Her illumination comes, ironically, when the electric company cuts off the power to her house, and she is forced to admit to her neighbour that her husband has lost his job. The neighbour, the wife of another unemployed worker, serves as the narrator of the story and spokesperson for the point of doctrine being illustrated. The story exposes the fallacy of bourgeois individualism in terms that recall Lenin's denunciation of ideological error as "infantile." "She was so young," says the narrator about Mrs. Dakin, "and she thought she could do everything by herself" (*RHLH* 172). At the end of the story the young wife has recognized her error and is resolved to convert her husband. "I'll tell Everett," she promises her neighbour. As in many of her early stories, Livesay combines socialist realism with feminism. In this instance, however, the feminism relates to class solidarity in the social struggle rather than to antagonism between the sexes. Livesay suggests that when working-class men are defeated by circumstances or their own weaknesses, the women must take action, not as a gesture of anti-male reproof or as an assertion of feminist power, but as a necessary act of intervention to maintain the momentum of the proletarian revolution.

In "Case Supervisor" (published under her own name in *New Frontier* July 1936), Livesay associates power and aggression with men and victimization with women, but she makes it clear that this gendered power structure is a consequence of the corruption of capitalism. The women in the story are oppressed both directly through their economic inferiority, and indirectly by being deceived into serving the capitalist system. In contrast to the sympathetic and politically knowledgeable narrative voice of "Six Years," the point of view of "Case Supervisor" is the deluded consciousness of the title character, Miss Chilton, a functionary in a welfare agency, who tries to evade her complicity in the failure of social institutions to relieve human misery. She takes refuge in the manufactured illusion of the cinema, and when that recourse fails she hides behind bureaucratic impersonality. In the latter strategy she follows the example of her superior, a woman who sees the agency's work in terms of budget priorities and procedural efficiency, and who invokes as her authority the "businessmen" on the governing board who complain about the inefficient management of the agency. Chilton, like her superiors, tries to keep the people on relief at a distance, to commodify them as "cases," or to perceive them as icons of bourgeois romanticism, like characters on a movie screen. But while she and her superiors retreat into some form or other of evasion, one of the younger social workers on Chilton's staff replaces the bureaucratic procedures with human generosity, by paying for the fuel of a poverty-stricken family out of her own earnings. In her expression of protest, Chilton addresses the young woman as "child," but it is Chilton and the bureaucracy behind her who are the symbols of historical immaturity. The young woman, by her act of personal commitment, brings the new era based on social justice one step closer to realization.

"Out West" (published only in *Right Hand Left Hand*) focuses on the familiar Depression situation of young unemployed men wandering across the country. The aimlessness of their lives is counterpointed by the confinement of the jail cell in which the story takes place. The aimlessness and confinement are offset by the idea of political awakening, however. From his more politically knowledgeable cellmates a young man named Sean learns the necessity of revolutionary struggle: "We will be castaways all our life unless we fight for our future" (188). The new "fight for the future" reminds Sean of his own father's commitment to the western ideal of subjugating the frontier; but the father was a dreamer whose ideal degenerated into the phrase "mebbe someday" (190). Similarly, his mother dreamed materialistic dreams of money, electric appliances, automobiles—all resolving into the words "some day" (190). The parents' words are echoed in the refrain Sean has heard from prospective employers when he looks for a job: "maybe next year things will pick up" (191). Sean has the advantage over his parents, however, of his intellectual vitality. He "devours history books," and his academic interest in the past not only contrasts with his father's vague frontier dreams, but underscores his openness to systematic historical knowledge, a prerequisite to Marxist enlightenment. While Sean's mother blames her son for his own failure, Sean has made a beginning toward understanding the real causes of the crisis that has engulfed his generation. For now, he is forced to defer to the "someday" illusions of his parents and the lies propagated by an officialdom that puts unemployed men in jail. "That letter won't be censored!" (195), his cellmate agrees as Sean writes his mother that he has found a job "out west," and is living in comparative comfort. He cannot have the socially created esteem of a "real job," but through camaraderie with his fellow victims he is discovering working-class solidarity, one of the first steps toward proletarian revolution. The story ends, however, not with a melodramatic gesture of rebellion, but with a tentative question, a hint of defiance, and a reminder of Sean's eagerness to learn:

> his generation—the crowd around him...would they go on taking it?
> He wanted to know. (195)

• • • • •

The subject matter and techniques of social and socialist realism also emerged occasionally in longer works of Canadian fiction in the

1930s, although it is difficult to find more than a few novels that might be considered social realist, socialist realist, or proletarian, within even the loosest meanings of these terms. The dearth of such work in both English and French Canada during the 1930s is attributable partly to the reluctance of Depression-era publishers to undertake books with a limited sales potential, and partly to the prevalence of anti-socialist sentiments. In Quebec, especially, writers of fiction tended to ignore the Depression. "Of the roughly 100 novels published in Quebec from 1930 through 1939," reports Emile J. Talbot, "only two deal with the Depression in a substantive way and only three or four mention it" (69). Writers interested in the theme of the struggle for economic survival, furthermore, tended to focus on rural Quebec rather than on the urban society that is the usual setting of Marxist or other socialist fiction. One of the few novels about industrial capitalism, Jehan Maria's *L'Autre...Guerre* (1931), as Talbot points out, condemns capitalism but offers no alternatives except possibly a retreat to the past. Throughout the 1930s Québecois fiction writers largely remained loyal to indigenous religious and nationalistic influences. When Communism and non-Marxist socialism enter into fiction plots at all, they are invariably represented in unfavourable terms. This is not to say that either the Catholic Church in Quebec or the writers who followed its ideological assumptions were completely uncritical of capitalism. In fact, both writers and clerics had harsh criticisms of the economic system that collapsed in 1929. But, as Talbot points out, they saw the basic conflict to be not between capitalism and some socialist alternative but between materialism and religion. The prevalent literary and spiritual response to the Depression, then, was to denounce allegedly atheistic ideologies like Communism, and to advocate not social revolution but spiritual renewal.

A similar kind of response is featured in the earliest published English-Canadian novel dealing in detail with Depression problems, Claudius Gregory's *Forgotten Men* (1933). The British-born Gregory (1879?-1944) came to Canada around 1900 to settle in Hamilton, Ontario, as a journalist. Of the three novels he published during the 1930s, only *Forgotten Men* concerns the problems of poverty and unemployment, which Gregory relates to the kind of Christian socialism expounded in Machar's *Roland Graeme: Knight*. Pursuing the Christian elements much further than Machar does, Gregory writes a parable revealing the consequences of a second coming of Christ in the modern world. Like Douglas Durkin's *The Magpie*, Gregory's novel is concerned with the dilemma of the imaginative and morally responsible individual at a time of historical crisis; but in contrast to Durkin's Craig Forrester, who in the end retreats from urban society to fulfill his own personal ideals, Gregory's Christopher Worth is a Christ figure who is effectually crucified by a world unprepared for the kind of moral challenge he brings. This Christ figure is a socialist who has detailed plans for the redistribution of the world's wealth, but his gospel has more to do with religion than with political economy. Through more than four hundred pages, Gregory clumsily and repetitively highlights his Christian parallels: the main characters have allusive or explicit New Testament names like Christopher, Peter, and John; the mother of the Christ figure is named Mary; the "Society of Forgotten Men" is made up of twelve members; in the end Christopher is betrayed by one of his own followers, whose name is "Jude," and so on.

It could be argued that the didacticism and redundancy of *Forgotten Men* is no different from similar elements that are regarded as authorized features in socialist realist fiction like Maguire's novel *O Canada!* or the short stories of Livesay. It might also be suggested that *Forgotten Men* builds its plot and ideological argument on a tradition of analogy between Marxism and Christianity that goes back at least as far as Sergei Bulgakov's 1907 essay *Karl Marx as a Religious Type*. Bulgakov, like most successive writers—including Northrop Frye—who have commented on Marxism from a Christian perspective, emphasizes that Marxism is not a new politico-economic revelation but just another religious system derived from Judeo-Christian traditions. But although such an analogy may be inferred from *Forgotten Men*, Gregory never alludes explicitly to Marxism. His aim is not to compare belief systems but to recall his readers to the Christian principles of self-denial and sacrifice and to a conception of human life that emphasizes spiritual rather than political and economic solutions.

A much more talented novelist, Morley Callaghan, turned in the 1930s to fiction dealing with the relationship between Marxist Communism and Christianity. Callaghan had, in fact, become interested in Communism in the 1920s, and dealt with it in some of his earliest attempts at journalism and fiction. At age eighteen, in his final year of high school, he sold his first piece of professional writing, "A Windy Corner at Yonge-Albert" (*Toronto Star Weekly* 6 August 1921), a description of the street-corner harangues of Christian evangelists, socialists, and "Bolshevists" that were regular features of summer evenings in downtown Toronto. Two years later, as a reporter for the *Toronto Daily Star*, he published two articles on the visit to Toronto of the prominent American Communist, William Z. Foster. The young newspaperman subsequently became interested enough to seek out local radicals. "I knew all the communists in town," Callaghan claimed in a 1985 interview about his early years, "and tried very hard to be friendly with them." Ultimately, he resisted the personal and organizational attractions of the movement, just as he resisted formal commitment to the other ideology that fascinated him, Christianity. "You always knew you were going to be used," he argued, "because they [the Communists] were like Christian and fundamental evangelists. Everything must serve the truth, or their truth" (qtd. in Boire 21). Callaghan's early tendency to relate political with religious movements is demonstrated in an unpublished short story, probably written about 1923, entitled "I Should Have Been a Preacher," which ridicules the confused attempts of a working-class character to spread the Marxist gospel through techniques borrowed from Christian evangelism. He also explores this confluence more briefly in his first novel, *Strange Fugitive* (1928), whose gangster protagonist enviously contemplates the oratorical and manipulative skills of street-corner Communist and Christian orators.

In the 1930s, Callaghan turned to more detailed explorations of the relationship between Christianity and Marxism, in his novels *Such Is My Beloved* (1934) and *They Shall Inherit the Earth* (1935). In *Such Is My Beloved*, a Roman Catholic priest who devotes himself to the attempt to redeem two prostitutes is compared to a Marxist medical student who sees life in terms of the impersonal forces of history. The student, Charlie Stewart, with the detachment of the physician he is to become, compartmentalizes his life and separates his personal feelings from the spectacle of human suffering. Marxist Communism is thus represented in the novel as coldly materialistic, detached, even inhuman. Catholicism, on the other hand, is spiritual-istic and sympathetic; but its adherents are liable to be incapable of dealing with the hard realities of a fallen world. Father Dowling's holistic commitment leads him to social alienation, to an intensity of the solitude and celibacy that are the requisites of the priest's life, and eventually to madness. *They Shall Inherit the Earth* similarly opposes spiritual experience to the materialism of Communism (as well as to other political and social responses to the Depression), but the spiritual experience in this novel is not related to the dogmas of Christianity. The central character, Michael Aikenhead, sees the private and public agonies of human beings as the consequences of a futile search for order in a meaningless world. "There's no use trying to hold on to anything," he reflects,

> it all gets broken in the same stupid, meaningless way. Anybody could run this god-damned universe better than it's run. No matter how you long for a thing, it doesn't matter. You get kicked around just the same. There's no order in anything human. Everything you love...it's all accidental. (154-55)

The Communist solution to the problem of universal chaos is introduced mainly as an object of satire. One of Aikenhead's acquaintances in the city is a former dentist turned "Marxian economist" (102). By reducing everything to "economic necessity," this character offers a faith that amounts to certainty, in contrast to Aikenhead's "bewilderment" (103). Rejecting such simple solutions as that of his Marxist friend, Aikenhead struggles toward the realization that the truth is within the self rather than in the actions of society. In the search for belief, he recognizes, some become Catholics, others become Communists, but "such people...only heaped the chaos in their own souls on whatever they touched. Such people were all like him in this, that they couldn't know peace or dignity or unity with anything till they were single and whole within themselves" (242). Aikenhead, unlike Father Dowling, is able to achieve a sense of unity and integrity within himself, and is thence able to reestablish unity in personal relationships. With this emphasis on personal and family contexts and its easy dismissal of such social problems as poverty and unemployment, *They Shall Inherit the Earth* could hardly be considered a socialist realist or "proletarian" novel. In a review for the *Daily Clarion*, Dorothy Livesay was prepared to approve of Callaghan's positive representation of the principal female character in the novel, but she denounced his preference for the personal over the public theme as a "familiar middle-class point of view." In emphasizing spiritual fulfilment over social awareness, Livesay concludes, Callaghan "drives down a blind alley" (review reprinted in *RHLH* 175-76).

Livesay was more favourably impressed with the novel by Irene Baird (1901-81), *Waste Heritage* (1939), which comes much closer to the ideals of socialist realism. Where Callaghan subordinates the political to the personal, Baird emphasizes the involvement of the individual in political action. Set in the summer of 1938, the novel deals with the aftermath of the sit-down strike of unemployed men in the Vancouver post office, and their march to the provincial legislature in Victoria. Unlike Callaghan, who in *They Shall Inherit the Earth* deals primarily with the situation of one unemployed middle-class professional young man and focuses more on his family troubles than his economic troubles, Baird uses her protagonist as the epitome of a whole generation of young adults whose lives have been blighted by the Depression. Through the frequent emphasis on rallies, marches, demonstrations, and group discussions, Baird suggests further that her subject is collective rather than individual. Baird's treatment of her subject is surprising, for nothing in her background suggests a politically radical outlook. Born in England, she came to Canada in 1919, married early, and settled in British Columbia as a housewife, mother, and part-time writer. Her first published book, *John* (1937), is a pastoral novel about a man who lives a life of obscurity in the British Columbia interior. In the summer of 1938 she was living in Victoria when she read in the local newspaper about the sit-down strike in Vancouver and the protest at the provincial legislature. As she wrote in a 1973 article describing the origins of *Waste Heritage*, she was suddenly seized with "the wild idea of trying to put the whole sorry mess between the covers of a book" (Baird, "Sidown").

The result was a remarkable experiment in combining undercover reportage with imaginative fiction. Although police and city officials in Victoria attempted to keep reporters and local residents away from the protest marchers, Baird persuaded a physician friend to let her accompany him on his rounds among the protesters. Silently allowing the officials and protesters to assume that she was a nurse, Baird watched and listened, picking up impressions of the physical appearance, attitudes, and speech idioms of the young men. Although this first-hand observation probably accounts for much of the effectiveness of *Waste Heritage* as realistic fiction, Baird was also inspired by the recent work of the American novelist John Steinbeck, particularly his *Of Mice and Men* (1937). Baird's novel was written too early to be influenced by Steinbeck's *The Grapes of Wrath* (1939), but she obviously wrote, as Steinbeck did in the latter novel, in hopes of affecting public opinion and political policy in a time of national crisis. Like Steinbeck, she tried to bring to her story a combination of objectivity and sympathy. "If someone unconnected either by sentiment or politics could write it," she declared in her 1973 reminiscence, "maybe, just maybe, Canadians would take notice" (Baird, "Sidown").

Canadians did not take much notice at the time, for in spite of favourable reviews the novel was forgotten as the public submerged the memories of the Depression in world war and subsequent crises. Baird moved on to write other, very different, works of fiction. In 1973 Dorothy Livesay described *Waste Heritage* as the "strongest novel of its period...to be produced in Canada" and helped Baird convince the Macmillan Company to publish a reprint (Baird, letter to Macmillan, Baird Papers). But in spite of her admiration for Baird's novel, Livesay did not regard *Waste Heritage* as the great Canadian proletarian novel. In a 1978 comment, Livesay compared Baird's fiction briefly with Callaghan's, then went on to express her reservations about both writers. Although Livesay had long since rejected the Communist Party, her comments indicate that she continued to believe in the artistic validity of the politically didactic purposes of socialist realism. The problem with both Baird and Callaghan, Livesay suggested, lay in the very feature that Baird regarded as her strength, the detachment from political commitment. "Although dealing with the unemployed, often in struggle or despair," wrote Livesay, "neither of these writers' work could be called political. They relied on realistic 'slice-of-life' techniques; and though decrying the evils of the social order they offer no solution other than personal salvation" (Livesay, Editor's Foreword, "I Was a Young Communist," *CV11* [May 1976]: *17*).

Whether or not *Waste Heritage* was "political" within Livesay's presumed meaning, it represented a considerable advance over earlier fiction that attempted to deal with the problems of the Depression. The novel opens with the aftermath of the violent police expulsion of unemployed men who had been occupying the Vancouver post office and art gallery, on 19 June 1938. The protesters are defeated and demoralized, and although much of the rest of the novel emphasizes their efforts to regather their collective strength, an atmosphere of futility hangs over these efforts. This atmosphere is especially conveyed through the words and actions of Matt Striker, the young protagonist of the story. His name is an allusion to collective protest, but it also invokes his inclination towards anger and violence. The opening episodes also emphasize the disorientation and uncertainty that overshadow the actions of Striker and most of the unemployed protesters. Arriving in Vancouver the morning after the post-office expulsion, Striker gropes his way through the almost deserted, debris-littered streets of the strange city. He has come to the west coast to "join up with the rest of the boys" because "I never got any place on my own" (27); after the Communist organizers have restored a measure of discipline and order among the men, Striker feels "the power of mass action" (114), but the feeling is sporadic, alternating with impressions of futility and anger. He has discovered the beginnings of political awareness in his perception that "invested capital" must "be swept away" (215), but he cannot develop the working-class consciousness necessary to apply this discovery to action. He is pained by the memory that his father was ostracized as a "dirty radical" (115), and angered by the employed middle-class people he meets who accuse him of being unwilling to work. He is driven not by proletarian class consciousness but by rage, vehement and often undirected, or perversely directed against his fellow victims.

The Communist activists in the novel are eager to incite collective action, but are repeatedly frustrated by the feelings of apathy, internecine hostility, and futility that obsess the men they are trying to organize. "Seems like nothing come out of any of it in the end," says Matt (315). This failure, furthermore, is not presented as the result of police and government suppression. Significantly, Baird begins her story after the most violent confrontation between protesters and police is over. The failure of the unemployed demonstrators is related not to the opposition of officialdom but to a larger context of futility. The novel questions the effectiveness of strikes, demonstrations, and other efforts of the alienated men to relieve the crisis. Optimism is liable to be expressed ironically, as in Matt's contemptuous repetition of Hep's words "maybe tomorrow" (317), which recall the older generation who unthinkingly rely on the future in Livesay's short story "Out West." The futility of the strikers' actions is underscored by the conclusion, when the brain-damaged Eddy brings catastrophe down on himself and his friend Matt through his stubborn conviction that a "one-cent sale" means that he can buy a new pair of shoes for one cent. The tragic redundancy of the whole experience in *Waste Heritage* is also underscored by the repetition of setting in the opening and closing scenes. The novel begins and ends in the railway yards, where the trains that carry Matt Striker and men like him back and forth across the country in their elusive search for social stability become symbolic of violent, meaningless death.

Ultimately, *Waste Heritage* expresses only pity for the victims of the Depression. As the title implies, a whole generation has been deprived of traditional human expectations of economic and domestic stability. The remote verbal echo between Baird's title and Callaghan's *They Shall Inherit the Earth* invites a comparison between the two novels, a comparison that can especially be applied to their respective treatments of the subject of love. In *They Shall Inherit the Earth* the Christian promise of fulfilment seems to apply ironically to the emotionally and economically disoriented characters, until the conclusion when Michael Aikenhead achieves his sense of internal order through reconciliation with his father and through his love for his wife and child. In *Waste Heritage* the young people of the 1930s lose everything, including the normal experience of romantic love. Matt Striker's affair with Hazel, while appearing to develop from a meaningless sexual encounter to a genuine emotional commitment, comes to nothing in the end, erased in the tragic conclusion.

But even if *Waste Heritage* fails to develop full confidence in the efforts of its workers to achieve social justice, it is still much closer to the ideals of socialist realism than Callaghan's novels or most other novels written during the Depression. Other Canadian fiction writers dealt with contemporary economic problems in the 1930s, but like Callaghan, most preferred to seek solutions in terms of the individual rather than of class-defined population groups. Ethel Chapman's *With Flame of Freedom* (1938), for instance, expresses sympathy for the socio-economic problems of the people of its rural and small-town settings, but focuses its main attention on the story of a young woman who is absorbed more by problems of personal identity and romantic entanglements than by the larger political and economic world. Frederick Philip Grove's *The Master of the Mill* (reportedly completed in 1938, although not published until 1944) reverts to a romantic anti-capitalism reminiscent of the work of Durkin and Sinclair, in the story of the rise and fall of an industrialist family and their monolithic flour milling operation in northwestern Ontario. Covering a time span from the nineteenth century to an unspecified post-1930s future, the novel is an attack on the subordination of humanistic values to machine technology. Only secondarily concerned with class and ideological conflicts, it invokes the cosmic perspective but not the wryly ironic tone of the novel *We* (1924) by the Russian Yevgeny Zamyatin.

Only one Canadian novel in the 1930s rigorously follows the formulas of socialist realism: Ted Allan's *This Time a Better Earth* (1939). Like Callaghan's and unlike Baird's, Allan's title expresses confidence in an ultimately ameliorative historical outcome. But in contrast to Callaghan's allusion to a submissive faith in transcendent benevolence, Allan implies a militant human determination to remake the world. *This Time a Better Earth* is the only Canadian novel about the Spanish Civil War contemporary with the events it describes, and the only Canadian socialist realist novel by a member of the CPC published during the 1930s. Writing while the conclusion of the war was still in doubt, Allan could be hopeful enough to reconcile the dark events in Spain with the Communist faith in ultimate victory.

Surprisingly, however, considering the political temper of the times, Allan's strongly partisan novel was issued by a trade publisher in New York, and won general approval of readers and reviewers with its fast-paced plot and appealing characters. But tolerance of its Communist ideology evaporated during the Cold War: never reprinted and seldom mentioned in literary histories, *This Time a*

*Better Earth* became difficult to find outside of a few university and research libraries. The neglect of the novel is regrettable, for Allan effectively integrates the techniques of socialist realism with such elements of novelistic appeal as battlefield adventure and romantic love. Narrated by Bob Curtis, a Canadian Communist volunteer with the Spanish Loyalist forces, the story introduces a group of characters who epitomize the cosmopolitanism of the international brigades, including an American intellectual, a French Canadian, a Jewish American, a black, and an Alberta coal miner. The early chapters chronicle the acclimatization and political indoctrination experienced by Loyalist volunteers on their arrival in Spain. The narrative reproduces a speech addressed to the volunteers about the importance of the united front against fascism, although Allan also slips in some of the accusations of Trotskyism which the Communist Party was currently using against other political groups to consolidate its control over the Loyalist armed forces. Through Curtis, Allan describes the aerial and artillery bombardments of Madrid, emphasizing the courage of the civilian population. He describes the exulting response to recent Loyalist victories, but makes no mention of the more frequent Loyalist defeats. He does, however, include expressions of concern about the strength of the fascist forces, the war's probable duration, and the lack of international support for the Spanish government. Allan includes a love story which, like the relationship between Baird's working-class lovers, ends in tragedy. But Allan's point is not that love is futile in a desolate world. In his conclusion, he emphasizes that in times of political crisis people must be prepared to sacrifice personal to political commitment. As the title implies, such sacrifices are necessary in the immense project of rebuilding the world.

# 5

# The 1930s

## Progressive Drama, Poetry, and Non-Fiction

*T*his *Time a Better Earth* demonstrated how socialist realism, using a Canadian subject with international and revolutionary implications, could reach beyond the limited readership of Party members and sympathizers toward a mass audience. Allan's novel came too late and its success was too short-lived to provide inspiration for other would-be novelists in the Canadian Communist community of the 1930s. But if a substantial output of proletarian novels did not materialize in Canada, more hopeful signs appeared early in the decade for the proletarian drama. Plays, of course, were not dependent on the vagaries of book publication. In the 1930s, furthermore, as the popularity of the cinema indicates, there was a huge audience eager for inexpensive public entertainment; at least some of this audience could be led by judicious playwrights and theatre companies toward an appreciation of serious political drama. The few Canadian social realist plays published—but mostly not produced—in the 1920s, such as Trevor Maguire's *Unemployment* and works by Merrill Denison, suggested that the Canadian proletarian drama might encounter the same difficulties as the novel. But the drama had the advantage of a new and distinctive literary/theatrical form. "Agitprop," like socialist realism, had emerged in Europe with the Russian Revolution, and by the 1930s was the dominant form of Communist-inspired drama. Alluding to the two related purposes of partisan political activity—agitation and propaganda—the epithet would seem to apply more precisely to direct and unmediated political action than to an art form. The aim of agitprop drama was to break down the barriers between art and life, to bring theatre into the streets, to merge stage conventions with the real experience of audience and actors. Yet at the same time it sought to achieve its aims by highly stylized, unrealistic stage conventions.

From a purely literary point of view, agitprop could be traced back to aesthetic principles expounded by Lenin. E. Cecil-Smith, in "Propaganda and Art" (*Masses* 9 January 1934), cites Lenin's emphasis on the necessity of dream as an element of both art and Communist ideology. The Communist dream of a better world is in Lenin's terms an "essentially realistic" vision of the future, but this vision authorizes, in the words of Cecil-Smith, "those caricatures, hyperboles, exaggerations, burlesques and absurdities which remove us from reality with the object of bringing us closer to it, by showing up some otherwise hidden point." It is in its reliance on "caricatures, hyperboles, exaggerations, burlesques and absurdities" that agitprop drama most frequently differs from socialist realist fiction. Agitprop drama has, in fact, only a very limited relationship to fiction—and, indeed, to all literature, for it is little suited to silent reading or to close textual analysis. In contrast, for instance, to the socialist George Bernard Shaw, who made elaborate distinctions between the acting and reading texts of his plays and added long ideological expositions in the reading versions, the typical agitprop dramatist wrote with stage presentation exclusively in mind. In a published text, agitprop often seems simple-minded and crude, not merely because of its dogmatic political message, but more precisely because the text exists as a skeletal blueprint for the directors and actors to build an elaborate construct of tone and gesture that will provoke the audience to emotional response during presentation and to recollection and contemplation of the subject matter afterward. This is true of all serious drama, but agitprop is more dependent than most stage plays on vivification of the written text.

In agitprop drama, furthermore, the emphasis is usually on collective and emblematic representations of human character and action. Socialist realist fiction is likewise ultimately concerned with making generalizations about workers and the class struggle, but these generalizations are approached through the mimetic depiction of individual character and specific situations. Agitprop drama often takes its plots from actual current events, but frequently abandons realistic characterization and narrative presentation in favour of caricature, personification, and choric dialogue and action. The first agitprop dramas appeared in Soviet Russia in the 1920s, originally produced by groups of students and workers. Sometimes dressed in the standardized clothing that identified their trade or social status and employing minimal stage properties, the actors appealed directly to their audiences, often inviting responses as orators might do in a political meeting. Characterization and plot were equally minimal: virtuous workers (muscular and articulate young men) successfully challenge the authority of sinister capitalists (overweight older men dressed in top hats, cutaway coats and spats); eloquent Communist orators win over hesitant workers to the Marxist-Leninist cause. This kind of agitprop theatre spread from Russia to Germany, and by the early 1930s had reached the United States and Canada.

The emergence of a Canadian "workers' theatre," and the kind of drama it produced, was first proclaimed to a comparatively wide public by E. Cecil-Smith in an article published in the *Canadian Forum* of 14 October 1933 while the magazine was under the editorship of Communist sympathizer J. Francis White. Distinguishing this new theatre movement from the amateur drama leagues and their escapist entertainment that dominated the sparse contemporary activity of the bourgeois Canadian stage, Cecil-Smith emphasizes the nationalism of Canadian agitprop. He also divides the new genre into three sub-genres: the mass recitation, the agitprop sketch which "borrows much from the school of symbolism," and plays that "utilize the methods developed by the 'realist' school" ("The Workers' Theatre" 68). Cecil-Smith might have gone on to point out that Marxist-inspired plays of the 1930s often used elements from all three forms, as well as other theatrical and literary devices adapted from the bourgeois stage. The first Canadian agitprop troupe, the Workers' Experimental Theatre (subsequently known as the Workers' Theatre) had emerged from the Toronto Progressive Arts Club in 1932. As the workers' theatre movement spread to Montreal, Winnipeg, Vancouver, and other centres, it must have raised the hopes of would-be playwrights within the Party. But the phenomenal popular success of these amateur groups did not ultimately result in a significant increase in either the stage production or the publication of original Canadian plays. When the theatre companies in their home cities and on tour encountered large and enthusiastic audiences, they began to think in terms of more elaborate productions, more professional scripts—and more probable success of imported plays with reputations already established abroad. After 1935 the Workers' Theatre was replaced by the Theatre of Action, a national united front troupe that emphasized in its repertoire such successes of the international (especially US) left-wing theatre as Clifford Odets' *Waiting for Lefty*, Irwin Shaw's *Bury the Dead*, and John Wesley's *Steel*.

Fragmentary information in the only comprehensive history of the Canadian progressive theatre movement of the 1930s, Toby Gordon Ryan's *Stage Left*, suggests that workers' theatre groups in Toronto and elsewhere produced several original plays by local writers. But few of these works found their way into print, and most are presumably now lost. The Montreal PAC put on a mass recitation written by "two members of the club" about the murder of Nick Zynchuk (37). The Vancouver Progressive Arts Players mounted a play about unemployment, *Twenty-Five Cents* by Eric Harris, which was a winner in the Dominion Drama Festival of 1936 (54). Harold Griffin, a Vancouver Communist journalist, wrote *Hostage* (1937), a one-act play about the Spanish Civil War, and *Embargo* (1938) about British Columbia's political and economic position in the Pacific (69, 71). Frank Love reported in 1939 that the city of Hamilton, Ontario, had "six producing playwrights," some or all of whom were working with agitprop forms (186). The original Canadian plays produced by the Workers' Experimental Theatre include the one-act *Deported*, written collectively by members of the troupe, performed in May 1932 but apparently never published, and *Solidarity, Not Charity* by T. Shapiro, a two-scene work published in pamphlet form as *Charity*. *Deported*, like Maguire's *Unemployment*, was a realistic domestic vignette, in this case involving foreign-born workers threatened with deportation, but ending in accordance with the socialist realist formula on a note of hope. *Charity* combines realism, caricature, and mass recitation to ridicule the "boss charity" doled out by a paternalistic bureaucracy and to affirm confidence in working-class solidarity.

Perhaps some day the texts of many other plays by forgotten authors will emerge from research into Canadian theatre history to enable a fuller survey of the art of Canadian agitprop drama. In the meantime, an assessment of the significance of this art for Canadian literary history must be based primarily on examples of the genre published in 1933-34 in *Masses,* and collected by Richard Wright and Robin Endres in *Eight Men Speak and Other Plays from the Canadian Workers' Theatre* (1976). Like the socialist realist short story, the typical agitprop play is usually brief, with a deliberate focus on one point of theory about modern society. These features are evident in Oscar Ryan's mass recitation *Unity* (*Masses* May/June 1933). Here, four capitalists speaking in sequence and in chorus mouth the clichéd apologies of their class concerning the Depression, blaming "international conditions," the USSR, and "agitators." Four workers respond, denouncing capitalism and fascism and extolling a united front against the class enemies of the proletariat. Ryan establishes a national context through occasional allusions to Canada and Canadians, but the theme is abstract and universal, and involves the refutation of the false unity expounded by capitalism and the celebration of the true unity of the working class. In line with his tendency to reduce the main theme of proletarian art to the class struggle, Stanley Ryerson in his one-act *War in the East* (*Masses* March/April 1934) simplifies the political situation in Asia to a wish-fulfilment episode in which Japanese soldiers turn against their officers and join forces with their Chinese working-class comrades. The decadence and deceit of capitalist and fascist power are epitomized by the "Mikado," who appropriately wears a mask and rants about the divinity of his regime, while revealing that he is hand-in-glove with unmistakably human militarists and financiers.

The art of Canadian Communist agitprop drama is best epitomized in the most ambitious and influential example, *Eight Men Speak*. Suppressed by police after its famous performance in Toronto on 4 December 1933, it was published in excerpt in *Masses* (January 1934), and in its entirety later that year in an edition prepared by the Toronto Progressive Arts Club. A defiantly inorganic collection of stage artifices and rhetorical conventions, the play was written by the team of Oscar Ryan, E. Cecil-Smith, "H. Francis" (Frank Love), and Mildred Goldberg. "Four of us volunteered to write it collectively," declared Ryan, who apparently coordinated the group. "We worked out a sketchy outline, and assigned scenes and acts among ourselves. Within a few weeks we had the first scripts to read, discuss and revise" (qtd. in T.G. Ryan, *Stage Left* 44). Written to exploit public indignation over recent events, the hasty composition might have resulted in a bad play. Yet in spite of its abortive run the play was a phenomenal stage success, and remains a memorable incident in Canadian theatre history.

Critical commentary on the written text can add little to the understanding of the play, but brief description of some of its rhetorical strategies might help place its significance in Canadian Communist literary history. The play is a prime illustration of Cecil-Smith's exposition of how agitprop combines realistic and non-realistic elements. Some agitprop plays, like Ryan's *Unity*, use only abstract situations and personifications to represent the struggle between workers and capitalists, but *Eight Men Speak* follows most examples of the genre in taking its subject from real contemporary people and events. In 1932, after a much- publicized trial under Section 98 of the Criminal Code, CPC leader Tim Buck and seven other Party officials were imprisoned in Kingston Penitentiary. During a prisoners' riot in the fall of the same year, a guard fired shots into Buck's cell. Since Buck was neither an instigator nor a participant in the riot the shooting was clearly an assassination attempt, possibly carried out under the order of prison or even government officials. Instead of providing the investigation the incident called for, however, the authorities laid charges against Buck, who was convicted as a participant in the riot. The guard who fired the shots was never even identified, let alone charged. Around these events the playwrights constructed a series of brief scenes. The central episode—originally intended to be the entire scope of a much shorter play—is an imaginary trial of the prison guard. The guard is defended by "Capitalism," the stereotypical fat, formally attired caricature; the prosecutor is a personification of CLDL, the Canadian Labor Defense League. Significantly, CLDL is represented as a woman, a reflection of the feminist influences in the Communist literary community that made this milieu so congenial to writers like Dorothy Livesay and *New Frontiers* editor Margaret Gould. The trial is preceded by scenes exposing the hypocrisy of the prison bureaucracy and the bourgeois society it serves, and extolling the courage and humanity of Buck, his fellow political prisoners, and their supporters. Essentially, the whole play is devoted to this kind of reversal of stereotypes: the authors' basic argument is simply that the accusations made against Communists, in the courts, the media, and public opinion, should properly be made against the accusers. It is the bourgeois government and its judicial and penal administrators, not the working class and its Communist organizers and leaders, who are the liars and criminals. Bourgeois society, as the play reveals in various scenes, is characterized by moral and religious hypocrisy, a sleazy and irresponsible obsession with voyeuristic sex, self-indulgent and simple-minded notions of art, and an ignorant fear of revolution which it can only relieve through brutality. Communism, represented by the eight victims of bourgeois injustice and especially by Tim Buck, stands for moral rectitude, intelligence, family values, and a commitment to genuine justice.

*Eight Men Speak*, like most non-realistic agitprop drama, reduces moral and political issues to black-and-white conflicts that resolve in the victory of Communism. As effective as this reductive method could be on the stage, by the mid-1930s this kind of agitprop began to decline in popularity with drama groups and audiences. This decline can be traced to several factors, including the vigorous opposition of police to agitprop theatre companies, and the willingness of Communists in the second half of the decade to form united front compromises with socialists, liberals, and other movements that preferred more moderate and subtle forms of socially critical art. In March 1937 the arts periodical *New Frontier* published a one-act play that epitomizes the liberal anti-capitalist counterpart to agitprop.

Mary Reynolds's *And the Answer Is...* avoids extravagant stage conventions in favour of a presentation much closer to social realism. The winner of a playwriting competition sponsored by *New Frontier*, Reynolds's work is more reminiscent of Baird's *Waste Heritage* than of the formulaic and partisan plays of the *Masses* writers. The theme is the hopelessness of the economic victims of the Depression, depicted directly through an accidental convergence of a representative group in a city park, and comparatively through a scene of hypocritical bourgeois women who talk vaguely about their social responsibility but use their own dishonest moral standards as a means of evading this responsibility. Among the poor people, the "man in the cap" expresses angry cynicism; a young couple who want to get married try to deny the hopelessness of their situation; an older man devastated by personal tragedy takes refuge in hysterical religious zeal; and in the midst of all this misery a supine figure on a park bench slips silently into death. There is no exposition of the economic problem, no explicit denunciation of capitalism beyond the ridicule of the bourgeois women, and no suggestion of prospects for the ultimate overthrow of the unjust social system. Like Baird in *Waste Heritage*, and like Trevor Maguire in his pre-Socialist Realism *Unemployment*, Reynolds suggests that for socially caused human misery there is no answer beyond the expression of grief and pity.

• • • • •

Of the various literary genres available to progressive writers in the 1930s, poetry especially flourished. Less popular with readers than fiction and drama, it was the most appealing to would-be writers. Labour journalists, or working people with only a casual interest in literary activity, might try their hands at doggerel that could be submitted to a wide choice of publications. The cultural periodicals *Masses, Canadian Forum*, and *New Frontier* featured poetry, as did most pro-labour newspapers and magazines such as the *Worker*, its successor the *Daily Clarion*, regional papers like the *B.C. Lumber Worker* and the *People's Advocate* of Vancouver, even specialized organs like the Canadian Labor Defense League's *Canadian Labor Defender*. Much of the newspaper poetry was designed to make a straightforward appeal to the naive reader, but a few poets tried to incorporate into their work the experimentalist forms and techniques associated with bourgeois modernism. Within the international Communist movement there was relatively little theorizing about poetry as a medium for progressive political ideals; such speculations were much more likely to be related to fiction and drama. The ideals of socialist realism might be applied vaguely to poetry, through assumptions that all creative literature should deal in a critical but politically positive way with the problems of the real historical world. The limited theoretical commentary that found its way into print raised the same sorts of questions as were applied to drama and fiction. Such questions included how the class struggle should be represented in terms of language and form, how modern proletarian poetry should relate to the bourgeois poetic tradition, and how (or even whether) proletarian poetry should try to reflect the national distinctiveness of its country of origin.

Some of these questions were confronted by "Maurice Granite"—probably a pseudonym for Oscar Ryan—in an article entitled "On Canadian Poetry" for the July/August 1932 issue of *Masses*. Like many mainstream Canadian poets of the 1920s and 1930s, Ryan sees the national poetic tradition as stuck in the Victorian age, but expresses doubts about the kind of anti-Victorian modernism practised by T.S. Eliot and his imitators. This kind of poetry, says Ryan, is too abstract and metaphysical. "The poet of today must sing about demonstrations of the workers in such a way that the workers will want to repeat his poems and march in the streets....Poetry must become the inspiration of the masses." Like their British and American counterparts, the bourgeois Canadian modernists of the 1920s and early 1930s espoused primarily aesthetic rather than political revolutionary ideals. In the preface to the 1936 anthology *New Provinces*, F.R. Scott recognizes that modern poets want to participate in the processes of restoring "order out of social chaos" (38), and the anthology includes a number of tentative socially critical poems. But in 1933, no Canadian poet influenced by international modernism outside the Communist Party was writing work that was intended to inspire the masses to revolutionary action. Ryan's model Canadian poet, consequently, is Wilson MacDonald (1880-1967), a somewhat ironic choice, since MacDonald achieved popular acclaim through his vestigial Victorian verse in the tradition of Bliss Carman, although by the late 1930s he was turning more frequently to poetry of social protest and political satire, from a leftist (although non-Communist) perspective.

As early as 1930, in fact, in a slim, self-published volume entitled *Caw-Caw Ballads*, MacDonald expressed his satirical reflections on the aspects of human nature that were leading western civilization to social and economic disaster. Representing various bourgeois functionaries—preachers, politicians, critics, clubmen, doctors, artists, lawyers—as crows, MacDonald exposes the pomposity and self-centredness that lead to social injustice. "The Political Crow," for instance, tells of how "[a] poor old crow/Who was hungry and lean" is thrown in jail for stealing "one white bean," while

> ...another bird
> Who had lots to eat,
> Stole sixty bushels
> Of corn and wheat.
>
> "This bird" cried the crows,
> "Has political bent."
> So they sent him to Caw-
> Caw Parliament. (14-16)

But MacDonald's cynical verses about the vagaries of human nature do not imply the possibility of revolutionary action. The poetry of Oscar Ryan, in spite of his professed admiration for MacDonald's work, is much more politically didactic and inclined toward a synthesis between modernist and traditionalist poetic forms. But if he is divided between modernism and traditionalism as far as form is concerned, he is in little doubt as to content. Poetry, like all proletarian literature, is to reveal the evils of capitalist society and the inevitability of working-class triumph. Although inclined to the limited use of indirection and linguistic incongruity, Ryan recognizes the proletarian poet's obligation to provoke a response from the untutored worker whose concept of poetry is most likely to be based on such musical forms as marching songs and patriotic anthems.

Ryan's poems of the early 1930s, published in *Masses*, the *Worker*, and other papers, reflect the general tension between form and content evident in his article on Canadian poetry. "Hunger" (*Masses* April 1932) invokes in three brief, metrically irregular blank verse stanzas the elemental sufferings of the Depression-era poor and the inevitability of proletarian revolution. The "children of hunger" proclaim their economic extremity with "coughs and curses" and "crude speech" as "they finger/the last loaf of bread." But

> Sometimes—
> it's good to finger
> the last loaf of bread,
> because hunger goes on
> like the hollow darkness
> of an empty
> terribly empty world.

This conclusion to the poem conveys a rather incoherent impression of irremediable desolation, but the intimation of the positive historical value of hunger provokes an unspoken reminder of the Marxist concept of the inevitability of revolution. The language is too uncertain to fulfill the political purpose, but Ryan is clearly trying to adapt modernist indirections and ambiguities to such a purpose.

He is more explicit with "Sky Scrapers" (*Masses* April 1932), a slightly longer poem that invokes colloquially worded images of high-steel construction workers risking their lives "for thirty cents an hour." Playing ironically with the capitalist cliché of "rising in the world," the poet calls on the worker to "go up," as he literally does, rising as the building rises in construction, to discover at the apex the spectacle "down below" of "thousands hungry/cold/naked/homeless." Two longer poems, "Estevan" (*Worker* 9 January 1932) and "This Is the Road" (*Masses* November 1932) invoke through dramatized voices and repetitive refrains the stultifying work routine, the danger and the exploitation suffered by miners and lumber mill workers. In "This Is the Road," the workers' revolutionary spirit emerges out of the destructive power of the mechanized industrial processes and converges with the beat of a drum that suggests the militancy of revolution.

Like the writers of socialist realist short stories, most of the poets who contributed to *Masses* aimed at providing unsophisticated read-

ers with a concise assertion of Marxist political principles and observations of society. Sometimes, as in some short stories of the 1930s,
the conclusion is pessimistic or ironic. Benjamin Katz's "Idle Stands
the Linotype" (*Masses* April 1932) is a free-verse elegy spoken by a
worker who contrasts the pleasure he took in his work in the past
with the misery of unemployment in the present:

> but the days of work are gone.
> cold and hunger,
> and men at missions
> waiting,
> for bowls of soup....

Maurice Zigler's "Proud Soldier" (*Masses* April 1932) is a sarcastic
tribute, also in free verse colloquialisms, to the soldier who is sent in
to attack striking workers. "Red Squad," by "S." (*Canadian Labor
Defender* February 1932) is a brief character sketch and physical
description of a brutal anti-labour cop, "Feet on table, swivel-
chair/back, cigar jammed into/a bovine jaw." Mona Weiss's "My
Fellow Stenos" (*Masses* July/August 1932) criticizes the lack of unity
and class-consciousness among workers, and their tendency to regard
each other with jealousy and contempt, largely on the basis of the
social roles imposed upon them by capitalism.

The contributors to *Masses* included the most prolific Canadian
writer of revolutionary Marxist poetry throughout the 1930s, Joe
Wallace. In the summer of 1933 Wallace finally gave up his job in his
brother's advertising agency under pressure from the company's
clients, and committed himself to a full-time career as a labour poet,
journalist, and activist. "I'm out of a job for the first time in my life,"
he wrote in *Masses* of May/June 1933. "No—that is far from the fact:
the real truth is that for seventeen years and more I have been out of
work. Now, for the first time in my life I've got a job" ("So I Quit").
Wallace's new job was that of itinerant activist, usually unpaid, for
the Communist Party. Over the next three years he worked in Ottawa
and Montreal for the Canadian Labor Defense League, lobbying for
the release of Tim Buck and other imprisoned Communist leaders. In
1936 he joined the staff of the *Daily Clarion* as a reporter, columnist,
and regular contributor of poetry. For the most part, Wallace

remained loyal to the rhymed and rhythmically regular verse forms modeled on the work of nineteenth-century poets like Longfellow and Burns, although he also used looser verse and line forms in his attempts to develop a colloquial proletarian voice. He could also be abstract and metaphysical, at least in his own idiosyncratic way, if not exactly in ways that suggest the direct influence of modernism. Even though he was ostensibly dedicated to a Marxist materialist view of history, Wallace remained loyal to the Roman Catholic beliefs of his upbringing. As a result, he shared with his beloved Victorian poets and with modernists such as T.S. Eliot and W.B. Yeats a concern for the search for values in a world where spirituality is decaying.

But his main purposes were to heroicize the workers and extol the importance of revolutionary militancy and solidarity. One of the first poems Wallace published after committing himself full-time to the Party was "Working Class Coinage" (*Masses* January 1932). Adopting a metaphor from the resource-based economics of industrial capitalism, he equates "gold, silver and steel" with "hunger, revolt and rebirth," the three basic experiences by which the proletariat will ultimately come into possession of its heritage. Another of his poems from the early 1930s, "Way of Life" (1933), presents a darker vision of revolutionary struggle. Comparing the worker to Christ on his way to crucifixion, Wallace emphasizes the alienation, suffering, and sacrifice of the individual revolutionary rather than the triumph of collective working-class strength. In "The Rebel" (1935), he again tries to characterize the individual rather than the collective revolutionary, but presents in contrast to the suffering Christ-figure of "Way of Life" a Wildean aesthete who is

> ...responsive to the evening orchards
> Where Eve's dark apple hangs enticing down,
> To mirth of music grown to melancholy
> Over wide waters blown.

"But time evolves a sterner quest to lure him"; the rebel abandons his self-indulgent extravagances and "puts his hopes and dreams and dear illusions/Beyond the barricade." The poem ends with a vision of a new life of "love and laughter" that the rebel will fight for but will not live to see (*JW Poems* 21-22).

In other Wallace poems, the proletarian revolutionary merges with the poet in a unified expression of the self-doubts and anxieties that he experiences in both identities. In "Sometimes the Smoke Lifts" the title image of a pause in battle blends with the rising of a curtain on a stage where the actor/poet, feeling momentarily cut off from the enigmatic god-like "actor-manager" who directs him, pauses to question the meaning and value of both his performance and the controlling power behind it. Wallace expresses even greater self-doubt in "De Profundis" (1936), where he abandons the subject of his public obligations to contemplate his inner feelings of guilt and inadequacy:

> For in my being is a sea
> Peopled with blacker infamy,
> With sensual pulp and brutal shell,
> Spawn of a self-created hell. (*JW Poems* 136)

Throughout his long literary career Wallace continued to assert in his poetry doubts about his spiritual status and to express generalized human anxieties such as feelings of loneliness and fear of death. But in the 1930s he devoted most of his efforts to poetry involving political and social issues. This poetry often includes nationalistic sentiments, such as those expressed in what became his most popular poem, "O Lovely Land" (1936), with its echo of the song that was to become the Canadian national anthem:

> O Canada, O promised land
> This is the dream our fathers planned,
> And tho' the rich have ravished you,
> We swear to make this dream come true! (*JW Poems* 5)

As he did in the 1920s, Wallace also continued to write epigrammatic, satirical anti-capitalist poems. In comparison to MacDonald's crow fables, Wallace's criticism of capitalism and its supporting bureaucracies usually features more sympathy for the victims, as can be seen in his "The Doll House" (1936):

> Hundreds of thousands
> Spent to make
> A mansion for a doll;
> What, spend that much

To clear the slums,
For children?
Not at all. (*JW Poems* 27)

The rhetoric of anti-capitalism and even of Marxism was by no means the exclusive property of poets who belonged to the Communist Party, especially in the late 1930s as more and more Canadian creative writers accepted the idea of a political "united front" involving socialists, Communists, and liberal democrats. Although his objections to Stalinism kept him aloof from the Party, the Vancouver author A.M. Stephen also wrote anti-capitalist satirical poems during the Depression, as he became more increasingly involved with Marxism and the ideas and policies of both revolutionary and evolutionary socialism in the 1930s. His "Keep Your Eye on Heaven" (newspaper clipping, c. 1932, Stephen Papers), was written in response to a news report of the RCMP finding a man starved to death in Calgary, the home town of Conservative prime minister R.B. Bennett, soon after Bennett was reported to have declared to an assembly of American clergymen that "Christianity was the remedy for all our social ills."

Hungry, son?
Been standing in the bread line?
Been tramping, looking for jobs?
Keep your eye on heaven.

Through its accumulation of such pious declarations intermingled with materialist hyprocrisies ("if we trust in God/...Stocks will go up/And Profits pour into our tills"), the poem ridicules the moral abstractions offered to Canadian economic victims throughout the 1930s.

Stephen was equally vigorous in his attacks on fascism and his critiques of the deteriorating international political situation, as in his monologue, "How Are You?" (*New Frontier* April 1936):

"How are you, this morning?"
I questioned a man.
He replied:
"In Spain, a bullet has shattered my brain.
In China bayonets have pierced my side.

In America, I am crying for bread at my mother's knee.
I am rotting in Canadian gaols.
In Europe, I am driven by hunger and despair to the
red shambles of war.
Thank you for asking.
I might be better than I am…this morning!"

The poet and editor Kenneth Leslie (1892-1974) also wrote
Depression-inspired verse with strong anti-capitalist and sometimes
explicitly Marxist reverberations. A Nova Scotian like his acquaintance Joe Wallace, Leslie was associated with a Halifax-based literary
milieu in the 1920s, and inclined toward nature-oriented mystical
and romantic poetry comparable to the early work of A.M. Stephen.
Like Wallace, Leslie was also inspired by both leftist politics and
Christianity—in his case, Baptist Protestantism. In the early 1930s he
moved to Boston, where he established a religiously oriented periodical of social criticism, the *Protestant Digest*. Leslie was one of a very
few politically progressive Canadian writers who spent much of their
literary careers in the United States, where he lived until the late
1940s, although most of his books of poetry were published in
Canada, and dealt extensively with Canadian themes. Considering
himself a Christian socialist, Leslie's strong sympathies for the victims
of the Depression and his antipathy to fascism drew him toward
Marxism and pro-USSR sentiments, although he remained outside the
Communist Party (Devanney, passim).

Leslie published many poems of social criticism in the *Digest* during the 1930s, but his best-known poem in this vein is "O'Malley to
the Reds" (August 1939). Like Wallace and Stephen, Leslie preferred
rhymed, emphatically rhythmical verse, especially for his poems of
social commentary. In over two hundred lines, mostly of dialogue
with a minimum of exposition and authorial commentary,
"O'Malley" dramatizes the respective attitudes of Communists and
Christians toward the labour-capitalist conflict and revolutionary
social change. Since Leslie himself, like Joe Wallace, was interested in
exploring the continuity between the two ideologies, both the
Christian and Marxist positions are presented thoughtfully and sympathetically. Surprisingly, however, the Protestant Leslie makes his
Christian spokesman a Roman Catholic priest. This is partly attribut-

able to local colour realism, since the "Reds" of the poem are Cape Breton coal miners of Scottish Catholic Highlander descent, but O'Malley's religion is also an important part of the larger thematic development of the poem. As Leslie makes clear through the priest's address to the miners, O'Malley represents not the reactionary and authoritarian Catholicism that was gaining notoriety for its support of fascist regimes in Italy and Spain. Rather, he stands for the egalitarianism and ecumenicalism that is part of the traditional meaning of Christianity.

O'Malley begins by taking a conventional Christian position and criticizing the strikers for devoting their energies entirely to negative and materialistic hatred and revolutionary destruction, while forgetting their spiritual obligation to "the One Within." Instead of hatred, they should commit their energies to Christian love,

> for only love can build a nest,
> and only love can spread
> rich hunger on your table,
> sweet rest upon your bed. (Leslie, *Poems* 172)

By way of reply one of the miners sings a traditional Gaelic lament about the ruthless expulsion of their ancestors from Scotland, a lament

> for the croft and runrig, for the nets drying,
> for the lost sheiling,
> grey gulls wheeling
> forever and crying. (173)

The strikers, he explains, are driven not by anger, but by sorrow for their heritage of suffering and loss, a sorrow such as that suffered by the crucified Christ, whose name has been appropriated by the pious hypocrites who exploit them. O'Malley recognizes that he and the strikers are not so spiritually far apart as he believed. Communists and Christians, he admits, should recognize their union in poverty and humility. The red flag, ultimately, is the

> flag of the "ancient lowly,"
> the hungry, dispossessed,
> the simple-hearted, holy. (178)

The poem ends with the priest's appeal to the miners to incorporate their Christian values into their struggle, but does not go on to suggest how this synthesis might be translated into the practicalities of negotiations between the miners and the employers. As in many of his socially critical poems, Leslie is concerned with emphasizing that in social conflict Christian ecumenical and ethical ideals should not be neglected in favour of a secular militancy.

Montreal poet A.M. Klein (1909-72) likewise turned in the 1930s to political poetry expressing a socialist perspective, but his position is frequently much more explicitly Marxist and more militant than that of Leslie or Stephen. Like F.R. Scott and other poets who were influenced by international modernist poetry in the 1920s, Klein turned to social criticism around 1936, as the economic and political crises in the national and international milieux produced intolerable levels of suffering among masses of populations. But Klein went much further than most of his non-Communist literary contemporaries along the road of Marxism. In several poems published in *New Frontier* and the *Canadian Forum*, he expounded the corruption of capitalism—especially the fascist-like police-state tendencies emerging in Quebec—and the possibility of proletarian revolution. Significantly, almost none of Klein's Marxist poems were included in the various volumes of his work published between 1940 and his death in 1972. His work in this vein was largely forgotten until Miriam Waddington wrote an appreciation of it in the *Tamarack Review* in 1967 and included some of the poems in her edition of *The Collected Poems of A.M. Klein* (1974).

As Waddington pointed out, Klein's radicalism was influenced by the socialist tradition in Yiddish literature, and much of his 1930s poetry is concerned with the sufferings of Jews under capitalism. But a more national or even universal reference emerges from some of this work, most notably from the ten-part, 250-line satire "Barricade Smith: His Speeches." Originally conceived as a verse play on "industrial strife" (Klein, qtd. in *Complete Poems*, ed. Pollock, 2:955), the fragments of the uncompleted drama were published in the *Canadian Forum* in four parts, August-November 1938. Through the bitterly ironic voice of a political rabble-rouser whose anonymous Anglo-Saxon name implies his connections to the dominant ethnic majority as well as to the working class, Klein sets forth his diagnosis of the ills of North American capitalist society, and his appeal for a complete revolution in human values. In verse forms ranging from doggerel trimeter through iambic pentameter quatrains, Smith hurls sarcastic challenges to his working-class listeners to wake up to the deceit and exploitation that the bourgeoisie imposes on them. Smith's speeches include many familiar Marxist arguments: the bourgeoisie preaches genteel standards of behaviour as a means of discouraging workers from revolution ("Of Violence"); politicians, teachers, and preachers delude the workers with false promises ("Of the Clients of Barnum"); popular culture has supplanted religion as the new opiate of the people ("Of Psalmody in the Temple"); and distinctions of political ideology have been replaced by oppositions of clothing styles ("Of Shirts and Policies of State"). In his angry zeal to convince the workers of their deception and exploitation under capitalism, Smith addresses his listeners as "rubes" and "suckers" who have been taken in by the hucksters of politics, education, and theology. His anger extends also to poets, who may not serve the masters of capitalist society directly, but are guilty of neglecting the real world in favour of "stars archaic" and "obsolete dew" ("Of Poesy," *Complete Poems* 2: 468). In their neglect of reality they are only comparatively less guilty than the purveyors of religion and entertainment, who are in the business of

> persuading the cockerel dung is beautiful,
> and the bespatted, spit is only rain. ("Of Soporifics," *CP* 2: 469)

Illusion, deceit, and hypocrisy dominate both the institutions of capitalist society and the behaviour of people in this society. In his emphasis on the folly of the people, Klein seems to doubt the Marxist faith in the ultimate triumph of the proletariat. The poem ends with an extended image of bourgeois decadence, "Of the Lily Which Toils Not," featuring the fictional ascent of a social-climbing adventuress to wealth and international notoriety. Earlier in the poem, however, Klein does assert the Marxist belief in the ultimate overthrow of capitalism, although he leaves vague the means and the timing of this overthrow. Inevitably, whether people are prepared for it or not, the new age will come, capitalism will be defeated, and people will one day recall

How they did on that day
If not create new heaven, at least abolish hell. ("Of Dawn and Its
Breaking," *CP* 2: 465)

Besides addressing the themes of poverty and social revolution in
Canada, Klein turned to the international struggle against fascism, in
"Of Castles in Spain" (*Canadian Forum* June 1938), a sequence of
three short poems about the Spanish Civil War. "To One Gone to the
Wars," dedicated to his friend Samuel Abramson who fought in the
Mackenzie-Papineau Battalion of the International Brigades, Klein
expresses his shame for merely theorizing about revolution while
Abramson committed himself to action:

'Tis you who do confound the lupine jaw
    And stand protective of my days and works,
As in the street-fight you maintain the law
    And I in an armchair—weigh and measure Marx. (*CP* 2: 473)

"Toreador" compares the war to a bullfight, in which the republicans
under the "scarlet banner"—like the toreador's red cape—imagina-
tively deliver a clean, efficient coup de grâce upon the bull of Fascism.
"Sonnet Without Music" issues a warning to the Spanish grandees
and priests as they glory in their wealth and position:

beware aristocrat, Don Pelph, beware!
The peon soon will stir, will rise, will stand,
breathe Hunger's foetid breath, lift arm, clench fist,
and heil you to the fascist realm of death! (*CP* 2: 474)

The Spanish loyalist cause elicited responses from several Canadian
poets, both Communist and non-Communist. As Klein's three poems
suggest and as Nicola Vulpe confirms in an essay introducing the
anthology *Sealed in Struggle: Canadian Poetry and the Spanish Civil
War* (1995), most of this poetry tends to be rather detached and
impersonal, based on reading and imagination rather than direct
experience. Unlike the British and American volunteer forces which
included many writers and intellectuals, "of the 1,600 Canadians
who are known to have served in Spain almost all were genuinely
working-class" (Vulpe 21). But the Spanish war provoked many
Canadian poets toward a political commitment they might not other-

wise have espoused. As Dorothy Livesay pointed out in a retrospective article "Canadian Poetry and the Spanish Civil War" (1976), more than any single event of the 1930s that they may have read about or witnessed in their own country, the war prompted Canadian poets to express social concerns (*RHLH* 255).

Some of the resulting poetry, furthermore, was of considerable power. In "Madrid," originally published in the *B.C. Worker's News* (9 October 1936) and reprinted in *New Frontier* (May 1937), A.M. Stephen draws upon his skill with rhymed quatrains to contrast the horrors of the fascist siege of the city with the traditional exotic and sensuous associations of the Spain familiar to tourists:

> Last night in old Madrid guitars
>     Twanged softly to a rose-lit tune
> And castanets, in slim brown hands,
>     Wove spells beneath an autumn moon.
>   . . . . . . . . . . . . . . . . .
> Tonight, in lanes of old Madrid,
>     Red death is arm-in-arm with hate—
> Hate of the creeping Fascist horde,
>     The beast that crouches at her gate.

The final stanzas of this poem, in socialist realist fashion, prophesy an ultimate spiritual and moral victory for the defenders of freedom:

> Though on twisted Nazi cross
>     They nail those hands that were so brave,
> The flower of liberty will spring
>     Triumphant from the martyr's grave.

The civil war poems of A.M. Klein's fellow Montrealer and colleague in the McGill group, Leo Kennedy, who likewise turned toward Marxist-influenced political commitment in the late 1930s, emphasize the gruesome details of battlefield violence. In "You, Spanish Comrade" (*New Frontier* November 1936), the republican fighters are reflected in the image of an eagle's sudden and merciless attacks on its prey. In a dramatization of the violent reversals of the battlefield, the bird is transformed abruptly into a "fallen" victim. But the poet proclaims confidently that the victim's bone, blood, and flesh will provide the foundations for a new life of "peasants turning earth" and "new children springing tall." In Kennedy's "Memorial to the Defenders" (*New Frontier* February 1937), images of the splintered bone, spurting blood, and violated flesh of republican workers fade into a vision of a war memorial erected in the future by "newborn men," a memorial that is also a vision of a revitalized society, "The People's Spain with freedom on its towers!"

L.A. MacKay's "Battle Hymn of the Spanish Rebellion," by contrast, rather than celebrating the republican cause, condemns the Spanish Falangists for defending Christianity with Muslim troops from North Africa and airmen from Germany whose barbaric saturation bombing implies the Nazi revival of Teutonic paganism:

> The church's one foundation
>     Is now the Moslem sword,
> In meek collaboration
>     With flame, and axe, and cord;
> While overhead are floating,
>     Deep-winged with holy love,
> The battle-planes of Wotan,
>     The bombing planes of Jove. (Vulpe 84)

At the opposite extremes of both poetic form and theme, Kenneth Leslie's "The Censored Editor" (*New Frontier* July/August 1937) is a long narrative, virtually a short story in verse, that tries to convey the complexity of the war in personal rather than mythic terms. Like his "O'Malley to the Reds," the poem does not rely on a simple commitment to one side of an argument, but tries to convey something of the spiritual subtleties in all human relationships and beliefs. A Spanish mother who has discovered her son's plot to betray his republican comrades follows the son to his meeting in the hills with his Falangist contact. Recognizing that her son's pride and ambition have overcome his sense of justice, the mother clings to the hope that he will redeem himself before it is too late. The themes of vanity and betrayal are conveyed in metaphors of desolation and sterility, reflected in the barren landscape in which the drama takes place. The conflict between mother and son climaxes in a dialogue which the poet ambiguously suggests may take place in the minds of the characters involved. The mother's parable of rock climbing in which one careless climber brings disaster on the group applies to her son's treason, but the poem deliberately avoids revealing the effect of the parable or the outcome of the whole episode. A clearly defined conflict between right and wrong is set forth but, like the war itself in 1937, the conflict remains unresolved. Although not an entirely successful poem, it is one of the few pro-Republican literary treatments of the war that relies on ambivalent dramatization rather than on chauvinistic assertions of the ultimate triumph of good.

Poets committed to the Communist Party were inevitably inclined to see the issues of the war in straightforward moral terms, but this moral dogmatism does not preclude the possibility of poetic subtlety. Joe Wallace's "Artists in Uniform" (1937) takes the title of the 1934 anti-Stalinist book in which American former Communist Max Eastman denounced the regimentation the Party allegedly imposed on its creative members. Wallace adopts Eastman's epithet and applies it literally to the writers serving with the International Brigades in Spain. Speaking in the voice of the fighting poets, Wallace envisages them as Christ-like heroes sacrificing their creative promise and their lives for their beliefs. But they make this sacrifice in a hope, backed by the assurance of their Christian faith, that their actions will be an adequate substitute for the poems they might have written:

> It may be that we shall die
> With half of our songs unheard,
> But it's been before,
> And may be once more,
> That the Deed becomes the Word.

The ultimate consolation, however, proclaimed in the last of the poem's three stanzas, is the life and beauty which their sacrifice will give to future generations:

> ...richly we're reconciled
> One hour to give
> Forever to live
> A rose in the hands of a child. (*JW Poems* 56)

The war in Spain inspired several of Dorothy Livesay's poems, including the short, sonnet-like lyric "Spain," an appeal for commemoration of the war dead whose sacrifices make possible the enjoyment of beauty and peace. The longer narrative poem "Catalonia" is an imaginative recreation of the front-line fighting, complete with soldiers' dialogue, descriptions of wounded men and the chaotic movement of refugees, ending with an expression of confidence that "another spring" will blossom out of the earth, "fertilized" by "the bones of young men." The war also provoked more personal poems, including the sonnet "Comrade," in which the speaker informs a lover that sexual love must give way to commitment to the revolution. This political commitment, the speaker continues, is not a rejection of the personal life but the establishment of a new kind of personal bond:

> ...sealed in struggle now, we are more close
> Than if our bodies still were sealed in love. (*RHLH* 262)

In the context of her long and prolific literary career, Livesay's Communist poetry is often dismissed as wrong-headed apprentice work. But although Livesay herself excluded many of these early efforts from her *Collected Poems*, she expressed neither disparagement nor regret for her years as a writer in the Communist Party. Unlike Klein, Livesay found at least temporary poetic and political fulfilment within the Party, although she often had to struggle to reconcile Party ideology with her conceptions of poetic form and language. Some of her very early Communist poems are rather repetitive and simplistic. "Pink Ballad" (*Masses* December 1932), for instance, merely repeats mechanically the Communist Party hard line against the "sunshine and socialist guile" of such Canadian democratic socialists as J.S. Woodsworth and Agnes MacPhail (221). Most of her poems of the 1930s likewise express her political zeal, but she also revealed early in the decade that she could adapt Communist ideology to more subtle representations of modern human experience. "A Girl Sees It!" (*Masses* March/April 1933), a dramatic monologue of about one hundred and fifty lines retitled "In Green Solariums" in subsequent reprints, deals with the exploitation, self-discovery and Marxist politicization of a young working woman. In blank-verse iambics that embody her calmness and fortitude, the speaker tells of being seduced by the son of the family for which she worked as a domestic, of bearing his child, descending through unemployment and poverty and gradually rising toward personal and political maturity. This potentially clichéd Communist fable takes on psychological depth as the speaker recognizes the yearnings of her own mind and body that contributed to both her sexual entrapment and her political liberation.

Livesay thus revealed early in her Communist literary career her interest in combining Marxism with a feminist commitment. Much of her 1930s poetry, however, features ungendered reflections on the politics of the decade. "Broadcast from Berlin" (*Masses* September 1933), for instance, based on news reports of riots between Nazis and Communists, is a relatively straightforward partisan comment on current affairs, enlivened by the incorporation of political symbolism:

> Eagles and mystic symbols have no place
> When men in every land together know
> (As one together understand)
> The hammer's swing, the sickle's harvesting.

Her poem "Anyox" (*Daily Clarion* 13 May 1936), applies similar idioms to the subject of exploited mine workers in British Columbia, unapologeticallly proclaiming a remote and supposedly insignificant mining town to be a new Athens or Rome. Other poems, such as "Yes!" (*New Frontier* May 1936), deal with the longing of the younger generation in the 1930s to find beauty in a world of conflict and alienation. "Doom Elegy" (July 1936) and "Man Asleep" (October 1936) depict sheltered youth awakening almost too late to the crises of fascist militarism.

Many of Livesay's poems of the 1930s also reflect her interest—like other Canadian Communist poets such as Oscar Ryan and on occasion Joe Wallace—in reconciling her political ideology with the idioms of poetic modernism. As Livesay reveals in *Right Hand Left Hand*, her conception of modernism, derived principally from reading T.S. Eliot, was drastically altered by the discovery of the politically radical poetry of C. Day-Lewis, Stephen Spender, W.H. Auden, and Louis MacNeice (153). This discovery is reflected in deliberately obscure allusiveness and incongruity, as in these interconnecting images of technology and sexuality in "Yes!":

> The steel-helmeted bird, relentless to Honolulu
> Pilot spanning belief's outdistance
> They lie low together, loving.

But while Livesay adapted the brief lyric and modernist syntactic convolutions to her Marxist purpose, she also began experimenting with a poetic genre that she later called the "documentary poem," and which she continued to explore after she left the CPC. These long poems (usually between one hundred and two hundred lines) used "descriptive, lyrical, and didactic elements" to develop theses about topical subjects, usually political (Livesay, "The Documentary Poem" 269). Her best-known work of this sort, "Day and Night," written while she was still a Communist, appeared in the first issue (1936) of *Canadian Poetry*, the journal of the Canadian Authors Association, edited by E.J. Pratt. A critique of the processes of industrialism that destroy workers in body and mind, the poem emphasizes the numbing succession of shiftwork time ("Day and night/Night and day") and the repetitive movement of assembly-line labour ("One step forward/Two steps back"). These refrains also echo the words and patterns of popular songs and dances, suggesting how the oppressive work routine is commingled with escapist popular culture, as it is in the opening scene of Livesay's short story "Case Supervisor." The poem evolves through imagistic variations and elaborations on these ideas toward a conclusion that suggests an impending climax that could signify either the complete perversion of human thought and experience or the workers' ultimate revolutionary overthrow of the old order:

> Day and night
> Night and day
> Till life is turned
> The other way! (Livesay, *Collected Poems* 125)

Perhaps because it leaves its political implications ambiguous and avoids an explicit Marxist declaration, "Day and Night" has attracted greater critical approval than Livesay's 1930s poetry as a whole. Indeed, readers may not even think of it as a Depression poem, since it was the title work of a collection of poems published in 1944, after Livesay had left the Communist Party. In the article on Livesay in the *Oxford Companion to Canadian Literature*, Frank Davey mistakenly describes the poem as "concerning workers' contributions to wartime industry" (675). Livesay herself, in her 1972 *Collected Poems* included it in a section entitled "Day and Night" rather than in the section "The Thirties." But it is one of three documentary poems of the Depression that Livesay wrote in the late 1930s. The other two, "Depression Suite" and "Queen City," are much more explicit as to political ideology.

"Depression Suite" proclaims the priority of human spiritual values over impersonal material ones. The poem is evidently set in Vancouver, to which Livesay moved in 1936, but the panorama of urban poverty and unemployment and the denunciation of capitalism are not restricted by geographic place. As in "Day and Night," the poem invokes the popular music of the decade, but now the sentimental tunes constitute only one of several forms of music that make up the impressionistic "suite." The succession of seven "songs" invokes such ideas as urban loneliness, routine mechanized labour, and the proletarian urge toward liberty. Various voices—a typist, an unemployed man, a disillusioned worker who hoped vainly to succeed by favouritism ("The boss was a friend of mine")—dramatize both the desperation and the idealism of the Depression's victims. The weak conclusion of the poem, however, is not an affirmation of revolutionary ideals, but a vague assertion of Life. In "Queen City," Livesay's ironic tribute to Toronto, the social message is established in an opening series of quatrains dedicated to the lost generation of young Canadians who have been socially alienated by the Depression. Imagistic stanzas invoke a "sea of faces,"

> Uniform, solemn
> Alert for the warning–
> Whom hunger outpaces. (*Coll. Poems* 80)

The poem opens out on a panorama of urban industrialism: "soot-grimed factories," "commercial steamers, fishing boats, / Oil-manned tankers" contrasted to "the wings of diving gulls." The panorama resolves into more glimpses of the human victims, itinerant unemployed and refugees from dust-bowl farms who are denied relief by urban bureaucrats. The desperation of these victims is expressed in a passage which is a slightly revised version of her earlier short poem "Yes!" As in "Day and Night" and "Depression Suite," fragments of words from popular songs punctuate the victim's search for relief

from misery. In the final section, the obscurity and supposed insignificance of the sufferers are underscored by the grandiose architecture
of the new Royal York Hotel, built by the Canadian Pacific Railway,
one of the corporate pirates denounced in Myers's *History of
Canadian Wealth*. The luxurious hotel is a travesty of a living organism, "with its elevator heart pumping life/Pumping gold from cellar
to summit." While the building stands "shooting above hunger" and
"friendly with the sun," the flesh-and-blood victims of the perverted
values of capitalism are reduced to shadows "under a cold wall." But
in the final stanzas these anonymous victims are identified with a
poetic "I" who proclaims the superiority of flesh and blood and
human creative power over stone walls:

> ...when I look at man again
> A thing scarce noticed by the sun, or mentioned in
> The social columns; when I see
> His legs, his overcoat, his hatless head
> His hands held steady and his clearlit eyes—
>
> Then I am tall as the Royal York,
> For I built it!
> The sun's distance is no chasm, for
> I harnessed him with Copernicus
> and Karl Marx, years ago! (*Coll. Poems* 85)

• • • • •

In addition to poetry, drama, and short fiction, the Canadian progressive literary output in the 1930s included a great deal of discursive prose. Much of this material was ephemeral journalism, but some
authors of political articles and pamphlets were conscious of their
participation in a literary heritage traceable to such writers as
Thomas Paine and John Stuart Mill. At the least, some Canadian journalists and pamphleteers shared the ambition of proletarian poets,
fiction writers, and dramatists to influence the masses through both
aesthetic and polemical means. Before the 1930s, Communist and
socialist expository writing in English was hampered by a stiff
bureaucratic style, probably influenced by European revolutionary
journalism and political theory, especially Russian and German,

which often appeared stilted in translation. But Canadian radical writers in the 1930s were eager to reach the masses by means of a popular style and idiom. Joe Wallace took to this kind of writing with particular enthusiasm. In *Clarion* columns variously titled "A World to Win" and "Between the Lines," he cultivated an autobiographical rhetoric, drawing general lessons about the political turmoil of the modern world from anecdotes about his own troubled childhood (26 November 1936) or his estrangement from his own children as a result of his political commitments (23 April 1938).

The published prose of Norman Bethune in the 1930s also reveals a vigorously idiosyncratic writing style. Of his many reports and commentaries from and about Russia, Spain, and China, two particularly demonstrate his abilities to disturb bourgeois complacency. His "Reflections on Return from 'Through the Looking Glass,'" delivered as a speech to a gathering of physicians in December 1935 and published early in 1936 in the *Bulletin of the Montreal Medico-Chirurgical Society*, conveys the incongruities and paradoxes of the USSR, based on his recent visit to that country. Providing virtually no specific details about what he saw in Russia, Bethune compares the country to Lewis Carroll's imaginary land where one must be prepared to believe "impossible things." Modern Russia, he suggests, like Alice's Looking-Glass Land, is just as real as—perhaps even more real than—the world the observer inhabits. Like Looking-Glass Land, the new USSR should not be dismissed as meaningless merely because it seems strange. Moving on to an even more vigorous metaphor, he draws on the professional experience of himself and his audience to compare the USSR with a woman in labour, and to remind them of the "pitiful, ludicrous, grotesque and absurd" as well as the beautiful qualities of his subject. "Creation is not and never has been a genteel gesture," he concludes. "It is rude, violent and revolutionary. But to those courageous hearts who believe in the unlimited future of man...Russia presents today the most exciting spectacle of the evolutionary, emergent and heroic spirit of man which has appeared on this earth since the Reformation" (Bethune, *Politics of Passion* 91-92). In contrast to the indirect and metaphorical method of the essay on Russia, Bethune describes in direct and abundant literal detail the plight of Spanish refugees from fascist bombings in his pamphlet *The*

*Crime on the Road: Malaga-Almeria* (1937). Atrocities are described with the understated conciseness of an eyewitness who is sated with visions of wartime violence. The essay concludes with a minimalist statement of the horror of the fascist bombing of the city of Almeria, where the refugees believed they had finally reached safety. "That night were murdered fifty civilians and an additional fifty were wounded. There were two soldiers killed" (Bethune 153).

Oscar Ryan adapts broader techniques, reminiscent of agitprop drama, in his pamphlets for the Canadian Labor Defense League. In *The "Sedition" of A.E. Smith* (1934) he defends a CLDL leader who has written and spoken on behalf of imprisoned Communists. Beginning with brief biographies, printed in parallel columns, of Smith and R.B. Bennett, Ryan contrasts the career of Smith from poor boy through Methodist minister to social activist with the political decadence of the millionaire Bennett and his public expressions of contempt for the working class. Thus establishing Smith as a champion of freedom against the "iron heel" tyranny of Bennett, Ryan goes on to enumerate the chronicle of government deceit and crime against the workers, including the attempted assassination of Tim Buck, the police murder of Nick Zynchuk, and the illegal mass deportations of radical immigrants, many of whom may have been sent to their deaths at the hands of fascist regimes.

The Vancouver poet and novelist A.M. Stephen, in spite of his refusal to join the Stalinist CPC, achieved approval from both Communists and socialists with his Marxist and anti-fascist pamphlets. His *Marxism: The Basis for a New Social Order* (1933) is a lucid explication of the "materialist conception of history" as opposed to the "sentimental and Utopian ideas" of non-Marxist socialist movements. Addressing himself to working-class readers, Stephen expounds the surplus value theory, the significance of the class struggle, and the modern evolution of capitalism toward fascism. Published by the *B.C. Clarion*, the official organ of the Socialist Party of Canada, Stephen's pamphlet demonstrates the ideological connections between the socialist and Communist movements in Canada, even at a time when the political parties representing these movements were extremely hostile to each other. As socialists and Communists came closer together in the united front period, Stephen emerged even more prominently as a spokesman for their common cause. Although he eventually affiliated himself with the newly formed social democratic CCF (Co-operative Commonwealth Federation) in preference to the Communist Party, he became increasingly zealous for Marxist political solutions and against right-wing ideologies and police-state policies. His *Hitlerism in Canada* (published 1936 by the Canadian League against War and Fascism) and his *Fascism: The Black International* (published 1936 by the *B.C. Clarion*) warn against the tendency of Canadian politicians and bureaucracies to take the side of the capitalist oligarchy in the class struggle. For the Communist-dominated League, Stephen makes an explicitly Marxist appeal, labelling fascism "the black spectre that is haunting Europe," and denouncing the fascist-like policies of the federal government toward the unemployed. The *Clarion* pamphlet, addressed mainly to the members of the CCF, is relatively restrained in its Marxist rhetoric, calling for a "united front of all radical parties" in a peaceful struggle against monopoly capitalism and the "world-wide rule of economic imperialism." "With the same courage and integrity as those who fought for freedom in 1837," Stephen concludes, "we may, by constitutional methods, and without loss of human life and property, stage the second Revolution in Canadian history and bring the blessings of peace and prosperity to our people under the new social order, in which the means of wealth production will be in the hands of the producers of wealth" (23).

Stephen's invocation of the nineteenth-century uprisings in Upper and Lower Canada seems an incongruous analogy to his appeal for peaceful constitutional change, but 1837 was becoming an increasingly prominent rhetorical rallying point for anti-capitalist writers in the late 1930s. Canadian progressive writers especially found parallels between the rebellions and the Spanish Civil War, parallels that were to be commemorated in the establishment within the International Brigade of a Mackenzie-Papineau Battalion. The parallels were recognized also in the first book-length work of Marxist historiography written by a Canadian, Stanley Ryerson's *1837: The Birth of Canadian Democracy* (1937). After graduating from the University of Toronto in 1933 and spending the summer as a Young Communist League activist and contributor to *Masses*, Ryerson went on to the Sorbonne, to earn a Diplôme d'Etudes supérieures with a thesis on the Sicilian peasant novelist Giovanni Verga (1840-1922). In his *Novelle rusticane* (1883) and other works of fiction, Verga depicted the exploitation of Sicilian peasants and villagers by the church, feudal landowners, and corrupt bureaucrats. The study of Verga's work undoubtedly fueled Ryerson's radicalism, and especially his sympathies with the French-Canadian industrial and rural workers, who were oppressed like Verga's Sicilians by the Roman Catholic Church and a corrupt government. After returning to Canada, he abandoned the study and teaching of languages and literatures in favour of journalism, the writing of Canadian history, and active engagement in "the revolutionary movement of this century" (Ryerson, foreword, *1837*, 11).

While teaching for the year 1934-35 at Sir George Williams College in Montreal, Ryerson joined the Communist Party of Quebec, where his administrative abilities and fluent bilingualism quickly propelled him into the positions of provincial secretary and associate editor of the French-language Party newspaper, *Clarté*. Subtitled "journal d'opinions et d'action populaires," and committed "au service du front populaire des droits du peuple," *Clarté* launched vehement attacks on the right-wing Quebec government and its ultra-nationalist and neo-feudalistic ideologies. Although frequently subjected to harassment by the Montreal City Police and the Sureté provinciale, including a raid on Ryerson's home in early 1938, *Clarté* managed to survive almost until the outbreak of the Second World War. In addition to his journalism and Party administrative duties, Ryerson completed his brief history of the 1837 rebellions. The 136-page book was published by Francis White, the former editor of the *Canadian Forum* who in 1936 established a small publishing company to produce books and pamphlets relating to the USSR and the international Communist movement. As Ryerson admits in a foreword, *1837* is not "a work of original research." He has attempted "as far as possible, to have the actual speeches and writings, letters and newspaper articles of the period, do the telling of the story" (10). His commitment to journalism and political activity, however, prevented him from spending the requisite months sifting through massive amounts of archival source material, so the quotations and basic narrative facts are adapted from published sources. But the facts are given an interpretation unprecedented in Canadian historiography.

As a Marxist and a Communist Party functionary, Ryerson recognizes his obligation to make his work consistent with both Marxist ideology and the expectations of a working-class readership. The latter consideration—plus, no doubt, the pressures to complete the work in time for the centennial of the rebellions—contributed to the brevity of the text. The expectations of his non-specialist readers also influenced his decision to exclude the scholarly apparatus of reference notes and bibliography, although there are enough implicit and explicit indications in the text to identify the most important of Ryerson's sources. To fulfill his aim of telling the story "as far as possible" through quotation and paraphrase from documents of the period, Ryerson makes extensive use of such readily available published sources as the *Durham Report* and William Lyon Mackenzie's *Sketches of Canada and the United States* (1833). He also draws on the work of earlier historians and biographers, especially work sympathetic to Mackenzie and Papineau, such as Charles Lindsey's *Life and Times of William Lyon Mackenzie* (1862, rev. 1926) and L.O. David's *Les Patriotes de 1837-1838* (1884). But he also acknowledges the work of hostile historians, particularly J.C. Dent, whose *Story of the Upper Canada Rebellion* (1885) Ryerson cites repeatedly to demonstrate the fallacies of the right-wing Tory tendency to conceive Mackenzie and Papineau as rabble-rousers and the rebellions as extremist responses to social and political problems that could have been solved by benevolent action from above.

Ryerson's analysis of economic conditions in the provinces (especially in his chapter "Land, Capital, State Power") demonstrates the thoroughgoing corruption of the administrative and land-owning classes of Upper and Lower Canada. As Gregory S. Kealey points out, Ryerson distinguishes his work from that of his predecessors by placing the events of 1837-38 in the context of the history of ideas related to revolution. The 1837 rebellion, from this perspective, is part of European ideological and political tendencies that can be traced back to the English Civil War of 1642-49, down through the American and French revolutions, the Chartist movement in England, the European revolutions of 1830 and 1848, and forward to the

Russian Revolution and the republican cause in the Spanish Civil War. But although he suggests parallels between 1837 British North America and 1937 Spain, Ryerson does not try to make his Canadian rebels into full-fledged proletarian revolutionaries. As the writings and actions of the leaders make clear, the uprisings were essentially bourgeois revolts against feudalism, part of the stage in the evolution of industrial capitalism which, according to Marx, precedes proletarian revolution (69). However, Ryerson does emphasize the fact that in the armed revolt the bourgeois leaders had to rely on the working class for the rank and file of their fighting forces. "In the Canadian struggle, as in the 1848 bourgeois revolution in France, the participation of these masses left its imprint on the program and character of the movement" (75).

Ryerson tells the story of the armed struggle with unsparing explicitness, emphasizing the ruthlessness of the British military leaders and the many disadvantages of the insurgents, including a lack of trained military leaders and of experienced and properly armed soldiers. But he also emphasizes the many positive aspects of the ill-fated conflict. In line with his beliefs as a pan-Canadian nationalist, he avoids the tendency of bourgeois historians to treat the events in Upper and Lower Canada as two distinct rebellions. Although he acknowledges important political and social differences between the two provinces, he insists that these differences were reconciled in the rebels' common motives and goals. To Ryerson, the events of November-December 1837 constituted one uprising, fought on two fronts. He also avoids the designations "rebellion" and "rebels" used by bourgeois historians, in favour of "revolution," "revolutionaries," and—mindful of the parallels with Spain—"civil war." Like other contemporary supporters of republican Spain, furthermore, he refers to the insurgent cause of 1837 as the cause of *democracy*. Enshrining the word in the title of his book, he suggests that it refers to both the bourgeois liberalism that will supplant the remnants of feudal oligarchy and the ultimate vision of equality in the classless society brought about by the proletarian revolution. Ryerson's aim, consistent with the larger Marxist Communist purpose of redefining "democracy," is to change the way Canadians think about and refer to the events of 1837 and the idea of revolution generally. His language occasionally lapses into melodrama—"The Canadian people, the working men and women who are the true Canada, are not forgetting!" (9)—but his tone is more characteristically governed by the prophetic strain of passages like the following: "the proletariat and farming people, the ruling majority of the future, made their voice heard; and the 'social democracy' proclaimed by Mackenzie was the gleam, cast far ahead, of the ultimate democracy of Socialism" (75).

The responses of most bourgeois historians to *1837*, as Gregory S. Kealey has demonstrated, were predictably unfavourable. The reviews of University of Toronto professor Donald Creighton and *Saturday Night* editor B.K. Sandwell denounced Ryerson for his attempt to appropriate Canadian history to the narrow Communist agenda. Liberal historian F.H. Underhill was a bit more positive, but none of the few reviews outside the Communist press recognized the importance of Ryerson's introduction of Marxism into Canadian historiography. Even if it is true that Ryerson focuses too narrowly on evidence consistent with Marxist conceptions of the class struggle and proletarian revolution, it must be admitted that his procedures as a historian differ from those of other Canadian historians only in the nature of his biases. As Kealey points out, his Marxist approach—besides being remarkably persuasive at many points, especially in its class analysis of nineteenth-century Canadian society—is a welcome antidote to the many bourgeois interpretations that have dismissed Mackenzie and Papineau as fanatics and the 1837 uprisings as comic-opera farces. Besides contributing to the elaboration of Canadian historical perspectives, Ryerson's book must be counted as the remarkably sophisticated achievement of a twenty-six-year-old author, as well as a significant contribution to Canadian literature of the 1930s. Like the best works of proletarian fiction and poetry, Ryerson's *1837* is a work that successfully transforms the ephemeral textures of human experience into comprehensible ideas and aesthetically appealing language. As Margaret Fairley's edition of the selected writings of William Lyon Mackenzie was also to do two decades later, Ryerson's book contributes to the enterprise of making the events of 1837, and the idea of a revolutionary "spirit of democracy," a respectable part of the Canadian progressive heritage.

# 6

## The 1940s

### War and Post-War

The 1940s brought new vigour to the literary activities of the Canadian Communist movement, as it did to creative writing and publishing generally in Canada. As if in compensation for the cultural failures of the 1930s, a number of novels appeared in the 1940s dealing with the social and economic problems of the Depression era. Many Communist writers benefited from this renewed interest in social realism as well as from widespread public toleration of the USSR and Marxist ideology during the war. At first, however, the outbreak of the Second World War was a disaster for the CPC. The Soviet-German Non-Aggression Treaty of 1938 produced dissension within the Party and aggravated the anti-communism of bourgeois politicians and police. Committed to the official line of the USSR and the Communist International that condemned the war as an imperialist power struggle, the Party found itself isolated from its former united front allies. In the fall of 1939 the Liberal government of Mackenzie King invoked the War Measures Act (passed in 1914) to issue a series of orders-in-council known as the Defense of Canada

Regulations, aimed at the suppression of various allegedly subversive organizations, including the Communist Party. Both the *Clarion* and *Clarté* were immediately banned; in June 1940 the CPC was declared illegal. Over the next year, more than one hundred Communists were arrested and interned in prisoner-of-war camps and jails, most without charge or trial (Whitaker and Marcuse 10). Tim Buck and other Party executives fled to New York and the clandestine protection of the Communist Party of the US.

The consequent apprehension and disorganization reached all segments of the progressive movement, including the literary community. In March 1941 Joe Wallace was included in a police round-up of Communist journalists. Dorothy Livesay in Vancouver tried to continue to function as a Communist, although the influence of her new husband as well as her own widening literary inclinations were drawing her away from the Party. Her decision to make the final break was hastened by the atmosphere of persecution and fear. "I was supposed to make contact with a comrade and meet him in a lobby somewhere," she reminisced years later. "But the second time I was to meet him he never showed up and that was the end" (notes of an interview with David Arnason, 30 May 1976, Livesay Papers). For other Communists and sympathizers, however, it was far from the end. To carry on the work of the exiled central committee, the Party set up a secret operating centre in Montreal, under the interim directorship of Stanley Ryerson and two other young Party members. In January 1940, only weeks after the suppression of the *Clarion*, the first issue of the weekly *Canadian Tribune* appeared. Edited by A.A. MacLeod, former president of the non-partisan Canadian League for Peace and Democracy, the *Tribune* was incorporated as an independent publication to avoid suppression under the government's emergency regulations. Although watched closely by police and even suspended briefly in 1941 by order of the Secretary of State, the paper grew in popularity and circulation, attracting the literary contributions of important writers, including Irving Layton, Miriam Waddington, and Dorothy Livesay. Eventually established as the official organ of the CPC, the "Trib" survived as the voice of Marxist-Leninist Communism in Canada for over fifty years.

With the German invasion of Russia in June of 1941, the government lost its principal excuse for the suppression of the Communist movement. Although the rabidly anti-Communist minister of justice Louis St. Laurent implemented various delaying tactics, all the internees had been released by the fall of 1942. Also in the fall of 1942 the exiled Party leaders and their interim substitutes surrendered to the RCMP and were shortly cleared of charges and set free. Although federal authorities would not lift the official ban on the Party, they did not oppose the formation of a Marxist-Leninist political organization under a new name. In August 1943 the former Communist Party of Canada was reconstituted as the Labor-Progressive Party (LPP), a name it retained until 1959. The Communists emerged from their period of internment and exile to find themselves in a new atmosphere of toleration, thanks especially to public approval of the Russian war effort. Even before the formal establishment of the legal party, a newly published literary work by a Communist attracted unprecedented attention. *Night Is Ended*, the first book of poems by Joe Wallace, appeared in early 1943 under the imprint of the leftist Contemporary Publishers of Winnipeg. Previewed in selections in the *Canadian Tribune* of 7 November 1942, the book featured a preface by the distinguished poet and University of Toronto professor E.J. Pratt, who described the poems as "genuine lyrics" and "emotionally dynamic." According to another prominent academic, E.K. Brown, the book was "an unusual and moving collection." Wallace's "martial" poems, said Brown, "are over-rhetorical and verbally not more than half-alive, but the melancholy personal pieces are often wholly admirable in their intensity, economy and clarity" (309). An anonymous reviewer in *Saturday Night* magazine described Wallace as "a poet of high distinction and accomplishment," and expressed outrage at the Canadian government's political persecution of Canadian citizens. "Shelley would have been interned under the Defense of Canada Regulations," the commentator observed ("Communist Poet" 3).

*Night Is Ended* featured poems from Wallace's whole Communist career, going back to his earliest publications in the *Worker* in the 1920s, but Brown was right in singling out the most recent works, based on Wallace's internment experiences. In his fifties and suffering health problems, Wallace had been hauled with other internees from one camp to another, ending up finally in a disused jail in Hull, Quebec. In spite of the indignities and petty persecution, however, Wallace remained defiant in captivity. One incident while he was being held at the Petawawa, Ontario, army base achieved something of a legendary status among Communists. On the occasion of an inspection of the camp by a British official, the commandant referred to the prisoners in Wallace's hut as "enemy aliens." "We are not enemy aliens," Wallace is reported to have said. "We're Canadian anti-fascists." For this alleged breach of discipline he was put in solitary confinement, an extreme reaction that sparked an inmate protest ending only when soldiers were called in and given orders to shoot if the protestors did not disperse (Repka and Repka 151-52).

As the title of *Night Is Ended* suggests, many of the poems present not an angry attack on capitalist society but a faith in ultimate social justice and personal vindication that is related to Wallace's Roman Catholic beliefs. The reconciliation of his political and religious beliefs is explicitly asserted in the poem "Catholics and Communists." In a cheerfully jingling rhythm and rhyme he insists that these beliefs are merely different forms of the same militant revolutionary faith:

> St. Thomas More (to prove my point
> I bring two famous men in)
> Utopia's author, now anoint,
> Would be at home with Lenin. (*JW Poems* 61)

Similarly, St. Joan of Arc, he suggests, might have led the defense of Stalingrad.

But as E.K. Brown observed, the real strength of *Night Is Ended* is in the "melancholy personal pieces." "How High, How Wide," for instance, is a concise and moving expression of Wallace's response to solitary confinement:

> My prison window is not large,
> Five inches high, six inches wide,
> Perhaps seven.
> Yet it is large enough to show
> The whole unfettered to and fro
> Of heaven.... (*JW Poems* 45)

In "I Rose When I Fell," the poet finds Christian patience and a renewal of idealism in the prison experience:

...this be said, through my prison bars
This be said of my sins and scars
This at least: that I reached for the stars
And I rose, when I fell, to my knees. *(JW Poems* 45)

The title poem, on the other hand, is a rousing appeal to the "Workingmen" of the world to awaken to the dawn of a new era that will see the defeat of "Poverty and pelf and plunder." In "Flame of the Future," the ultimate triumph of the "people" is expressed in terms of the reconciliation of spiritual and romantic ideals:

A people in arms, we fight on as one,
The flame of the future inside us!
While the glorious dead march on ahead,
And the women we love beside us. *(JW Poems 48)*

Wallace's hopes for the future could have applied to the renewed cultural prospects of the progressive movement. In 1943 the LPP established its own publishing company, Progress Books. The first editorial director of the company, John Stewart, was a University of Toronto journalism graduate with several years working experience with the trade journals of Maclean's Publishing Company and the *Toronto Star.* Appointed also to the staff of the *Tribune,* Stewart would later edit the newspaper and chair the LPP's National Cultural Commission ("Meet the Staff" 10). Although devoted mainly to Party policy statements, ideological pamphlets, and reprints or translations of Russian and other foreign publications, Progress also published original Canadian scholarly and literary works. Its first prospectus of possible future titles and topics (CPC/LPP Archives, NAC) includes biographies of eminent Canadians, one of which was to be a life of Norman Bethune by journalist and novelist Ted Allan. Allan was indeed working on a biography of Bethune, but the completed work did not appear until 1952, and then not under the imprint of Progress but of the commercial publishing house McClelland and Stewart. The first book published by Progress, however, was an encouraging sign of a commitment to Canadian culture. Stanley Ryerson's *French Canada: A Study in Canadian Democracy* appeared in September 1943.

Although researched and mostly written while Ryerson was much occupied with the direction of the underground party, *French Canada* was a careful and provocative analysis of Quebec social and political history. Like another work that appeared in the same year, journalist Bruce Hutchison's *The Unknown Country*, Ryerson's book aimed at encouraging a sense of national pride and unity among Canadians amid the uncertainties of war. But unlike Hutchison's travel-book view of the whole country, Ryerson's work was a socio-economic analysis of the region that was unknown to most English-speaking Canadians. In an important sense, *French Canada* is a sequel to his *1837*, for it is devoted to revealing the militant spirit of democracy among French Canadians that unites them with their anglophone compatriots. Beginning with an introductory chapter on the courage of the francophone Canadians involved in the Dieppe raid of 1942, Ryerson traces this kind of courage back through Canadian history, relating it especially to the insurrections of 1837 and the Northwest rebellions of 1869 and 1885. By invoking the Dieppe raid, Ryerson shows as he did in *1837* how even the military defeat of a determined people can contribute to a moral and ultimately a political victory.

In its early chapters, *French Canada* emphasizes the heroes of the nineteenth and early twentieth centuries who struggled for self-determination and/or Canadian unity, including Papineau, Louis-Hippolyte Lafontaine (one of the political promoters of responsible government), A.A. Dorion (one of the early advocates of federal union), the "founder of Manitoba" Louis Riel, and Sir Wilfrid Laurier, first francophone prime minister of Canada. This traditional "great man" approach to history is complemented by an emphasis on the achievements of the Québecois masses and their rise out of feudal subjugation toward political power. Throughout the book Ryerson emphasizes the common aims of French and English Canadians in the pursuit of freedom. Conversely, he condemns contemporary Quebec racist isolationists like Abbé Groulx and fascist sympathizers like Henri Bourassa, as well as the English-Canadian representatives of international capitalism who keep the Québecois in economic subservience. "The Toronto Tory and the Quebec corporatist meet on common ground: hostility to the democratic peoples' movement, denial of our democratic heritage" (36). "Every failure on the part of English Canada to fight consistently, hand in hand with the French Canadians, for the fullest democratic rights of the minority nation has meant the weakening of Canadian democracy and Canadian unity in general, and the reinforcement of reactionary influences" (85).

Ryerson bases his appeal for Canadian ethnic unity on the need to resist both national and international fascism, and on the indications of the Quebec people's rejection of the old feudalistic political and ecclesiastic machine. The proto-fascist Union Nationale of Maurice Duplessis that governed Quebec between 1936 and 1939 was the climax of a long anti-democratic chronicle going back to the Conquest. Like Gustavus Myers in *A History of Canadian Wealth*, Ryerson uses official government statistics and reports to chronicle the exploitation of Quebec workers through starvation wages, child labour, and inadequate housing, education, and medical facilities, all for the sake of maintaining bloated profits for international corporations and autocratic power for a bureaucratic minority. But the electoral defeat of the Duplessis machine in 1939 and the advent of a Liberal government under Adélard Godbout seemed to herald a new era for the people of Quebec. Ryerson relates this new era especially to French-Canadian support for the war effort. In spite of the defeatism of a fascist minority, Ryerson insists, Quebec francophones realize that "victory for Canada and the United Nations…will stimulate tremendously the growing, powerful democratic forces in French-Canadian life" (220). He also invokes indications of an emerging liberalism within the Catholic Church as further evidence of the hopeful prospects for post-war Canada. "There is every reason to believe that liberal Catholic trends will become more influential in Quebec as democratic victories are won" (223).

The critical response to *French Canada* was much more positive than the reaction to his earlier *1837*. A review signed "L.P." in the *Canadian Forum* of January 1944 objects to the Communist polemics and jargon, and takes emphatic issue with Ryerson's criticisms of the CCF, but concludes that "the book as a whole is interesting and stimulating" (236). B.K. Sandwell in the *Canadian Historical Review* of June 1944 complains of Ryerson's anti-Catholic bias that blames Quebec's economic problems on the greed of ecclesiastics, but he recognizes the overall value of Ryerson's contribution to a historical topic that by the 1940s remained ill-served by anglophone Canadian scholars (201). Ryerson's critics recognized also that *French Canada* is a wartime book, full of optimism about the prospects for Allied victory and a transformed post-war world that will be able to eliminate the conditions that gave rise to fascism and the war. It does not go all the way towards envisioning a Marxist Communist future for Canada, but it does suggest that the Labor-Progressive Party will play an important part in post-war Canadian politics. Its confidence in the political perspicacity of working-class Québecois turned out to be sanguine, since the Duplessis regime was returned to power in 1944 and Quebec settled into almost two more decades of neo-feudalistic social and political conditions. But at a time when most writers tended to regard Quebec as either a quaint or lamentable anachronism, Ryerson invoked a remarkably modern and hopeful image of French-Canadian society. The author and Progress Books, furthermore, found the book worth reprinting in 1980, at which time Ryerson asserted that the first edition had sold ten thousand copies. Although Carl Berger in his 1976 survey of *The Writing of Canadian History* insisted that *French Canada* and *1837* "made little impression on historians" (184), Gregory S. Kealey argued in a 1982 reconsideration of Ryerson's work that *French Canada* "still reads well...in the context of World War II conditions and French-English antagonisms" (108).

Ryerson indicated his belief that the political and social history of Quebec was inadequately understood by the Québecois themselves when he produced the slightly revised translation *Le Canada français: sa tradition, son avenir* (1945). A new and realistic image of Quebec stressing its socio-economic decadence and anti-democratic politics had only recently begun to emerge in French-Canadian fiction to challenge the sentimental pastoralism of Louis Hémon's *Maria Chapdelaine* (1916). *Trente arpents* (1938; English translation 1940) by "Ringuet" (Philippe Panneton) emphasized the oppressive influences of vestigial feudalism and exploitative modern capitalism on the rural life of the Quebec habitants. In his 1944 novel *Au Pied de la pente douce* (English translation 1948), Roger Lemelin would apply a similar realism to urban Québecois working-class life. Hugh MacLennan's novel *Two Solitudes* (1945) would explore from an anglo-Canadian perspective the tensions between the two ethnic communities. In this vigorous new literary exploitation of the history and contemporary situation of French Canada, Ryerson's book was a groundbreaking work. *French*

*Canada*, however, differs from most of the fiction in its optimism. While the novelists depict an ethnic community trapped in its unreflecting acceptance of a decadent way of life, Ryerson sees the anachronistic social institutions of Quebec as hostile impositions on a naturally individualistic and freedom-loving people.

While Ryerson was applying Marxist principles to the interpretation of Canadian political and social history, Margaret Fairley was doing similar work in the anthologizing, critical study, and promotion of Canadian literature. As a member of the Toronto university circle associated with the *Rebel* and the *Canadian Forum* through the 1920s, Fairley was strongly influenced by the pro-Marxist and Russophile teachings of A.T. DeLury and *Forum* editor J. Francis White. Her loyalty to less militant forms of socialism continued to be reflected in her *Forum* articles and reviews, but her emerging sympathies with the Marxist conception of the proletariat are evident in a 1931 review of an oral history of English working women, in which she objected to the condescending attitude expressed in the "introductory letter" of Virginia Woolf. "Mrs. Woolf is amazed to discover high moral qualities in these unexpected places," Fairley commented ("Short Notices" October 1931: 34). In 1932 Fairley's political evolution was abruptly accelerated when her husband accepted an appointment as head of the Department of German at the University of Manchester in England. The Fairleys and their children settled in nearby Buxton, where Margaret Fairley was much stirred by the poverty, unemployment, and radical activism of the region. Influenced also by an acquaintance with Barbara Niven, editor of the British *Daily Worker*, Fairley joined the Communist Party of Great Britain. In 1936 the University of Toronto lured Barker Fairley back with the offer of the headship of the Department of German. Soon after their return, Margaret Fairley joined the CPC.

Fairley immediately began to produce book reviews for *New Frontier*. With the financial collapse of the magazine in 1939, she might have begun writing for the CPC newspaper the *Clarion*, but was forestalled by the government's anti-Communist initiatives. The suppression of the *Clarion* after Canada's declaration of war prevented her from becoming a contributor, and also saved her from the possibility of arrest and internment as a staff member of a subversive publication. Although under police surveillance as a known Communist, she was not arrested, and in 1940 was appointed book review editor of the *Canadian Tribune*. On the *Tribune* she developed her serious commitment to Canadian literature. The *New Frontier* editors had taken advantage of her recent years spent in England to give her mostly British books for review. On the *Tribune*, at first, she continued to write about British and other foreign publications, but opportunities to pursue Canadian topics soon developed. Fairley had been interested in Canadian literature ever since her year as a lecturer at the University of Alberta in 1913-14, where she came under the influence of the chair of the English Department, E.K. Broadus. Like Fairley, Broadus was an immigrant to Canada, having been brought up from Virginia in 1908 to establish the English program at Alberta. A scholar of nineteenth-century British poetry as well as a creative writer influenced by early twentieth-century modernist trends, his imagistic poems had appeared in Harriet Monroe's *Poetry*. Taking an enthusiastic interest in the cultural development of his adopted country, Broadus brought his literary tastes and critical acumen to the editing of *A Book of Canadian Prose and Verse* (1923). Fairley's admiration for this anthology is indicated by the enthusiasm with which she continued to recommend it years after it had gone out of print (Fairley, "Our Heritage").

"Much of the best of Canadian literature has been either directly inspired by the Canadian scene or has reflected the effort to recreate the historic past," Broadus observed in his preface (vii). The anthology includes a section entitled "The People," with selections representing "a picture of the past and a panoramic view of the varied aspects of Canadian life to-day" (viii). Although Broadus obviously uses the word "people" with no political connotation, there is consistency between his conception of "Canadian life" and Fairley's Marxist views. Her ideas on Canadian culture, like Broadus's, emphasized an inclusive historical tradition that ranged from early colonial social record to modernist literary experiment, although she inevitably favoured those texts that could be reconciled with the Marxist conception of the struggle for democratic rights and the liberation of the worker from exploitation. In various *Tribune* columns during the war, Fairley reviewed a wide range of Canadian books, including a reprint of Anna

Jameson's *Winter Studies and Summer Rambles*, Dorothy Livesay's *Day and Night*, Emily Carr's *Klee Wyck*, and Joe Wallace's *Night Is Ended*. She also reviewed the first two issues of a new literary magazine, *Contemporary Verse*, edited in Vancouver by Alan Crawley ("Speaking of Books," 15 November 1941, 28 February 1942). Crawley's magazine was the first important periodical devoted to the work of Canadian modernist poets since the *McGill Fortnightly Review* in the 1920s. In her reviews, Fairley gives a generally open-minded response to the work of Anne Marriot, Leo Kennedy, and other contributors to *CV*, even including the Trotskyist Earle Birney and the defector from the CPC, Dorothy Livesay. But she finds in some of these writings a "fear to face the realities of the times in which we live," and suggests that Livesay's work expresses a "thwarted sense of life."

After almost four years of reviewing Communist and non-Communist Canadian writing, Fairley began planning a new anthology that would provide a unified view of the Canadian literary tradition. Stanley Ryerson had demonstrated in his two books the centrality of democratic "people's" movements in Canadian political history; Fairley hoped to begin the process of rewriting the country's cultural history along similar lines. In October 1944 she resigned from the *Tribune* to devote more time to the preparation of the proposed anthology. In 1945, shortly after the end of the war, Progress Books issued her *Spirit of Canadian Democracy: A Collection of Canadian Writings from the Beginnings to the Present Day*. Made up of very brief prose extracts interspersed with lyric poems, the volume was divided into three sections: "From the Beginnings to 1850," "From 1850 to 1930," and "From 1930 to the Present." Intended to illustrate the evolution of democratic traditions rather than of literary forms and techniques, the prose selections are taken from speeches and essays, books of history, fiction and travel, and newspaper and magazine articles. The poems include work by nineteenth-century socialists and social critics like Archibald Lampman and Alexander McLachlan, poets of social protest active in the 1930s such as Joe Wallace and A.M. Stephen, and a few younger poets, both Communist and non-Communist. In keeping with its pan-Canadian perspective, Fairley's anthology includes authors from all the regions of Canada, with many of the Quebec selections appearing in the original French.

Designed as a potential school text, the book suffers from an ambiguous sense of audience. Some of the selections provide rather simplistic or aphoristic versions of complex ideas, while others are too sophisticated to be easily accessible to younger readers. The primary strength of *Spirit of Canadian Democracy* is that it provides a concise survey of the evolution of progressive political ideals in Canada through the writings of politicians, educators, journalists, historians, and literary artists. By "progressive" Fairley meant particularly the commitment to social cooperation that by 1945 Communists, social democrats, and many liberals envisaged as the sequel to the ruthless individualism of the capitalist system that had led to depression and world war.

Fairley especially reveals her faith in progressive ideals in the long final section covering the years 1930-1945. Among the literary items in this section Fairley includes critical and satirical poems by socialist poets F.R. Scott, Leo Kennedy, and A.M. Stephen, a dialogue about the power of collective action from Baird's *Waste Heritage*, and Joe Wallace's nationalistic poem "O Lovely Land." Poems about the Spanish Civil War by Kennedy, Wallace, and others are followed by poems of the Second World War, including an excerpt from E.J. Pratt's heroic "Dunkirk," and Dorothy Livesay's atmospheric invocation of anxiety and hope on the home front, "West Coast." Of particular significance are several previously unpublished or ephemerally printed poems of the Second World War. One of the most notable of these is "Airman," by the Irish-Canadian Seamus Haughey, a survivor of the Mackenzie-Papineau Battalion, killed in action while serving with the Royal Canadian Air Force (RCAF) soon after publication of his poem in the *Toronto Star* in 1943. Haughey's poem transcends its conventional form and language and its remote echoes of W.B. Yeats's "An Irish Airman Foresees His Death" to celebrate the ideas of acceptance and commitment:

> When peace descends once more like gentle rain,
> Mention my name in passing if you must,
> As one who knew the terms, slay or be slain,
> And thought the bargain was both good and just.
> (Fairley, *Spirit* 196)

The Toronto musician Marcus Adeney, whose poems appeared regularly in *Canadian Poetry Magazine* in the 1930s and 1940s, contributed to Fairley's anthology the previously unpublished "Sirens (Worker's Lament)." This fifty-line blank verse meditation is based on the convergence of the strident factory signal that calls workers to their jobs and the "stark and empty horror" of air-raid warnings. Invoking the traditional god of humanity rather than the materialistic idol that has established its reign over the modern world, the speaker proclaims a belief in a better future. In the present state of the world spiritual values are suppressed, but if workers keep the faith a time will come when "sirens wail no more man's helplessness" (*Spirit* 210).

The prose selections in the modern section of *Spirit of Canadian Democracy* convey impressions of the pervasiveness among Canadian artists and intellectuals of the progressive view of their country's future. An excerpt from H.M. Cassidy's *Social Security and Reconstruction in Canada* (1943) urges the importance of establishing government-backed guarantees to the "men in the fighting forces" that they will not return to the economic conditions of the 1930s. A passage from an unpublished book by J. Francis White argues that the war should teach Canadians the superiority of collectivism over nineteenth-century individualism. From Jim Wright's patriotic war novel *All Clear, Canada!* (1944) a speaker denounces the "lone wolf" ideology as antiquated and undemocratic: "We have to learn to live and work together to improve ourselves and our community" (244). A selection from Marcus Adeney's *Community Centres in Canada* (1945) advocates the "cooperative society of responsible human beings" as opposed to the "free market economy" with its amoral anarchism that brought the world to depression and war (254). *Spirit of Canadian Democracy* indulges in no extravagant praise of either Marxism or the Soviet Union. Its basic commitment is to an ideal of social justice, freedom, and communal harmony, based not on any narrow political ideology but on the consensus of intelligent and imaginative observers about the disasters that unrestricted individualism has brought on the modern world. Fairley's book also provides suggestive glimpses of the Canadian progressive cultural tradition of the past, and the possibilities for the development of this tradition in the future.

Among its prose items *Spirit of Canadian Democracy* includes a brief paragraph from a new book published by Progress entitled *Sin and Science*. The author, H. Dyson Carter, had contributed a few short stories and articles to *New Frontier* under the name John Karr in the 1930s. Dropping the pseudonym in 1939, he began writing for mainstream newspapers and magazines. By the end of the war he had published five books and dozens of articles, and was well on his way to being the most prolific and literarily significant writer associated with the Canadian Communist movement in the post-1940 decades and possibly in the movement's entire history. In a career that spanned more than fifty years he was to publish over twenty books and pamphlets and achieve international renown as a fiction writer as well as a commentator on the USSR and the relationship between science and society. Born in St. John, New Brunswick, in 1910, Carter was the son of Salvation Army officers who in 1912 were appointed superintendent and matron of the Provincial Detention Home for Juveniles in Winnipeg. "I literally grew up in reform schools," Carter wrote in 1946, "taking grade schooling along with delinquent boys and girls" (Thomas 20). Besides being influenced by this early exposure to Christianity and to young victims of the economic and sociological imbalances of capitalist society, Carter's life was shaped by a severe physical handicap. He was born with *osteogenesis imperfecta* (O.I.), an incurable hereditary disease that makes bones brittle and inclined to break easily, especially in childhood. Like a more famous sufferer from O.I., French painter Henri Toulouse-Lautrec, Carter was an intelligent and imaginative child. Frequent bouts of hospitalization and convalescence in traction and wheelchair provided him with considerable time for reading and thinking about human suffering, both physical and social. According to an autobiographical article he wrote in 1945, Carter's parents were proponents of the social gospel; the Christian socialist founder of the CCF, J.S. Woodsworth, was a friend of the family (Carter, "Dyson Carter Explains"). Young Carter's intellectual interests also turned very early in life to the physical sciences. The natural processes of augmented bone calcification in adolescence, plus vitamin D treatments, enabled him to enroll in the University of Manitoba, where he majored in chemistry. In spite of the many interruptions to his formal education during childhood, according to the University of Manitoba yearbook *Brown and Gold* (1931) he completed his BSc at age twenty, graduating at the top of his class. The following year he acquired an MSc in physical chemistry. During his university career he also became enthusiastically committed to creative writing and to political activism. By the mid-1930s he was a professional engineer, a published writer of articles and stories, and possibly an active though secret member of the Communist Party.

Carter's early involvement with the Party must remain a matter of some uncertainty, for the fullest source of information about his early years is a work of fiction. His novel *This Story Fierce and Tender* (1986) appears, however, to be a factually reliable account of his childhood and early adult life. The year of birth, family background, and medical problems of his protagonist, Elgin Morley, can be verified by external evidence as identical to Carter's. Carter likewise gives his own educational experience to his fictional character, and credits him as the author of books and articles very similar in title and subject to Carter's own. Carter's education in Communist doctrine began, according to his autobiographical novel, when a university librarian with an interest in radical politics put into his hands a translation of Joseph Stalin's Speech to the Sixteenth Congress of the Communist Party of the Soviet Union (1930) (*This Story* 415-20). Stalin's speech is a defence of the USSR's system of Five-Year Plans, buttressed by an assertion of faith that the economic crisis in the West was a sign of the approaching end of capitalism. Soon afterward Carter read Lenin's *State and Revolution* (written 1917), and embarked on a wide-ranging program of study of Marxism-Leninism, and of the progress of science in the USSR. This, as he wrote several years later, "led me far afield. Into history, philosophy" ("Dyson Carter Explains"). Carter was possibly unique among Canadian Communist intellectuals in coming to the Party through the reading of Stalin before he had encountered Lenin, or even Marx. This unorthodox beginning obviously had a great deal to do with his almost obsessive admiration for the USSR, an admiration that emphasized achievements in science and technology and the dogmatic scientific socialism of the Stalin era.

After completing his MSc, Carter served as a lecturer in physical chemistry at the university, then as a researcher at the Winnipeg

Cancer Institute and in the physical chemistry/metallurgy laboratory of the Hudson Bay Mining and Smelting Company. Registered as a professional engineer in the province of Manitoba in 1936, and as a member of the Canadian Institute of Chemistry, he subsequently practised as a consulting chemical engineer (Biographical note, Inventory, Carter Papers, NAC). In an account of his literary beginnings that he wrote in 1942 for the dust jacket of his first novel, Carter claimed he began writing short stories when the editor of a literary magazine mistook him for someone else and solicited a submission from him. He also claimed that he subsequently wrote "a dozen blood-and-thunder stories," a "novel which he burned," and more "short fiction under five different names." As "Jack Parr" he began in 1936 contributing socialist realist short stories and science articles to *New Frontier*. Through the late 1930s and early 1940s he was also publishing stories under his own name in *New Advance* (the magazine of the Canadian Young Communist League), *For People Everywhere* (a New York left-wing youth periodical) and the American pulp magazine *Argosy*. In 1939, Vanguard Press of New York published his *If You Want to Invent*, a monograph for a popular audience outlining the procedures and pitfalls of securing patents. Based on Carter's own experiences developing new methods and apparatus in his physical chemistry experiments, the book warns would-be inventors against the large industrial trusts that suppress the initiative of the individual inventor by controlling the patent rights of their employees and contract researchers.

Also in 1939 Carter began contributing popular science articles under his real name to the mass media, including the *Winnipeg Free Press* and *Winnipeg Tribune* as well as the national magazines *Maclean's, Saturday Night, Star Weekly* and *National Home Monthly*. In the late 1930s he began a book-length work of historical geography which urged the development of Hudson Bay as a mercantile seaport for the Canadian wheat-farming regions, and as a base of naval defense against a possible invasion of North America. *Sea of Destiny* (1940) was very pro-Russian, especially in its contrast between the USSR's development of its arctic and Canada's neglect of its northern territories. Subtitled "The Story of Hudson Bay—Our Undefended Back Door," the book was also anti-German, suggesting that Nazi submarines and battleships might exploit the Bay as a major point of vulnerability in North American defences. Reviewers were impressed by this knowledgeable introduction to a neglected feature of North American history and geography, although the isolationist *New York Times* dismissed Carter's "alarmist" prophecies that the European war might be carried into the arctic (Baldwin 16).

As a regular science writer for the *Star Weekly* and *National Home Monthly*, Carter received roving commissions to visit military, industrial, and medical facilities across North America to report on the latest war-related technological advances. The subjects of his articles included methods of reducing air pollution, the development of synthetic fabrics, new agricultural procedures to increase food production, jet propulsion and the possibility of space travel, television, automatic piloting devices, and many other recent or projected developments. In 1942 he gathered together a series of these articles to be published as *Men, Machines and Microbes*, with a foreword by the editor of *Saturday Night*, B.K. Sandwell. In the same year Carter began writing a series of dramatized radio broadcasts for the Canadian Broadcasting Corporation (CBC) that popularized current scientific and technological issues relating to the war. He also wrote several articles and pamphlets on Soviet scientific and military achievements, the most popular of which was *Russia's Secret Weapon*. Serialized in newspapers across the country and published as a pamphlet in 1942, *Russia's Secret Weapon* reveals that the greatest Soviet strength is not an item of ordnance but a scientific spirit based on "love and heroism." Russia's positive attitude to science is contrasted to the attitudes prevailing in fascist countries, where science is merely an instrument of tyranny.

As a climax to his prolific literary activity during the war years, Carter completed his first novel, *Night of Flame*, published in 1942 by Reynal and Hitchcock in the US and by George J. McLeod in Canada. Like many Canadian writers of the time, Carter located the action of his novel in the United States to ensure cross-border sales. Set in Chicago, *Night of Flame* uses a hospital setting—like the 1936-37 *New Frontier* stories "East Nine" and "Exit R.N."—to depict the class conflict that the author regards as the primary symptom of a sick capitalist society. As in the two stories, Carter in *Night of Flame* contrasts the wasteful luxury of the wing of the hospital set aside for wealthy patients with the squalid facilities for industrial accident cases. But the political implications of *Night of Flame* are overshadowed by the second half of the novel, which describes in suspenseful documentary-like detail the outbreak and progress of a fire in the hospital, caused by the neglect of safety standards. Although the criticism of capitalism is still evident in the cynical motives of hospital administrators, the novel focuses on the tragedy of the fire and only hints at the possibility of social revolution. *Night of Flame* also devotes a good deal of attention to plot strands involving a liaison between a badly injured young patient and a nurse, the unrequited passion of an older woman for a much younger man, and a doctor's struggles to free himself from an obsessive relationship with a wealthy woman. Although Carter was mainly interested in the psychological implications of these relationships, his highlighting of romantic elements drew attention away from the socio-economic theme and perhaps contributed to the modest popular success of the book. Reviewers stressed the realism of the story, and did not mention the economic conflict underlying the hospital's social structure. Positive notices in the *New York Times* (24 May 1942) and the *Saturday Review of Literature* (6 June 1942) sent the book into a second printing, a notable achievement for a first novel.

The war years were thus a time of remarkable professional and personal success for Carter. In 1943 he married a public health nurse who shared his interests in medical science and politics. His wife Charlotte was to become his collaborator on several books and pamphlets. Although he still did not publicly declare himself a Communist, after the Russian victory at Stalingrad Carter made a cross-Canada lecture tour on behalf of the Russian war effort, sponsored by the LPP. In the last year of the war Carter began a ten-year association with Progress Books, who published his *Sin and Science*, in which Carter continued his idealization of Soviet technological and social achievements. According to this brief volume, the USSR had virtually eliminated such social evils as alcoholism, prostitution, and venereal disease, as a result of eliminating the capitalist obsession with individual financial profit. By the end of the war he was a modestly successful novelist, a popular science journalist eagerly read across

Canada, and a well-known publicist for the achievements of the USSR in war, science, and technology.

• • • • •

The wartime rapprochement between the Western allies and the Soviet Union encouraged other Canadian Communist writers to celebrate the Russian war effort and the possibilities for post-war cooperation between capitalist and socialist countries. Journalist and poet Harold Griffin, a member of the CPC since 1935 and editor in 1942-44 of the weekly *People* of Vancouver, emulated Carter's successful *Sea of Destiny* with *Alaska and the Canadian Northwest: Our New Frontier* (1944). In the spring of 1943 Griffin travelled by military and construction transport over the recently completed right-of-way of the Alaska Highway from its starting point at Dawson Creek, BC to Whitehorse, Yukon, where he proceeded by air to Fairbanks, Alaska. Like Carter in *Sea of Destiny*, Griffin in his book avoids obvious Marxist or anti-US sentiments. Part travel narrative and part economic analysis, *Alaska and the Canadian Northwest* devotes considerable attention to the soldiers and civilian construction workers who built the road, but the heroes of his story also include research scientists, engineers, and managers. Griffin does criticize the multinational corporations such as the oil and steamship companies, whose short-sighted pursuit of monopolistic profits has retarded northern industrial progress in the past. But the main thesis of his book is the new spirit of cooperation between government and private enterprise, civilian and military, employers and workers, and North America and the Soviet Union.

Griffin's book was well received in the United States, by reviewers who seemed unconscious of or indifferent to the author's political sympathies. The *Nation* (3 June 1944) described it as "a cogent account" of the building of the Alaska Highway, absorbingly written." The *New York Times* (5 March 1944) praised the author "not only for his vision but also for his grasp of the geographical, historical and economic trends" at work in the North. The *Weekly Book Review* (25 June 1944), without mentioning the author's advocacy of future US-Soviet cooperation, admired Griffin's "vision of the North as the great frontier of tomorrow, where we can practice as well as preach international cooperation" (*Book Review Digest* 1944-45: 301-302).

Pursuing the wartime ideal of the anti-fascist united front, the LPP encouraged its writers to reach out to the non-Communist media and public, and tried to recruit non-Communist writers to its own publishing outlets. In 1945 the Party's Progress Books, which had heretofore handled only non-fiction works in history, politics, and related areas, announced the forthcoming appearance of its first novel, Dorothy Dumbrille's *All This Difference*. Dumbrille (1897-1984) was not a Communist, or even remotely connected either by inclination or association with progressive politics. Born in southeastern Ontario, she had lived most of her life in Glengarry County, whose history and folkways she celebrated in fiction, poetry, and collections of popular folklore. Her first novel, *Deep Doorways*, a romantic cross-generational chronicle of a Glengarry family, was serialized in the Montreal *Standard* in 1941, but not published as a book until 1947 (*Creative Canada* 2: 82). Since only very sparse remnants of Progress's business files remain from the 1940s, the circumstances of Dumbrille's connection with the publisher must be a matter of conjecture. Possibly the company followed common practice and took an advertisement in the *Canadian Bookman*, the official organ of the Canadian Authors Association, inviting authors to submit fiction manuscripts. Having been disappointed in her search for a publisher for her first novel, Dumbrille would have leapt at the chance of interesting this new company in her latest work. Or it may be that a Progress representative made contact with Dumbrille through the CAA, for the historian of the CAA claims that the association was "infiltrated" by Communists "particularly after the USSR had turned against the Nazis, and become an ally" (Harrington 282). The pejorative "infiltrated" implies a conspiratorial purpose that probably did not exist, but Margaret Fairley, Harold Griffin, and other LPP intellectuals did join the CAA as part of the effort to promote Communist and non-Communist cultural unity.

Progress was undoubtedly attracted by the thematic similarities between Dumbrille's novel and one of its most successful books, Stanley Ryerson's *French Canada*. Although set in eastern Ontario rather than Quebec, *All This Difference* is concerned with French-English relations, and especially with the respective attitudes of French and English Canadians to the war. Like Ryerson's history,

Dumbrille's novel asserts the need for tolerance and compromise in the relationships between the two ethnic groups, while advocating solidarity in the war against fascism. Centring on the romance between the French-Canadian Raoul Faubert and the Scots-Canadian Wencie MacMillan, the novel uses the two lovers to develop a contrast between the francophone and anglophone communities. The MacMillan family's small weaving business, stimulated by war contracts, reflects the anglophone commitment to an industrial society; Raoul's father, Gabriel Faubert, obsessed with land and maintaining his paternalistic authority, personifies francophone patriarchal agrarianism. But both communities are committed to traditional ideals and a resistance to change. In spite of her romantic attraction to Raoul, Wencie muses resentfully on the francophone migration into eastern Ontario: "Many of the farms around were being bought up by the French people. Soon Glengarry would be entirely changed" (34). Gabriel Faubert, in a drunken Luddite response to the threat to his way of life posed by the wartime expansion of industrialism, attempts to burn down the weaving mill. All the French and English, including the two lovers, are similarly divided by the war. With her brother and other young English-Canadian men in the army, Wencie cannot countenance Raoul's refusal to volunteer and his insistence that the struggle against fascism is of no concern to the French Canadians.

"We are going to have to move together…and realize we are one in the very essence of our being," says the local anglophone Catholic priest, "or we will not survive as a nation" (55). An older villager, Katie Macdonnell, although sympathetic to the priest's plea for ethnic unity, can see nothing but irresolvable problems in Canada's future. The novel as a whole offers an ambivalent conclusion: Raoul finally enlists in the army, but before he can report he dies in an attempt to rescue Wencie's small nephew, who has fallen into the mill race. Dumbrille, like many of her characters—especially her women— seems to want to believe that the French and English communities can come together, but she can find no satisfactory dramatic way of asserting this belief. Perhaps remembering the conclusion of George Eliot's *The Mill on the Floss*, she tries to evade resolving a complex problem novel by means of a tragic catastrophe.

In a *Tribune* review, Stanley Ryerson approved of the "honest" and "moving" story, but condemned the novel's social analysis. Dumbrille, he insisted, sees the problem of ethnic conflict entirely in terms of the need for tolerance and education on the personal level, without regard for the social and economic system that promotes the conflict. In her portrait of the crofter and agrarian societies of Glengarry, further- more, she completely ignores the larger urban-centred, monopoly-rid- den industrial capitalist society beyond the village. This neglect of the larger context, says Ryerson, "is the more important...because [Dumbrille] makes a very real attempt to deal not simply with the lives of members of the upper bourgeoisie as is the case in 'Two Solitudes' by Hugh MacLennan, but with those of ordinary folk, of the people" ("Novel 'All This Difference' Seeks Roots"). Apart from the question of Dumbrille's inevitable neglect of the Marxist conception of her sub- ject, the failure of her novel can undoubtedly be attributed to the fact that it had the ill luck to appear only a few months after MacLennan's successful novel on the same theme. Like Ryerson, another reviewer in the *Tribune* complained that *Two Solitudes* was primarily concerned with the French-English conflict in a bourgeois context, and its repre- sentation of the working class was "remote and generalized" (Roberts). But even this Communist reviewer described *Two Solitudes* as "a fine new novel," recognizing a psychological and sociological complexity that Dumbrille's sentimental plot and characterizations lacked.

While Progress published the work of a writer who was uncon- scious of socialist realist formulas and *Tribune* reviewers gave guarded praise to MacLennan's bourgeois view of Canada, Com- munist literary theorists continued to call for a revival of the princi- ples of socialist realism. In April 1946, the LPP theoretical journal *National Affairs Monthly* published an article on "Canadian Literature: Trends and Limitations," which insisted that Canadian lit- erature "is monopolized by a middle-class intelligentsia" that does not allow the Canadian worker to "play more than an incidental role" (119). The spokesperson for this position was not the rigorously orthodox editor of the magazine Stanley Ryerson, but a new recruit to the Party, twenty-three-year-old Nathan Cohen. Cohen was soon to leave the LPP and pursue a successful career as a theatre critic, but while he was in the Party, like many young Communists, he was committed to hard-line principles. While Canadian literature of the 1940s, says Cohen, is dominantly concerned with the realistic depiction of "economic injustices," most authors have little awareness of the cause of these injustices or of the role of the working class in bringing about redress. As examples of writers who lack the proper political consciousness, Cohen cites some of the poets who had begun to espouse liberal and social democratic causes in the 1930s, including Klein, Pratt, Ralph Gustafson, and Margaret Avison, as well as several novelists of the war years and the immediate post-war period who turned to social realism. Besides citing Dumbrille's *All This Difference* and MacLennan's *Two Solitudes,* Cohen mentions Gwethalyn Graham's *Earth and High Heaven* (1944), a novel set in wartime Montreal which deals with the problem of antisemitism. As Cohen observes, however, most of these bourgeois social realists conceptualize modern problems in individualist rather than collective terms, and focus on the middle classes rather than the proletariat. Graham's Jewish male protagonist, for instance, occasionally expresses his anxiety about the future of modern capitalist society with its economic inequities and its tolerance of undemocratic and imperialist regimes, but the political conflicts of modern life are ultimately subordinated to the novel's love story and relentlessly middle-class perspective. "Canadian Literature: Trends and Limitations" ends with an appeal "for Communists to consider taking the initiative in the cultural fields which are now almost exclusively dominated by reactionaries and social democrats" (120).

If post-war social realist novels failed to fulfill the aesthetic ideals of Marxism as Communists like Cohen understood them, they still constitute a significant development in Canadian fiction. Often dealing with the 1930s, these novels lacked the journalistic immediacy of Baird's *Waste Heritage* or Allan's *This Time a Better Earth,* but had the advantage of a historical hindsight that could reveal the clear links between the failures of capitalism and liberal democracy on the one hand, and the rise of fascism and the outbreak of the Second World War on the other. Selwyn Dewdney's *Wind Without Rain* (1946), for instance, takes place between 1935 and 1943, and deals with the introduction of regimentation and centralized power in an Ontario high school. Dewdney's authoritarian school principal suggests analogies to political demagogues like Hitler and Mussolini, and dramatizes the anti-liberal tendencies emerging in Canadian education, particularly the uncritical acceptance of regimentation and utilitarianism which Dewdney traces to United States influences. Another novel about education, Joyce Marshall's *Presently Tomorrow* (1946), is less an Orwellian fable than Dewdney's, but emphasizes both the imminent danger of fascism and the need for positive social and cultural ideals. Set in a private girl's school in the then-predominantly anglophone Eastern Townships of Quebec, the action takes place over a few days in the summer of 1933, just months after Hitler's ascension to dictatorial power in Germany. International turmoil is both remote and ominously present in the lives of four young women about to graduate from the school and a young Anglican priest who briefly interconnects with them. The priest's struggles with sexual, spiritual, and political anxiety are complemented by the political naiveté of one young woman who has become an adherent of the pseudo-fascist Oxford movement, the insecure bravado of another, and the sensuality of a third. The priest and the fourth woman, an aspiring writer, share the narrative perspective which gradually reveals vaguely hopeful prospects for the future through strategies of social commitment and political resistance.

Alberta novelist Christine van der Mark (1917-69), in *In Due Season* (1947), depicts the marginalized lives of white and Métis subsistence farmers in the Peace River district during the 1930s. Her central character struggles to support her children and maintain her homestead after being abandoned by her ne'er-do-well husband, but *In Due Season* is not a feminist critique of male irresponsibility. Lina Ashley's determination to survive evolves into a materialistic obsession with money and land which in the end leaves her isolated and unhappy. A Christian Scientist, van der Mark was not interested in a Marxist or other socialist perspective, but like Marshall in *Presently Tomorrow* she uses allusions to 1930s politics to create a backdrop of crisis and change that applies to both the social context and the life of her protagonist. The choric comments of other settlers to the effect that "isolationism is a thing of the past" (266) and the world "is sliding toward an abyss" (273) refer explicitly to the international situation and implicitly to the lonely obsessions of the central character.

The urban proletariat rather than the rural peasantry forms the subject of *The Rich Man* (1948), by Henry Kreisel (1922-91). Like van der Mark's *In Due Season*, Kreisel's novel is a story of individual self-delusion and vanity, set against the international politics of the 1930s. An Austrian-born Jewish Canadian eking out an existence as a presser in a Toronto garment factory returns to Europe on a visit, where his attempts to pass himself off as wealthy in a country dominated by the corruptions and intrigues of fascism bring disaster on himself and his relatives. In a review in the *Canadian Tribune* Margaret Fairley praised *The Rich Man* as "the first working-class novel written in Ontario" ("Young Canadian's First Novel" 10).

Although its emphasis on the proletarian experience and the evils of fascism might have appealed to the anti-bourgeois aesthetics of Cohen, Kreisel's novel still fell short of the didactic purposes expected of a rigorously defined socialist realism. The same judgement might be applied to much of the French-Canadian fiction of the 1940s, including many of those works now regarded as classics of Québecois realism. Moving beyond the rural focus of such earlier works as *Trente arpents*, novelists in the 1940s turned their attention to the urban working class; but like Ringuet, most of them were inclined to emphasize the sordid details of the lives of their characters, without attempting any profound political or economic analysis of modern society. Realistic fiction of this sort included two novels, Roger Lemelin's *Au Pied de la pente douce* (1944) and Gabrielle Roy's *Bonheur d'occasion* (1945), which Ben-Z. Shek singles out as particularly revealing examples of Québecois "social realism." Both works focus on the recent past—Lemelin sets his story in the closing years of the Depression, Roy sets hers mostly in the war years—and both dramatize the alienation of Québecois working-class people trapped by an exploitative anglophone-controlled economy. The entrapment and alienation of working-class people—especially young people—within a hierarchical urban society were established subjects of radical proletarian fiction by the 1930s. The work of both Lemelin and Roy are reminiscent of, perhaps might even have been influenced by, such American literary works as James T. Farrell's *Studs Lonigan* (1932-35) or Sidney Kingsley's *Dead End* (1935). Even more directly, Roy and Lemelin are indebted to nineteenth-century French natural-

*Progressive Heritage*

ism, especially in their emphasis on the documentation of social decay through the relentless accumulation of detailed evidence, and in their reluctance to draw any but the most negative conclusions from this evidence. Both authors visualize the kind of economic conditions in 1940s Quebec that Stanley Ryerson reported in his *French Canada*; but both also emphasize the futility and sense of entrapment that characterize the lives of working-class Québecois.

Lemelin's visualization includes impressions of gradation in the poverty of the inhabitants of the "Lower Town" of Quebec City, but these impressions only accentuate the implication that the people of whom he writes do not constitute a homogeneous proletariat who might act collectively in their own interest. As the novel shows, in fact, their social organization is rife with internecine rivalries. Their political ideals, he emphasizes, are limited to a narrow ethnic nationalism, and their moral values are set by an autocratic church, which has an interest in keeping its adherents in a state of subjugation. Lemelin's title, in fact, suggests not only the gradation of social strata in its reference to the sloping hill of Quebec, but also the fixed position of the social elements, like parts of a human body, interconnected in mutual dependence yet rendered immutable by the very nature of the organism as a whole. Roy's *Bonheur d'occasion* likewise emphasizes the deterministic circumstances of its characters' lives. The working-class Montreal slum of St. Henri, dominated by the looming monuments of industrialism (cotton mills, grain elevators), is a prison in which each individual is isolated, alienated as in a cell. In the course of the novel, various characters discover the illusion of the dream of escape, as well as the futility of relying on family, friendship, or a sense of community. The novel is indirectly about the tendency of industrial capitalism to suppress freedom and justice, but Roy seldom makes the anti-capitalist message explicit, except through one character, Emmanuel Letourneau, whose tentative and semi-articulate radicalism even Roy deemphasized, by cutting some of his speeches in later editions of the novel (Shek 82).

In contrast to the non-partisan social realism of Roy and Lemelin, at least one Québecois novelist in the 1940s applied Marxist ideas to a contemporary Canadian milieu. *Neuf jours de haine* (1948) by Jean-Jules Richard (1911-75) was also the only Québecois novel to deal in any detail with the experiences of Canadian soldiers in the Second World War. After serving with the Canadian infantry in France during 1944-45, Richard returned to Canada to join the Quebec LPP and to write an anti-fascist and pacifist novel dealing with the contagious effects of battlefield hatred, which becomes nakedly animalistic, consumes the combatants, and calls into question the capitalistic society that has brought about the war. The narrative follows the members of a Canadian platoon on D-Day plus eight days chosen from their experiences as they proceed deeper into Europe over the following year. Significantly, Richard chose to write not about a French-Canadian army unit such as the famous Royal Twenty-Second Regiment. His platoon has a few Québecois in it, but his soldiers represent a conglomeration of ethnic and regional backgrounds. The narrative is told in the spare diction and sentence structure reminiscent of Charles Yale Harrison's First World War novel, *Generals Die in Bed*. The focus is less on external action, however, than on the emotional experience of the soldiers, especially the hatred that consumes them. As the author makes explicit in an early passage, their hatred is an extension of their fear: fear of the dark, of death, of their military superiors, and of their own instincts and reflexes (41-42). The soldiers even hate their own feelings of hatred, which weaken and deceive them, by overriding their capacity to reason, the faculty that makes them human. In the violence and hysteria of battle, the hatred is also focussed on the Nazis, but this hatred becomes intermingled with an antipathy to the whole of Europe, with its traditions of militarism and political corruption. Ultimately, the hatred evolves toward a pseudo-existentialist reaction against "la divinité absente" (260).

Developing a more explicit Marxist thesis, Richard reveals also how the soldiers in battle discover the fallacies of class distinctions that bourgeois society imposes on them. They see for themselves that the officers arbitrarily placed over them are weak and often cowardly yet arrogant in their assumption that their bourgeois origins endow them with a right to command (42). The soldiers dimly perceive that the military campaign is being directed not by the officers or even by a remote political authority, but by the propaganda machine of the bourgeois news media, which continues in war its established control of the working-class mind (98-99). Like the soldiers in *Generals Die in Bed*, the men of Richard's fictional platoon have been lured to war by this kind of propaganda, which urges on them the duty to defend the British Empire and save civilization, while at the same time appealing to their desire for adventure (120). Like Harrison's novel, *Neuf jours de haine* exposes the social and political falsehoods that lead to imperialist wars and the consequent suffering of the proletariat who are forced to fight these wars. Richard's badly neglected work deserves recognition in both French and English Canada, not only as an important response to the appeal for a socialist literary alternative to the bourgeois realism of the 1940s but also as one of the best novels to come out of the Canadian military experience in the Second World War.

# 7

# The 1950s
## Post-War to Cold War

The proliferation of English- and French-Canadian social realist novels in the 1940s was only one of several indications that national cultural activity might be entering into a new and vigorous era. The bureaucratic as well as the artistic community contributed to the positive prospects. In 1945 the Canadian Arts Council had been established as an autonomous administrative body for the promotion and financial support of the arts. The CAC was part of the general concern for the preservation and promotion of the arts in Canada, a concern to which the federal government responded in 1949 by establishing a Royal Commission to investigate the status of arts, letters, and sciences, headed by Vincent Massey. As a legal political party, the LPP was anxious to get involved in these initiatives. In 1943 Stanley Ryerson had been appointed the Party's director of "education and publicity," a phrase replacing "agitation and propaganda." In December 1946 he organized a Party conference under the auspices of *National Affairs Monthly* on the writing of Canadian history from a Marxist perspective. Reporting on the conference in the *Tribune* of 11 January 1947, Ryerson announced plans for the research and writing of short "people's histories" of Canada, the Canadian labour movement, and the Communist movement. Margaret Fairley was to chair the committee on the projected history of Canada (Ryerson, "Our Country's History"). Further meetings in Toronto and Montreal in May 1947 resulted in decisions to broaden the scope of activities to encompass the arts in general, and to establish an LPP National Cultural Commission, with local commissions in the two cities and proposals for organizations in other cities ("The LPP and the Arts," mimeographed bulletin, CPC/LPP archives). A follow-up bulletin issued by the commission in June 1948 called for organized resistance to the inundation of Canada by Hollywood movies, US radio programs, and pulp magazines. John Stewart, chair of the commission, repeatedly urged in the *Tribune's* editorial columns that Party members take more energetic cultural initiatives. In February 1949 Tim Buck's address to the LPP's national convention included a special appeal on behalf of support for cultural activity. All in all, as the 1940s came to an end, the LPP's various reports, proclamations, and appeals suggested that in culture as in politics the Communist movement in Canada was moving forward vigorously.

But in spite of the many expressions of optimism in the Communist community, early and prominent signs began to appear of the revival of irreconcilable hostility between capitalism and Communism. Margaret Fairley's anthology *Spirit of Canadian Democracy* was ignored by reviewers and denounced by bourgeois cultural and political leaders. Dyson Carter announced his membership in the LPP in 1947, and was shunned by the newspapers and magazines that had welcomed his popular science articles. Joe Wallace, whose book of poems *Night Is Ended* had been so sympathetically received by reviewers who expressed disgust with the government for imprisoning him under the War Measures Act, now had to take a job as a janitor to make a marginal living. The new atmosphere in which Canadian literary Communists found themselves was a reflection of the widening international conflict between Communism and capitalism. In the April 1945 *Cahiers du communisme*, prominent French Communist Jacques Duclos denounced the policies of the US Party leader Earl Browder, who was transforming the American Party into a "political association" with the avowed purpose of working for peaceful social change in conjunction with liberal bourgeois organizations. Also in 1945, after succeeding to the US presidency Harry S. Truman repudiated Franklin D. Roosevelt's policies of friendship and cooperation with the USSR. Joseph Stalin expressed his suspicions about capitalist intentions in Europe and Asia, and his determination to pursue Soviet interests through the militant propagation of Communism. In a famous "Iron Curtain" speech in Fulton, Missouri, on 6 March 1946, Winston Churchill proclaimed the beginning of the Cold War. Less than a year after the surrenders of Germany and Japan, the opponents of fascism had rearranged themselves into two hostile armed camps, and the Communist movements in capitalist countries were reverting to their roles as the irreconcilable antagonists of bourgeois regimes.

The Canadian Party had a dramatic induction into the Cold War atmosphere. On 5 September 1945 a young Russian cipher clerk walked out of the Soviet embassy in Ottawa with a bundle of papers that allegedly revealed the existence of an elaborate USSR-sponsored spy network in which several Canadians were implicated. Historical opinion varies considerably about the significance of Igor Gouzenko's defection and the subsequent arrests and trials of alleged spies. Reg Whitaker and Gary Marcuse, in their study of the roots of the Cold War in Canada, suggest that Gouzenko's revelations were inflated in importance and exploited by police, intelligence services, and governments for the ultimate purpose of discrediting the Canadian and international Communist movements (52-53). "The damage done by the spy trials," writes Merrily Weisbord in a similar vein, "is not to be found in the 'secrets' given or in the augmented power of the Soviets, but in the way the trials were used: to inaugurate the Cold War, to justify the arms race, to strengthen the secret service, to smash the militant unions, to repress dissent, and to leave the world teetering dangerously on the edge of brinkmanship" (172-73). On the other side, Robert Bothwell and J.L. Granatstein, who produced an edition of excerpts from the tapes of Gouzenko's debriefing and the interrogation of witnesses by the Kellock-Taschereau Royal Commission, believe that Gouzenko's revelations about Russian espionage in Canada were significant enough, in the light of Soviet threats against world peace and security, to justify the Commission's and the RCMP's vigorous (and frequently illegal) actions.

But whatever the political significance of the Gouzenko affair, the Cold War atmosphere that it initiated had unmistakable effects on the public perceptions of the Communist movement and on the LPP's efforts to establish itself as a conventional political party with a stake in Canadian culture. Cultural activists within the LPP felt the consequences as the wartime flood of Party members and sympathizers began to drain away in the new atmosphere of fear and police repression. The *Canadian Tribune*, encouraged by the expansion of its circulation during the war, tried to set up as a daily in 1947, but the newspaper had to revert to a weekly tabloid format after six months, during which it lost one hundred thousand dollars (Elliott 238). In January 1949, the American novelist Howard Fast spoke at Massey Hall in Toronto to warn listeners that the repressive anti-Communist measures currently being imposed in the US could have repercussions for Canadians ("Trial of 12 Communists"). In March, 1949, a Cultural and Scientific Congress for World Peace held in New York was denounced as a Communist front operation, since its supporters and participants included such leftist-tinged artists as Fast, Aaron Copland, W.E.B. Dubois, Dashiel Hammett, Lillian Hellman, Thomas Mann, Arthur Miller, and Paul Robeson. Two attendees from Canada, Margaret Fairley and the Vancouver-based British singer John Goss, were ordered out of the US by the Immigration and Naturalization Service. Barker Fairley, who was an officer of the Canadian-Soviet Friendship Society, was allowed to stay and finish his term as visiting professor of German at Columbia, but in October he was refused re-entry into the US to deliver a scheduled series of lectures at Bryn Mawr ("Culture Sessions"; "Toronto University Professor"; Programme, Cultural and Scientific Congress for World Peace, Fairley Papers).

But in spite of dwindling Party membership and the post-war renewal of anti-Communism, cultural activists in the Party pressed doggedly on in their efforts to respond to the National Cultural Commission's calls for more and better artistic endeavour. LPP branches in the major cities followed the NCC's urging to form writers', artists', and drama groups, counterparts of the Progressive Arts

Clubs of the 1930s. Like the PAC—and many non-Communist organizations of would-be writers—the Writers' Groups especially devoted themselves to the establishment of literary magazines. Even before the formation of the NCC, local Party branches had made attempts at establishing outlets for their writers. The St. Lawrence-St. George LPP club of Montreal, for instance, in 1945 produced a small literary journal entitled *En Masse*. Montreal was an active centre of English-Canadian literary initiatives throughout the 1940s and 1950s, initiatives that included such influential periodicals of modernism and early postmodernism as John Sutherland's *First Statement* (1942-45) and *Northern Review* (1945-56), Patrick Anderson's *Preview* (1942-45) and Aileen Collins's *CIV/n* (1953-55). It was, in fact, the founding editor of one of these magazines who established *En Masse*. In his autobiography, British expatriate Patrick Anderson (1915-79) referred to his LPP membership as "an escapade in my life that has left scarcely anything behind it, not even a sour taste" (*Search Me* 151). He appears to have belonged to the Party from 1943 to 1945, when after the collapse of the independent *Preview*, he founded *En Masse*, which he edited from March to October. His wife, Peggy (Doernbach) Anderson, withdrew the magazine from affiliation with the LPP when she took over the editorship in late 1945, but the magazine folded after two more issues.

Patrick Anderson's many other achievements as an editor and poet make his flirtation with Communism a significant link between bourgeois and Marxist literary activity in Canada. Anderson's own contributions to *En Masse* avoid the dogmatic assertion of Communist ideology. His "St. Henri" (March 1945), for instance, is a wistful lament for suffering humanity with ironic reflections on the inability of either Marxism or poetry to relieve the suffering. His editorial column, "Notes from the City" (April 1945), calls attention to the spectacle of "dull unhappy lives" in a Montreal controlled by corporate trusts and monopolies, but suggests that this spectacle at least presents an important aesthetic challenge to the Canadian writer. In his own response to this challenge he identifies with Archibald Lampman, "our only Canadian poet, working back there in Ottawa in the Eighties and Nineties amongst the hypocrisy of graft—horror of inimical environment and also its extreme fascination." Anderson's own poetry of "horror and fascination," with its roots in the Victorian Canadian tradition and its affinities with the British modernism of W.H. Auden, might have constituted a contribution to the progressive poetic tradition as significant as Dorothy Livesay's. But Anderson gave up *En Masse* after two issues and moved on to other literary ventures, leaving only intimations of new possibilities for Communist creative literature.

These possibilities were renewed briefly by another Montreal venture, *Canadian Writing*, published by the Montreal Writers' Workshop of the LPP, and founded in 1950 by another British expatriate, Maurice Whitbread. As an editorial in the first issue established, the magazine was committed to a more traditional conception of socialist realism than *En Masse* had been. Rejecting "writers who deal with mystical beings in a mystical world," the anonymous editorial called for writing about "the two central concerns of modern man, namely peace and a secure livelihood." *Canadian Writing* would also seek working-class writers, as opposed to intellectuals who "view life from an ivory tower." *Canadian Writing* introduced a few promising young writers, including D.S. Daniels, a war veteran and member of the militant Canadian Seamen's Union, who was later to achieve modest success as a playwright outside the Party. Most of the sincere but undistinguished poems, short stories, and articles in the magazine, however, reflect an intellectualized rather than a working-class perspective, and an amateurishness that probably reflects the youth of most of the authors. Lacking broad or innovative appeal, *Canadian Writing* was able to secure only a minimal audience, and folded after two issues.

While little magazines emerged and quickly expired, the Party newspapers continued to provide outlets for creative writing. In francophone Montreal, the weekly *Combat* appeared in 1947 as a substitute for the long-defunct *Clarté*. Edited by Pierre Gélinas, *Combat* struggled for survival throughout the 1950s against the repressive Union nationale regime of Maurice Duplessis, finding space for only occasional cultural news, poems, and fiction. In Toronto, writers had access to the *Canadian Tribune* and to a new weekly paper for young people, *Champion*. Sponsored by the National Federation of Labor Youth (NFLY), the successor to the Young Communist League,

*Champion* began life in 1951 under the editorship of D.S. Daniels. Subsequent editors included Ben Shek and Kari Levitt, both of whom went on from NFLY membership to distinguished careers as university professors. Literary contributors included Margaret Fairley, who published some of her early research on William Lyon Mackenzie, and Nancy Doyle, a Winnipeg writer whose short stories on Canadian historical themes included "Coals of Fire" about Egerton Ryerson, and "The Glory and the Grief," about the Winnipeg General Strike. Doyle's short stories also appeared in the *Tribune*, beginning with "Rachel," a fictional sketch about an anti-fascist Polish woman immigrant to Canada, published in conjunction with an editorial appeal for more "stories about the Canadian people, about Canada; stories about the fight for peace, about the struggles of labor, about our history" (2 October 1950: 17).

As in the 1930s, Party culture leaders and writers regarded the short story as potentially the most important literary genre in the propagation of socialist realism. In the 30 April 1951 issue of the *Tribune* Margaret Fairley introduced a significant variation on the socialist realist short story, an eight-thousand-word narrative entitled "The Autobiography of a Working Woman." Although purporting to be "as told to Margaret Fairley," the story has a sophistication of style and structure, political interpretation, and literary allusion that suggests Fairley took a substantial part in composing the narrative. British-born like Fairley herself, the anonymous narrator tells a discursive story of an impoverished and abused childhood in northern England of the 1890s, immigration to Canada as a farm worker and bondservant, and an itinerant life of poverty and toil through the Depression and two world wars. The woman's political education comes about not through a sudden exposure to Marxism but through a gradual evolution from Victorian ideas of the inevitability of social inequality to the recognition of the common interest and collective strength of the working class. This experiment in worker autobiography was part of a larger project. As Fairley wrote in a *Tribune* article of 27 February 1950, she wanted "to collect and publish a series of first-hand accounts of the real making of Canada," through narratives of "clearing of the land, told by early settlers" and of railroad, construction and other workers ("Want Stories"). Fairley's public

appeal brought her an abundance of stories, which she began to combine with narratives of Canadian pioneers that she had collected from
archives and old publications, with a view to bringing out an anthology tentatively entitled "With Our Own Hands." Although she published several articles based on her collection, by the time of her death
in 1968 she had not completed the anthology, which remains in manuscript among her papers.

Fairley's failure to complete "With Our Own Hands" was in part
the result of her heavy commitment to other work. In May 1951 the
LPP called a second national cultural conference, in which speakers
related the problems of establishing partisan literary outlets to the
commercialism and US domination of Canadian culture. According to
the report of the conference, "Canadian cultural development is
being sacrificed on the altar of the American dollar....With the servile
cooperation of our government, two-thirds of everything we read,
almost 100 per cent of everything we see in our theatres, by far the
greatest proportion of what is broadcast, is stamped with the trade-
mark of Made in USA" (CPC/LPP Papers, NAC). The conference outlined ambitious plans for Party-sponsored drama groups, choirs,
courses of lectures on English-Canadian literature, and a national
cultural magazine. Fairley threw herself enthusiastically into the
magazine project. With a committee of volunteers, she produced a
prospectus, which emphasized the political significance of the proposed magazine:

> Aware of the great dangers in and to Canada of fascism and war,
> it will speak through the creative arts, for peace and national
> independence, and will combat the war-inciting, dehumanizing
> "Yankee dollar culture" that is part of the economic and politi-
> cal domination of our country by the United States, and which
> has nothing in common with the real culture of the American
> people....It looks to the new civilizations arising in the Soviet
> Union, the People's Democracies of Europe and People's China
> where one-third of mankind, free from centuries of bondage, is
> building great new cultures dedicated to peace and brotherhood
> of all mankind. (Printed prospectus, CPC/LPP Papers, NAC)

Although edited in Toronto, *New Frontiers* was supposed to appeal
to readers and potential contributors from all regions and ethnic

groups in Canada. The magazine was also intended to fill a gap in the Canadian literary scene. Most of the new literary magazines established in the 1940s were politically nonaligned publications, favouring writers moving in the direction of modernist technical experimentation. *New Frontiers*, on the other hand, was committed to the unity of culture and politics within the Marxist socialist realist tradition. The magazine was attractively produced, approximately 6" x 9" in size with glossy covers featuring reproductions of socialist realist works of art, photographs of eminent artists, or of ordinary people at work or leisure. In an editorial statement in the first issue, Fairley expressed the new magazine's commitment to cultural activity that would foster world peace and encourage rapprochement between Canada and the Soviet Union. She also emphasized, as she had in *Spirit of Canadian Democracy,* an inclusive definition of the Canadian cultural heritage that would take into account the efforts of francophones, immigrants, native people, and the younger generation. She stated that the magazine's goal was to "publish stories, poems, songs, pictures, and critical, historical and scientific articles revealing the Canadian and world significance of the aspirations of our people towards a genuine democracy in which alone they can find a free, peaceful and plentiful life" (n. pag.).

Fairley and her collaborators wanted to compensate for the shortcomings not only of other magazines but also of the Canadian government, which had recently promised much and delivered little for national culture. In her inaugural editorial, she warned that Canadian culture "cannot thrive if it is choked by a flood of the cynical, degenerate products of U.S. commercialism" (n. pag.). In another article in the same issue, she attacked the recently published Massey report for its subservience to a political status quo based on the Cold War agenda of the Americans. The report, she insisted, "makes Canadian culture responsible to the Department of External Affairs and so to the U.S. State Department and its war plans" ("Massey Report" 19). But as Fairley realized, the liberation of Canadian culture from American influences could not be achieved simply by railing against the adversary; *New Frontiers* would have to reveal evidence of a distinctive and aesthetically valuable Canadian progressive cultural tradition. She also realized that it would have to be a pan-Canadian magazine, with relevance to all regions of a geographically vast and ethnically diverse country. She tried to encourage regional input by including representatives on the editorial board from the western provinces, the maritimes, and Quebec. Most of the associate editors and contributors were Toronto-based, however, and a literary content that was both regionally diverse and aesthetically significant was slow in developing. In the first issue the editorials and critical articles were of greater interest than the creative contributions. These articles included a translation of a commentary on the fiction of Roger Lemelin and Jean-Jules Richard by *Combat* editor Pierre Gélinas, and an essay by the painter Frederick B. Taylor, "Towards a Socialist Art," a defense of socialist pictorial realism based on a recent trip to the USSR. The poems, by contrast, tended to be formally simple sentimental effusions, including a reprint of Joe Wallace's "O Lovely Land," and Mary Holmes's salute to the magazine itself, "Shout Aloud, New Frontiers."

The responses of non-Communist newspapers and magazines to the new periodical were predictably surly, as the editor herself revealed by reprinting some of them in the second issue. "*Saturday Night* resents our interest in early Canadian culture," she acknowledged; "the *Toronto Telegram* wants no first-hand reports from behind the 'Iron Curtain,' the *Saskatoon Star-Phoenix* rejects left-wing literature as 'pretty poor stuff' and criticism of the Massey Report (especially when documented) as 'scurrilous'" ("A Light and a Weapon" n. pag.) But the *New Frontiers* editors were much less interested in pleasing the right-wing media than in developing a readership among workers and intellectuals in the politically progressive community. The second issue (Spring 1952) tried to establish the connections between modern progressive art and the historical traditions of working-class culture with a poem on Louis Riel, a scholarly reprint of a French-Canadian folk song, and an article that attempted to re-establish the Canadian roots of the Paul Bunyan legend which had been appropriated by US popular culture, and even to facetiously suggest a connection between Bunyan legends and the USSR through apocryphal Siberian folk tales. Also featured was a reprint of a speech delivered at the recent World Peace Council in Vienna by the eminent Polish physicist Leopold Infeld, who had spent the war years at the University of Toronto, and an article on Gogol by Australian Communist novelist James Aldridge (b. 1918), whose recent sojourn in Canada provided the setting for his novel *The Hunter* (1951). The third (Fall 1952) issue, like its predecessors, remained stronger in expository and polemical prose than in literary art. Fairley's editorial dealt with the topical controversy over the "Symphony Six" musicians who were fired from the Toronto Symphony Orchestra because American immigration officials imposed a vague subversive label on them and refused them entry to play in the US. A historical article on the Depression in the Saskatchewan dust bowl was complemented by a contemporary piece on Korean women protesting against the war in their country. Other items included a reprint of Norman Bethune's famous essay "Wounds" and a first-person proletarian narrative similar to Fairley's "Autobiography of a Working Woman."

The Winter 1953 issue included two original pieces of short fiction that held out the possibility of new standards in the Canadian socialist realist short story. Dorise Nielsen (1902-80) was an English-born former teacher and former member of the CCF who served as an independent MP for Battleford, Saskatchewan (1940-45), and as a member of the national executive of the CPC/LPP since 1940. Her book *New Worlds for Women* (Progress, 1944) outlined the prospects for women in the work force and political life in post-war Canada. Her short story "The Dance," in spite of being her only venture into creative writing, is a remarkably effective socialist realist adaptation of an otherwise conventional initiation story. Nielsen uses the autobiographical narrative of a young schoolteacher fresh from England attending her first dance in a Saskatchewan farming community to highlight the solidarity of working-class experience and the elemental cycles of work and healthy leisure. Nancy Doyle's "The Right to Live," by contrast, uses a tragic situation to emphasize the importance of women's role in the peace movement. One of the few works of Canadian fiction to apply anti-war opinion to the Korean conflict, the story explores the thoughts and emotions of a mother who has lost a son in the war, and asserts the need for women to question and oppose the male-oriented cultural assumptions that lead to war. Although not free of sentimentality and redundant didacticism, the story in both its subject matter and feminist perspective stands out in the rather arid field of Canadian short fiction in the early 1950s.

The Fall 1953 issue was equally innovative. Again taking up subjects that non-Communist literary magazines of the 1950s ignored, the issue featured writings by and about ethnic and aboriginal writers. The articles included a bio-critical study of the Canadian-Icelandic poet Stephan G. Stephansson, and a report on an opera recently staged by Cowichan native people of Duncan, BC. Going beyond North America, the issue published an interview with and critical commentary on the Turkish Marxist poet Nazim Hikmet, an article on the Ukrainian poet Taras Shevchenko, and the translation of a story by a Chukchi (Siberian Inuit) writer studying at Leningrad University. Included also was a review article on a new film from the United States, *Salt of the Earth,* made by an independent company that included blacklisted Hollywood actors and technicians, concerning the resistance of Mexican-American miners and their wives during the Empire Zinc strike in New Mexico, 1950-52. By 1954, *New Frontiers* was having remarkable success at unearthing new fiction, criticism, and graphic art of high professional quality which could not otherwise get exposure in the political atmosphere of the decade. The Spring and Winter 1954 issues featured excerpts from a new novel by William Allister, *The Prisoners,* based on Allister's experiences as a prisoner of the Japanese after the fall of Hong Kong. The Summer 1954 and Spring 1955 issues included excerpts from *Asbestos on Fire,* a translation of Jean-Jules Richard's *Le Feu dans l'amiante.* Other highlights of 1954-55 issues included further editorial criticisms of the Massey Report and the delays involved in the establishment of the Canada Council; a photographic essay on the relief sculptures of working-class scenes by a Sudbury miner; an article on cultural exchanges between Canada and Eastern European countries; and a report by Margaret Fairley on her recent visit to Rumania, Poland, and Hungary. These countries, Fairley discovered, were remarkably vigorous in preserving their cultural heritage, especially their folk art and the work of artists of earlier centuries—areas of achievement in which Canada in the 1950s showed neither bureaucratic nor scholarly vigour. Fairley used the magazine to promote Canada's cultural heritage through regular reprints of neglected nineteenth-century literary texts, and through modern articles on such figures as William Lyon Mackenzie, Thomas MacQueen, and Pauline Johnson.

Yet in spite of its diverse content and the increasing distinction of the literary submissions, New Frontiers had little success attracting a broad readership. An unpublished "Statement of Purpose" prepared after the second issue acknowledged the magazine's weaknesses in appealing to the working masses and its heavy reliance on Party members as both writers and readers. This statement also indicated a primary source of the problem, however, by rededicating New Frontiers to "the critical theoretical fight as [sic] against US cultural domination and its ideological agent, cosmopolitanism," and the critical-theoretical fight for realism (including socialist realism) and against formalism. The opposition to cosmopolitanism and formalism set the magazine squarely against the prevailing tendencies of both the producers and consumers of bourgeois culture in the 1950s, and reflected the paradoxes of international Communist political and cultural strategies during the Cold War. Communist opposition to bourgeois idea and practice was consistent with Stalinist hard-line policies, but was in conflict with the Leninist ideal of achieving the Party's aims by means of infiltration and appropriation of bourgeois institutions and procedures. The commitment of New Frontiers to a narrowly defined socialist aesthetic would inevitably lead to the magazine's alienation from many readers and writers whom it might have hoped to attract.

In order to win the attention of non-Communist readers, the magazine editors tried to get out into the community and become involved in cultural debate and dialogue, but their sectarian aesthetic positions tended to provoke strong opposition from non-Communists. One public indication of this opposition emerged in March 1952 from Vancouver, where the regional associate editor of New Frontiers, Harold Griffin, participated in a symposium on Canadian culture. Griffin spoke in defence of "people's art" and the importance of resistance to the "cold-war culture of the U.S." But his remarks provoked a vigorous dissenting opinion from Dorothy Livesay, now expressing her alienation from the Communist movement by insisting that "the artist must stand above the [political] struggle" and concentrate on "knowing himself" [sic] ("Magazines Meet"). There was even resistance to New Frontiers within the Communist community. In a letter of 2 November 1955 Tom McEwen, editor of the Pacific

*Tribune,* complained about *New Frontiers* to Charlie Sims of the *Canadian Tribune.* "You can't give the damn thing away in the clubs let alone get members to read it," McEwen insisted. In a brief to the National Cultural Commission he criticized the magazine as "too 'highbrow', ivory-towerish and obscure, with little in keeping with the living struggles of a virile, pioneer people" (CPC/LPP Papers, NAC). McEwen's own origins and literary credentials were remote from the ivory tower: a Scottish-born blacksmith, he had learned journalism by reading and contributing to union and Party publications in the 1920s, and had modeled his own attempts at verse primarily on the works of Robert Burns. Suspicious of academically trained, Toronto-based scholars like Fairley and others on the *New Frontiers* staff, he accused the editors of neglecting regional and historical working-class perspectives on culture.

McEwen's accusations reveal the conflict between proletarian and intellectual perspectives that is the perennial dilemma of the promoters and practitioners of Communist-inspired cultural activity. Fairley herself was aware of this conflict, and did her best to reconcile opposing points of view by an inclusive editorial policy that accepted sophisticated critical and historical articles as well as plain-speaking rhythmically simple poems. The work of the ever-popular Joe Wallace appeared in almost every issue, and the magazine published two chapbook collections of his poems, *All My Brothers* (1953) and *Hi, Sister, Hi Brother!* (1956). Wallace was still turning out much the same kind of poems he had been writing since the 1920s, which gave *New Frontiers* a direct link with the Party's populist literary past. Surprisingly, however, Wallace's poetry also had highbrow appeal, for it suited a critic no less sophisticated than Northrop Frye, who, in spite of his general disapproval of Communist-inspired culture, praised both of Wallace's new books in his annual reviews of Canadian poetry in the *University of Toronto Quarterly.* Describing Wallace as a "skillful and astute versifier," he insisted that it was "most important to keep the tone of genuine anger and contempt at hypocrisy alive in our poetry, no matter where it comes from or for what motives it is uttered" ("Letters in Canada," 1953 and 1956). But neither Wallace's popularity nor Frye's praise of his poetry could keep *New Frontiers* afloat. The magazine continued to lose money and to draw the disapproval of readers both within and outside the Party. After reducing its size and simplifying its format, it folded with the Summer 1956 issue.

*New Frontiers* had emerged at a time when a politically leftist cultural magazine should have been able to reach a small audience beyond the LPP and its sympathizers. There was a lamentable lack of good literary and general arts magazines in Canada in the mid-1950s, and no other periodical interested in exploring the connection between culture and politics. John Sutherland's *Northern Review* had a slight Marxist tinge, reflected in Sutherland's critique of the worst excesses of capitalism and of cosmopolitan pro-US influences on Canadian culture. But lack of financial support and the editor's unpredictable health and temperament contributed to the demise of the *Northern Review* in 1952. *New Frontiers* might have hoped to capture part of *Northern Review*'s readership, but by 1952 most bourgeois Canadian intellectuals accepted the cosmopolitan cultural attitudes promoted by pro-US Cold War politics and postmodernist anti-political aesthetics. Fairley wanted to re-establish the link between fine arts and leftist politics just at a time when the Canadian cultural community and general population were particularly hostile to Marxist and Soviet Russian opinions. The triumph of cultural cosmopolitanism and anti-political aesthetics is reflected in the emergence of the *Tamarack Review* (1956-82) almost simultaneously with the end of *New Frontiers*. But Fairley and *New Frontiers* had at least demonstrated that a good Communist culture magazine could survive for five years, even in the midst of the Cold War. The magazine had given exposure to Canadian and international writers and artists who would otherwise have been ignored in Canada of the 1950s.

• • • • •

Although critics and biographers tend to gloss over his years with the LPP and date his literary career from the early 1960s after he had left the Party, the most important writer launched by *New Frontiers* was undoubtedly Milton Acorn (1923-86). Acorn's literary beginnings as a Communist and his contributions to *New Frontiers* and the *Canadian Tribune* are worth examining as illustrations of how the allegedly limited Marxist aesthetic can nourish a major artistic talent. When *New Frontiers* printed his first published poem Acorn was thirty years old and had been trying to establish himself as a poet for almost ten years. After being invalided out of the Canadian army in 1943 as a result of either an injury on board a troop ship, a psychological trauma, or both, Acorn had returned home to his native Prince Edward Island to pursue his related interests in poetry and radical politics (See Lemm 54-58). The Island in 1943 was not a propitious place for radicalism. That year marked the beginning of the decade-long administration of a Liberal government under Premier J. Walter Jones, a wealthy farmer whose political platform included a determination to defend the province's "traditional way of life" by a program of power-sharing between government and large corporations, and by blaming labour disturbances on "communist agitators" from the mainland (Sharpe 188). In spite of this atmosphere, or because of it, there were many disaffected young Islanders like Acorn, growing in numbers after 1945, who were eager to absorb radical ideas. Soon after returning from his abortive war, Acorn took out a subscription to the *Canadian Tribune* from which he probably got his early education in both Communism and modern Canadian poetry.

At first, however, Acorn was inspired less by the young modernists like Layton and Waddington who were appearing in the *Tribune* in the 1940s than by the Party's perennial favourite, Joe Wallace. "One day I opened the Canadian Tribune," Acorn wrote years later, "and there was a picture of Joe the poet, with a group of things he dared to call poems. They were not....My reaction was...'well, if that fellow can be called a poet...so can I.'" In spite of this retrospective satire, however, Acorn referred to Wallace's poetry as "sometimes totally inspired," and his own early work shared Wallace's emphasis on traditional form and subtle but explicit political commentary, as well as the older poet's fondness for combining Marxist and Christian imagery (Acorn, "In Wry Memoriam" 38, 40).

Acorn apparently began submitting short poems to the *Tribune* in the late 1940s. These early efforts must have been very weak indeed, for they failed to satisfy even the *Tribune*'s none-too-exacting standards, but he kept scribbling and submitting, thereby gradually discovering what and how he wanted to write. By the early 1950s, Margaret Fairley could recognize in Acorn an original poetic voice. His first published poem appeared in the fourth (Winter 1953) *New*

*Frontiers*, the same issue that included Dorise Nielsen's short story "The Dance." Attributed to "A., a Prince Edward Island poet," "Grey Girl's Gallop" is a long satirical work written mostly in anapestic tetrameter rhyming couplets, about a trotting horse that defies the rules imposed upon her by her "masters," and forfeits the race by breaking stride and then abandoning the race altogether. In this fable of innocent individualism rebelling against exploitative economic power, Acorn presents racetrack gambling as the epitome of investment capitalism—"Some call it business but I call it stealing!" (37)—and compares the race to the artificial competitive spirit that capitalism imposes on society to ensure a submissive loyalty to the profit motive. The horse's act of rebellion leads to the moral of the fable:

> When life was imparted
> To men and to horses both races knew this
> "A thing is well done that is done for its own bliss
> Or else done for life—living now or begotten."
> Most horses remember:
> Most men have forgotten. (40)

*New Frontiers* accepted two more of Acorn's poems for its Fall 1953 issue. These successes plus his urge to get into a metropolitan cultural milieu prompted him to move to Montreal in the summer of 1953. In the city he was unsuccessful in finding more than occasional work to support himself, but here his career as a Communist writer flourished, especially when he encountered the person who was his second important literary and ideological contact after Joe Wallace. Louise Harvey (1912-83) was in socio-economic background at the opposite pole from the working-class status that Acorn claimed for himself. The daughter of J.C. Smith, late president of the Shawinigan Water and Power Corporation, Harvey had been educated at Wellesley College in Massachusetts, and had returned to Montreal to marry into a family as socially distinguished as her own. But when Acorn met her Harvey was divorced and pursuing a career as a poet, editor, writer of short stories and feature articles, and militant Communist. In the late 1930s Harvey had contributed socially critical articles and poems to the *Canadian Forum* and *Saturday Night* while serving as a member of the Montreal Committee to Aid Spanish

Democracy, which sponsored the blood transfusion unit organized by Norman Bethune for the benefit of the republican side in the Spanish Civil War. About this time she joined the Communist Party, and during the years of illegality she served as liaison between Communist MP Dorise Nielsen and the Party's operating centre in Montreal. After the war she was a founding member of the Montreal LPP writers' workshop that published the two-issue *Canadian Writing* to which she contributed poetry and fiction under the pen name "Linda Joslyn." Her short story, "Oh, My Lovely Kimi" in the second issue, is arguably her most notable work, featuring the then-neglected topic of the wartime confinement and forced removal of Japanese Canadians on the Pacific coast. Contrasting the vulnerability of the Asians with the insensitive, economically based power of European Canadians, the story emphasizes the capacity of the victims for forgiveness and mutual dependence within their own wounded but durable community.

In 1953 Harvey stood as an LPP protest candidate for the riding of St. Antoine-Westmount in the federal election. It was during or soon after the summer election campaign that Acorn and Harvey met, probably at an LPP club meeting. Although ten years older than Acorn, Harvey seems to have fallen in love with the young Islander. As members of their LPP club's literary group they provided mutual support and submitted their poems to each other for criticism. There is little evidence that Acorn paid attention to Harvey's detailed critiques, several of which are in the Acorn papers at the National Archives. But her complaints of Acorn's obscurity may have encouraged him in the use of colloquial diction and simple poetic forms. More important, Harvey was the first of a series of sympathetic literary friends who encouraged Acorn in his determination to become a poet. Harvey's own poetry published in *New Frontiers* and the *Tribune* tended to be very explicitly polemical, encompassing meditations on current political issues. Partly as a result of Nielsen's influence, she was especially committed to the peace movement and the struggle for women's rights. Her first poem in *New Frontiers*, "To My Daughter" (Spring 1953), is a brief secular prayer in which she envisages a future free of economic strife where her child will be able to fulfill her life as a woman. "Woman's Song" (*Tribune* 2 November 1953) is a tribute to the LPP-sponsored Congress of Canadian Women, as well as a confident salute to the emergence of a new age of equal opportunity. "From Door to Door" (*New Frontiers* Fall 1954) conveys a similar vision of women joining men in the march toward a world of peace, work, and joy.

Most of Harvey's poems are simple and explicit articulations of her quiet faith in the future. Acorn's Communist poetry makes its points by more subtle means, and encompasses a wider variety of form and subject matter. The theme of rebellion against money power is incorporated into a comic animal fable in "Grey Girl's Gallop." "Jack and the River" (*New Frontiers* Fall 1953) is a dialogue between two workers that idealizes their status not by directly defining their position in the socio-economic scheme but by attributing to the title character a poetic sensitivity to nature. "Norman Bethune, Died Nov. 13, 1939" (*New Frontiers* Fall 1953), inspired by the 1952 biography of Bethune, is a tribute to the Party's larger-than-life hero. A sonnet with a rigorously traditional structure of rhythm and rhyme, the poem is a dramatic monologue ostensibly spoken by Bethune's real-life Chinese interpreter, Tung Yueh-ch'ien. Bethune is portrayed in Christlike terms in relation to his followers, who express only awe and grief as their leader dies. The speaker sees himself as "a bruised and helpless child" against Bethune's "angelic fire and pity." Bethune's final comment in reply to the appeal of his grief-stricken interpreter, "No Tung—you live—and make improvements," increases the impression of the remoteness of the divine Bethune in contrast to the human disciple, who can absorb little from his master beyond the general lesson to carry on the struggle.

In "To Coté's Statue of Louis Riel" (Spring 1954), Acorn similarly sees a revolutionary hero in collectivist and Christlike terms. The poet apostrophizes the Métis rebel through the representation of him by the working-class wood carver Jean-Baptiste Coté (1834-1907). An artist best known for the wooden saints, apostles, and Virgins that he carved for churches throughout Quebec province, Coté conceived a calm and pensive Riel, dressed in his prairie leggings and fur coat, gazing with meditative dignity rather than striking a militant revolutionary pose. "A quoi pense-tu, Bonhomme Riel?" Acorn asks. In answer to his own question he conceives a saviour who agonizes over the sufferings of his people, and whose "early thought" ("early" because predating the time for inevitable revolution in the Marxist sense), led him to "the British gallows-tree." The poem combines Christian and Marxist ideology to focus on the suffering and death that are part of the prelude to ultimate revolution.

In "Of Martyrs" (Winter 1955), a tribute to the anonymous victims of capitalist exploitation, Christian imagery and ideas are similarly put to the service of Marxism. Acorn's first venture into free verse, the poem consists of six five-line unrhymed stanzas of uneven line lengths, with a rhythmic pattern that arises from the uneven stress on key words:

> I often think of martyrs
> and when I do the cosmos shakes
> and with that pity I can touch their time
> can feel their flesh
> for they were the most loving of folk.

In the following stanzas Acorn goes on to envisage the anonymous revolutionary heroes marching and singing, and finally passing through "the door of their deaths," leaving "the song of their lives" to be taken up by dedicated partisans who follow them.

But by 1956, Acorn was beginning to see the ideals of collectivism in skeptical terms. "A Pretty-Near-March-Song" (Spring 1956) offers deliberately naive, doggerel-like rhyming quatrains about robins, oak trees, and melting snow. The birds, trees, and snow, furthermore, are all personified, represented as reluctant to accept the coming of spring. The robin sings, but wishes that the weather were warmer; after thinking the matter over, the trees "decide they ought/to wait a bit" before budding, even though they will later "grieve" for the additional spring weather they might have enjoyed. The snow longs for a "prophet" to tell it whether to go or stay. The poem is about the political indecision of people who lose opportunities because they lack the self-confidence to take revolutionary action. As they waver, or long for a "prophet," they justify their indecision by approving the deceptive comfort of the status quo:

> And they admire those winter-streamlined, strange
> windfluted forms that they rest frozen in.

They defend their passivity further by claiming that any change for the sake of achieving mere "worldly aims" would be an "aesthetic sin." The creation of beauty, their inaction implies—whether the beauty of nature, art, or social reform—must wait for the proper moment. At the end of the poem, Acorn verbalizes the robin's song ("All this shall pass, shall pass, shall pass, shall pass") to suggest how would-be revolutionaries merely sing songs or chant slogans about change rather than doing anything to effect it.

Although Acorn later praised this poem to his friend and fellow poet Al Purdy, he never included it in a collection, perhaps because he thought it was too concerned with internecine Party squabbles to be of lasting interest. The implied criticism of the indecision of his fellow LPP members, including the "singers" of the writers' group, indicates Acorn's restless dissatisfaction with the Party by 1956. Meanwhile, however, he had finally broken into the *Tribune* with the poem "The Dead" (11 April 1955), a tribute to Canadian soldiers who lost their lives in the Second World War. Between 1955 and 1957 the *Tribune* featured eight of his poems, mostly simple lyrics dealing with social problems such as unemployment, worker safety, and the post-war housing crisis. His final poetic contribution to the paper, published in the issue of 22 April 1957, was "Callum," the second of the two Communist works he described to Purdy as among his best. "Callum" consists of four stanzas of irregular rhythm, rhyme, and line length, written in the colloquial worker's voice of "Jack and the River." But the new poem deals with the tragedy rather than the idyll of proletarian experience, for Callum is a "novice miner" who is forced to work in a dangerous location and falls "a hundred and forty feet" down a mine-shaft. The catastrophe is presented very briefly, however; the poem concentrates on Callum as an image of male beauty and mystery:

> eyes a lake you see rocks on its bottom;
> voice a loop
> with music in what it said
> that tangled inside your head.
>                   "Callum" was his name,
> pronounced as if he'd signed it on the sun;
> from "the island" he came...
> don't know which one.

The dead miner, like the revolutionaries in "Of Martyrs" or the soldiers in "The Dead," is another victim of industrial capitalism. But unlike "Of Martyrs," "Callum" stresses not the historical continuity of the sacrifice from one generation to another, but the obscurity of the individual life and death. Callum will remain forgotten, like all the anonymous victims of capitalism. Only the speaker in the poem can express his love and admiration, by preserving the name of the dead man in the only way available to him:

> Look anywhere
> at buildings bumping on clouds,
> at spider-grill bridges...
> you'll see no plaque of stone for men killed there
> but on the late shift
> the drill I'm bucking bangs his name in code...
> "Callum"

Callum's anonymity is related especially to his obscure origins. "Where the island is I'll never know," the speaker admits, indicating that he can never fully understand and identify with the martyred man. The probability that the mysterious Callum comes from the same "island" as the poet himself underscores Acorn's sympathies with the victims of capitalism, but the speaker's professed ignorance of the island suggests conversely an alienation that reflects the elusiveness of class-structured solidarity.

Acorn's growing skepticism about the effectiveness and practicality of the LPP's activities extended to his thoughts on the Party's aesthetics. In a letter to the editor of the *Tribune* published 3 June 1957, a little more than a month after the appearance of "Callum," Acorn objected to the Communist tendency to define art as that which is acceptable to the public, and insisted that the whole position of the LPP on culture needed to be reappraised. Acorn's dissatisfaction with the Party particularly singled out the weekly paper, the medium that ironically had a great deal to do with his joining the Party in the first place. In a letter to the editor published in the issue of 28 October 1957, he criticized the *Tribune's* "witless adoration of all things Soviet." Acorn's unhappiness with the *Tribune* was only one sign of his impending break with the LPP. In 1956 he published his first chapbook of poems,

*In Love and Anger*, choosing to underwrite the publication himself rather than have it appear under the auspices of the Party. His dissatisfaction with Communism is explicit in "My Love a Fierce Altruist," the opening poem of the collection. In an undated letter responding to Louise Harvey's complaints about the poem's obscurity, Acorn explained that it was about Harvey herself. The woman Acorn portrays is fierce in her single-minded dedication to humanitarian causes, pursuing these causes with "glum and introspective stare," stepping out like a tightrope walker into a "perilous black abyss" that she seems to appropriate solipsistically (Acorn, *I Shout Love* 27). The brief (eight-line, two-stanza) poem exposes with ruthless irony an idealism that ignores not simply physical obstacles but the very medium and atmosphere in which the idealism must be transformed into action. Either, as in "A Pretty-Near-March-Song," the Communists procrastinated, offered excuses, and did not act at all, or they acted with a blind indifference to reality that could only lead to disaster. In later accounts, Acorn related his departure from the Party to the changing political situation in Quebec. According to his 1977 article on Joe Wallace, the Supreme Court defeat of the so-called "Padlock Law" in Quebec in 1957 enabled the LPP to operate more openly, and a rapid increase in Party membership led to increasing friction between old and new members, then to mass resignations. "I just let my membership lapse," Acorn claimed ("In Wry Memoriam" 41). These circumstances may have been factors, but more prominent influences were his dissatisfaction with the Communist conception of poetry, the limited opportunities for publishing that were available to Party members, his changing relationship with Louise Harvey, and generally his erratic personality that tended to impulsive reaction against people, institutions, and routines he felt were restricting him.

In letters to Dorise Nielsen dated 27 November 1957 and 23 January 1958, Harvey revealed that over the winter of 1955-56 Acorn had a "nervous breakdown," became "utterly callous" toward her, and proved himself "a horror and an incubus who kept haunting me quite literally" (Nielsen Papers NAC). Whatever psychological demons impelled Acorn toward this destructive behaviour, it is evident that he was trying in his characteristically aggressive way to break away from the Party and the restrictions of his relationship with Harvey. For the rest of his life, Acorn referred to himself as a "Marxist" and a "Communist," and even joined various breakaway Marxist groups for intervals, but his sojourn with the old-line Communist party was relatively brief. "I found certain sections of the Communist movement difficult to work with," he admitted in a 1962 essay, but he was willing to describe the Party fifteen years later as "the nearest thing to my spiritual home I ever found" ("I was a communist" 38; "In Wry Memoriam" 41). For about three years, however, Acorn was a committed member of the LPP and a regular contributor to the *Tribune* and *New Frontiers*. His literary apprenticeship as a Marxist revolutionary poet provides a good example of how the Party was hospitable to creativity at a time when English Canada had little to offer its would-be writers in the way of publishing outlets or a congenial cultural environment. If the Party was too dogmatic in its politicization of culture, thanks especially to Margaret Fairley and *New Frontiers* it could still appeal to writers like Acorn who believed in a culture of political engagement.

Another important young writer featured in *New Frontiers* and committed to progressive political ideals was Alberta-born George Ryga (1932-87). Although Ryga's formal involvement with the LPP was even briefer than Acorn's, like Acorn he was strongly influenced by the Communist movement and continued to regard himself as a Marxist after he left the Party. Unlike Acorn, however, Ryga partly inherited his commitment to Communism. His father, born into a prosperous Kulak family in Ukraine, became an admirer of the Russian Soviet regime and was forced to immigrate to Canada partly because of the hostility of anti-Communist Ukrainian nationalists. As a homesteader in Alberta in the early 1930s he joined the CPC, and passed his political beliefs on to his son (Hoffman 59). Young George's political education was also influenced by his boyhood reading, which included the radical romanticism of Percy Bysshe Shelley and Robert Burns. In 1949, at a summer school on creative writing at the Banff School of Fine Arts, he came under the influence of an instructor from the United States, Burton James, a Marxist (Hoffman 44). By 1953 Ryga was a member of the LPP's National Federation of Labor Youth, and over the next few years his poems appeared in *Champion*, the *Tribune*, and *New Frontiers*. In 1956 he was an NFLY delegate to Communist-sponsored youth congresses in Poland, Finland, and Bulgaria, where he met other writers, including the American poet Martha Millet, whose work had been reprinted in the *Tribune* and *New Frontiers*. On a visit to London he met Marxist theatre director Joan Littlewood and her husband Ewan McColl, whose experiments with an updated form of agitprop may have influenced his conception of the drama (Hoffman 86-87).

Although Ryga's interests in drama and fiction had been greatly stimulated by his studies at Banff, it was through poetry that he made himself known as a writer in the Communist community. Under the influence of his reading he had taken to writing verse in adolescence, and his first literary successes were poems published in his local paper, the *Athabasca Echo*. His first published poem after joining the NFLY was probably "My Hands" (*Champion* 21 May 1953), which gave its title to his first, self-published book, *Song of My Hands and Other Poems* (1956). Most of his early work, such as "To Youth" (*Champion* 31 May 1954), dedicated to the national convention of the NFLY, and "Song of the Wilds" (1 July 1955) was traditional in form, and expressed sentimental responses to nature and angry complaints against social injustice which reflected his continuing debt to Shelley and Burns. His first poem for *New Frontiers*, "Federico Garcia Lorca," however, attempted to move in more comprehensive poetic directions. Although a fairly conventional elegy, probably inspired by one or more of the many tributes to the Spanish poet that had appeared over the years in Communist publications, Ryga's poem synthesizes some of his thematic and formal preoccupations. A free-verse, partly dramatic poem featuring the imagined last words of the Spanish poet as he faced a Fascist firing squad, the elegy suggests something of the universal tragedy of the creative artist. The established political power, Ryga suggests, perennially condemns as madness behaviour that arises out of processes of nature and human history:

> Mad? Then so were the souls
> Of our fathers,
> Whose lovely books you burned
> In the village court.
> Mad as my poems,
> Whose verse froze upon your lips
> In fear,

When they hushed with sword and flame
The songs of free men.
I go, but let my madness live
In the hungry hills,
And not in the sunless dungeon.
(*New Frontiers* 3 [Spring 1954])

Political oppressors condemn the impulse to freedom as "madness," but for the poet such madness is a yearning for a limitless world of nature in which people can realize their dreams. Ryga's application of this idea to all poets, including himself, is evident in his adoption of the title *Hungry Hills* for his first novel, originally published in 1963, based on his own youthful struggles toward freedom and self-fulfilment in the Depression-era countryside of Alberta.

By comparison to the Lorca piece, "They Who Suffer" (*New Frontiers* Fall 1955) is a much more conventional socialist realist poem. This one-sided dialogue in rhymed quatrains laments the poverty, hunger, and unemployment that pervade the modern world, and ends with a conventional expression of confidence in the revolutionary millennium:

But mark my words, John,
　A people bled white
　By those who own all, John,
May awake overnight!

Then remember the breath John,
　Of a morning in May;
　More sweet is the air, man,
Of the worker's great day!

"The Strike Is Over" (*Tribune* 14 February 1955) is a more specific vision of the "worker's great day," expressed in a concise paradigm of struggle and victory. The striking workers who speak chorically in the poem are oppressed by the bosses and their stooges, and alienated from nature:

For many months we have not seen
The summer sky with billows bound,
Nor daffodils upon the ground.

When vulgar curses fill the air
From hired thugs with glassy eyes,
One does not see the blue of skies.

But when the strike is over, the workers are released from the sunless dungeon of exploitation into the clear air of freedom:

How keen the breath of Canada;
How full the note the thrushes give—
When man has won the right to live!

In "Prairie Wind" (*Tribune* 29 August 1955), the vision of freedom is given a more regional focus, in the context of the Communist theme of the human conquest of nature. In this tribute to his native province, Ryga urges a traveller to discover Alberta not "in maps or printed books," but in the prairie wind "that whistles o'er a lonely grave." The traveller should then look to the cultivated fields and to "the many towns/where brick and smoke and steel abound" to contemplate the efforts of workers who "froze and bled" to build this industrial civilization. The poem ends, like "They Who Suffer," with an expression of confidence in the socialist future. As in most of his poetry, Ryga identifies this confidence with the unity between nature and freedom:

Traveller! When you see Alberta,
Where prairie winds and sun range free;
Remember those who found and built her—
Think of what she yet will be!

In the same year that Ryga collected many of these and similar poems in *Song of My Hands*, he left the LPP, partly in revulsion against the Soviet suppression of the Hungarian revolution and partly because, like Acorn, he was anxious to practise his art in a more open literary milieu. His one book written while a member of the LPP, then, was apprentice work. His best work, published from the 1960s to the 1980s as he expanded into the writing of novels, short stories and plays, reveal a widening conception of the artist's commitments to society, nature, and art, although it retained elements of political conscience that connect Ryga to the post-1960 literary New Left.

• • • • •

Besides introducing the poetry of Acorn and Ryga, *New Frontiers* published excerpts from two new socialist realist novels. The complete French-language version of Jean-Jules Richard's *Le Feu dans l'amiante* ran serially in the Quebec LPP's monthly periodical *Combat* in 1954, but because of his Communist affiliations the author was finally obliged to self-publish the novel in book form, in 1956. In 1954-55 two translated excerpts appeared in *New Frontiers* under the title "Asbestos on Fire." Based on the bitter 1949 strike in the Quebec asbestos mining fields, *Le Feu dans l'amiante* begins with an emphasis on violence and chaos reminiscent of the atmosphere of Richard's earlier *Neuf jours de haine*. "C'est encore une fois la fin du monde," the opening words announce, referring to one of the regular times for blasting in the open-pit asbestos mine, when the people stay indoors or scurry for cover as stones and asbestos dust pelt down on the town. The opening episode is the only one to dramatize the horrendous working conditions of the miners, but it establishes how both the workers and their families constantly live, like front-line soldiers in battle, on the edge of violence and death. Possibly inspired by nineteenth-century naturalist fiction like Émile Zola's *Germinal*, Richard also emphasizes the animalistic qualities of the lives of his characters, who are trapped in primitive cycles of work, eating, and casual sexual encounters. Richard makes clear in the course of the novel, however, that the workers of the fictional Quebec town of Johnsonville are oppressed not by vague impersonal cosmic forces but by all-too-human and readily identifiable people and institutions, including the feudalistic Union nationale provincial government and its police; the multinational corporation, personified by the American mine manager, James Donohue, and the half-American, half-francophone foreman, Romeo Johnson; and the local parish priests of the Roman Catholic Church.

To oppose the forces that tyrannize them, the people of Johnsonville at first seem to have little more than a belligerent pride in their cultural identity, and even this pride is rarely expressed, except by older characters like Mme Marier, who dares to object even to her priest's use of the term "Canadien français." "C'est nous autres les Canadiens," she insists. "Les Canadiens purs, pas français" (160). The English-speaking people, on the other hand, Americans, English-

Canadians, and British, she lumps together contemptuously as "Anglais." But as Richard suggests elsewhere in the novel, this claim to ethnic purity is illusory, for the Québecois are the products of many diverse influences. In describing the boisterous atmosphere of a community dance, he calls attention to how the people's behaviour reflects elements not only from old France but also from other parts of Europe, from Britain, and even from the United States, where many of them have served as migrant workers. The real unity of the French Canadians is not to be found in ethnicity or an idealized past, Richard insists in defiance of a favourite theme of the nostalgic school of Québecois literature, but in the class unity of the proletariat. For this reason, Richard particularly laments the fact that francophone police, originally men of proletarian origin, should be sent in to intimidate the strikers. Similarly, the novel at first deplores the oppression of the workers by another group of their own people, the Roman Catholic clergy, who advocate obedience to civil and economic authority. But Richard shows how the Catholic priests during the strike are gradually won over to the workers' cause, partly out of institutional support for their Catholic syndicalist union, and partly out of revulsion against the irreverence and arrogance of the *anglais* company bosses as well as the sadistically violent behaviour of the police.

Besides showing how the strike evolves from an illegal protest of a few workers to a mass movement supported by almost the whole community, Richard relates the action of the novel to elemental biological and spiritual cycles. The sexual awakening of the innocent young Odette Marier, and her gentle seduction by the pro-union activist Gilles Morency, could be read in terms of a symbolism common in Marxist-inspired socialist realist fiction, with Odette's pregnancy suggesting the emergence of a new age, or perhaps even suggesting parallels with the salvation theme of the Christian nativity. But Odette's baby dies soon after birth, so—again, as in other socialist realist works—redemption remains a hope or a promise to be fulfilled in some distant future. While the revolution is still to be realized, the primary fact of the worker's theology is not salvation but crucifixion, as dramatized especially in the agonizing death from asbestosis of the miner Sylvain Brisson, whose Christlike face haunts Odette in her waking experience and her dreams. But although Odette's pregnancy is socially condemned as immoral and thwarted by the atmosphere of violence and sterility, she is the true personification of motherhood and creativity in the novel, as opposed to the false mother, the lawful wife Jeanne Brisson, who abuses her children—just as the corporation and the Quebec government betray their obligations and abuse the workers, as Richard explicitly suggests (268).

At the end of the novel, the strikers have either won or lost the battle, depending on one's point of view. A six-month work stoppage, as the mine manager reflects, can actually be turned to the company's advantage, providing time to take inventory and clear out stockpiles of unsold asbestos. After settling the strike partly by police and scab violence and partly by giving the workers a small raise, the company can reduce dividends to stockholders and raise prices, under the pretext of being victimized by unions (280). From the workers' perspective, however, even a small rise in wages represents a partial victory for them, and perhaps more important, they have learned something of the strength of collective action. Ultimately, the workers must become as strong as the company, Odette observes, and to achieve such strength it is necessary to unite (282). As time passes, as more battles are fought and partially won, the workers will reach higher, just as the hill of slag, the cast-off product of industrial processes, reaches up toward the sun which each day lights the world anew (287). The final words of the novel return to the beginning, and replace the opening image of cosmic death and annihilation with an image of hope and immortality: "Car le monde guerira puisqu'il ne peut pas mourir" (287).

In 1954 *New Frontiers* also published two part-chapters from a novel by William Allister (b. 1919), under the title "The Prisoners." The complete novel was published in England in 1961 as *A Handful of Rice*. Based on the author's experiences as a prisoner of the Japanese after the fall of Hong Kong, Allister's novel appeared in excerpt in the same year as Pierre Boulle's *Bridge over the River Kwai* and in book version one year before James Clavell's *King Rat*. Thus sharing a subject with two best-selling novels, *A Handful of Rice* might also have achieved wide popularity. But Allister's perspective differs markedly from those of Boulle and Clavell. Boulle was primarily interested in comparing the codes of honour of the British and

Japanese, while Clavell focused on the theme of survival, which he relates to the selfish individualism that people display in crisis situations. In *A Handful of Rice* Allister uses the prison camp experience to demonstrate the workings of the class struggle and the potential strength of collective action. Conceiving the prison environment as a microcosm of the capitalist power hierarchy, the author uses some of the actualities of Japanese administrative methods to develop a parable of the capitalist system. The Japanese, who leave much of the day-to-day operation of the camp to the officer-prisoners, are like finance capitalists who delegate administrative responsibility to a managerial class which uses its power to tyrannize the workers. The officer-prisoners also organize themselves into a hierarchy in which the boldest and shrewdest rise to the top. Captain Welland, "a husky Canadian Flying Officer who had flown with the R.A.F. in Malaya" (36), bypasses his ineffectual senior officer to seize executive power, justifying himself by insisting on his affinities with his Japanese captors. "These aren't the regular Jap Military with their hammy displays or racial ranting," he insists; "they're essentially business men—like myself" (40).

Welland's idea of "business" involves conniving with Japanese officers to use the forced labour of the enlisted prisoners in a scheme to sell camp food supplies on the black market. The enlisted men, like an exploited proletariat, are overworked and cheated not only of their rightful compensation, but even of the bare means of subsistence, while Welland invokes the infamous euphemism of wartime Japanese imperialism to pretend publicly that everyone—prisoners and captors, officers and enlisted men—are benefiting from the efficient operation of the "Greater East Asia Co-Prosperity Sphere" (48). The enlisted men, meanwhile, must resort to stealing rations to survive. When their thefts are discovered, their own officers hand them over to Japanese guards for punishment in order to maintain the worker discipline necessary to their profit-making schemes. The novel thus exposes with mechanical but thorough specificity the corrupt aims and methods of capitalism. Like many socialist realist novels, *A Handful of Rice* relies on rather stereotyped representative characterizations, including a working-class French-Canadian prisoner whose physical strength and common sense qualify him as a proletarian leader; a Jewish urban proletarian; a cynical intellectual; and a junior officer who might have served as a model and leader to the worker/ soldiers, but whose moral weakness leads him to accommodate himself to the corruption of his superiors. The Japanese officers are aloof and enigmatic, seemingly as remote as shareholding financiers from the daily routine of business, while their soldiers are identifiable with the police goons that capitalist governments and corporations use to maintain a submissive work force.

In the end the enlisted prisoners are driven by desperation to defy the guns of their captors and organize a strike. Like other triumphant resolutions in socialist realist fiction, there is a measure of wish-fulfilment fantasy in the men's success. The striking prisoners not only manage to maintain solidarity among themselves against the threat of death, with the help of a convenient Chinese-speaking prisoner they even persuade local coolies not to serve as strikebreakers. If Allister's resolution departs from credibility, however, it is qualified by ambiguities. The strikers succeed in breaking the tyranny of only one man, Welland; they do not essentially transform the system or defeat the power of capitalism. That power continues in the person of the ruthless Japanese officer who has been Welland's superior both in his managerial capacity and his black-market operations. More pointedly, the novel does not end, as *King Rat* does, with the Japanese military surrender as a ready-made resolution to the conflicts of the prison-camp microcosm. As in Richard's novel, the conclusion of *A Handful of Rice* can only point toward a distant victory. Allister implies that the reader can be confident that the victory is coming, but in terms of the metaphor of the capitalist-worker struggle, the successful strike represents only one small episode in the slow and painful rise of workers toward freedom and power.

• • • • •

A survey of Canadian socialist realist works in the 1950s should also include the long-awaited biography of Norman Bethune which had been announced by Progress Books during the war. Written by Ted Allan in collaboration with fellow journalist Sydney Gordon, *The Scalpel, the Sword* (1952) was published by McClelland and Stewart rather than Progress, and became one of the best-selling works of

Canadian literary Communism. The authors and publisher hoped to restore to mass popularity the reputation of a Canadian whose fame had reached far beyond the Party in the late 1930s but had been badly obscured by the Cold War. Allegedly based on documents and eyewitness interviews, but using novelistic techniques such as extrapolated or hypothetical dialogue and inferences about thoughts and feelings, the work was regarded as a legitimate, if sometimes rather too imaginative, biography. In 1998, however, historian Larry Hannant revealed that sections of the book were adapted from a Chinese novel, *The Story of Doctor Bethune* (1948) by Zhou Erfou ("Doctoring Bethune" 79). In their foreword the Canadian authors acknowledged that they had been "immeasurably helped by the lengthy published chronicle written by the Chinese writer Chou En Fou on Bethune's work in China" (vii). The wording implies that Zhou's book (virtually unknown in the west in the 1950s) was a factual rather than a fictional work. But Allan and Gordon's deception does not completely invalidate their work, for the borrowings from Zhou are assimilated into a great deal of original research. *The Scalpel, the Sword* still qualifies at least as biographical fiction, and as such has particular relevance to the development of progressive creative literature in Canada. As a socialist realist novel, *The Scalpel, the Sword* is a study in hero worship, an attempt to create a larger-than-life Canadian mythic figure comparable to nineteenth-century iconoclasts and rebels like Louis Riel and William Lyon Mackenzie who were idealized by twentieth-century Communists. But Allan and Gordon make Bethune more than a Canadian rebel: his exploits in Spain and China raise him to the status of a hero of international Communism. Bethune's status is enhanced further by the fact that unlike his nineteenth-century predecessors he was not merely a prefiguration of the Marxist-Leninist hero, but a card-carrying member of the Party that was destined to lead the proletarian revolution.

Like Joe Wallace and Milton Acorn, Allan and Gordon use Christian imagery in their delineation of the Communist conception of heroism. The first section of *The Scalpel, the Sword*, entitled "Death and Birth," underscores the Christlike structure of Bethune's life by suggesting the dramatic primacy of the circumstances of their hero's death, his almost miraculous achievements as a healer, and the immortality he achieves in the memories of his disciples. In the early chapters, set in Canada and the US, the authors emphasize Bethune's solitude, isolation, and emerging transcendent power. His successful treatment of his own tuberculosis creates further suggestions of his miraculous healing abilities. In the Spain and China sections of the book Bethune triumphs over fascism—the political and militaristic counterpart of disease and death—by his establishment and administration of blood transfusion and field hospital services. To avoid detracting from the triumph theme, Allan and Gordon gloss over the ultimate Republican defeat to emphasize Bethune's departure from Spain as a publicist for the anti-fascist cause, and the merging of this assignment with the beginnings of his mission to China. The war in China provides the authors with an unambiguous theme of victory, with which Bethune is identified even in his premature death. As the legendary Pai-Chu-En, Bethune becomes the immortal source of heroic inspiration for the New China. In more specific Marxist terms, Bethune is presented as the culmination of the human forces that make history. As a scientist, his achievements in developing new surgical instruments and techniques contribute to the project of controlling nature for the benefit of the masses of humanity. As a tireless and self-sacrificing devotee to duty, he dramatizes the Communist ideal of the submergence of individualism in the common good.

Thanks to its publication by a non-Communist company, *The Scalpel, the Sword* was reviewed widely, although the reviews were mixed. The *New Yorker* (27 September 1952) and the *Saturday Review* (8 November 1952) applauded the biography of a "remarkable" and "extraordinary" man, but the *New York Times* (30 November 1952) dismissed the book's "one-sided, left-wing approach" and its "dated" subject matter. In Canada, *New Frontiers* was predictably enthusiastic, although the notice written by Bethune's old friend Dr. Daniel Longpré of Montreal was not really a review but a brief personal reminiscence of "a great Canadian doctor, a universal hero" ("Life of Bethune" 40). The social democratic *Canadian Forum*, on the other hand, published only the designated reviewer's brief refusal to review a book that "was obviously written to bolster up Communism" (November 1952). In spite of this kind of hostility, however, as Larry Hannant reports, the book sold thirty-five thousand copies in Canada, "a bestseller by domestic standards" and "more than 2-million copies" abroad, mostly "in Soviet-bloc countries" ("Doctoring Bethune" 79).

The success of *The Scalpel, the Sword* might have encouraged the LPP cultural community to believe that, given the right subject matter, the socialist realist aesthetic could achieve mass appeal even in the midst of the Cold War. By emphasizing affinities with non-Communist realist writers, furthermore, the Communists could represent socialist realism as an extension of a prominent tradition in modern literature, just as the LPP was trying to promote its political doctrine as a legitimate left-wing extension of the Canadian political continuum. More rigidly Marxist literary critics, on the other hand, insisted that socialist realism was irreconcilable with non-Communist artistic theory, just as Marxist political theorists envisaged the ultimate disappearance of all political systems based on capitalist economics. In the mid-1950s Georg Lukács renewed socialist realist complaints against both the apolitical modernism of early twentieth-century bourgeois writers and "social" or "critical" realism. "The modernist," complained Lukács, "identifies what is necessarily a subjective experience with reality as such, thus giving a distorted picture of reality as a whole," while the "critical realist" tends "to emphasize the contradictions [in capitalist society] rather than the forces working toward reconciliation." "Socialist ideology," by contrast, enables the writer "to give a more comprehensive and deeper account of man as a social being" (*Meaning* 51, 114-15).

The irreconcilability of socialist and social realism was invoked in a *Tribune* review of BC novelist Hubert Evans's *Mist on the River* (1954). Evans combines the experience of native Indian cannery workers with the theme of capitalist exploitation to create a poignant and potentially tragic exposé of ethnic prejudice and social injustice. Reviewing the novel in the *Tribune* of 22 November, Harold Griffin praised Evans's denunciation of the Canadian government's "false paternalism" which restricts native people to circumscribed economic and geographical environments while authorizing their treatment as second-class citizens. But the inexcusable weakness of the novel, Griffin continued, "is that it exposes the evils but indicates no real solution. It closes on a note of hope, but the hope is given no tangible form." The desired "tangible form" according to Griffin, is worker organization. Evans makes no mention of the activities of such associations as the Native Brotherhood of BC and the fishermen's union, preferring to formulate his subject in terms of the sufferings of the individual victim of a racist capitalist society. So even though *Mist on the River* is "one of the finest Canadian novels yet to appear," it fails in Griffin's view because "nowhere in the novel is the conclusion of organization and struggle drawn" ("An Outstanding Canadian Novel").

A more enduring commitment to socialist realism and the theme of organization and struggle during the 1950s can be seen in the work of Dyson Carter. In his writings published before and during the Second World War, Carter adhered to an anti-fascist united front ideology that assumed some consistency between capitalist and socialist political and cultural aims. Seeing no reason why he should not address himself to both the bourgeois reading public and the limited community of readers of progressive publications, he contributed articles to mass circulation newspapers and magazines, while publishing several books and pamphlets with Contemporary of Winnipeg (the same left-wing company that brought out Joe Wallace's first book of poems) and the LPP's Progress Books. Soon after the end of the war, however, it was evident to Carter that the bourgeois political and cultural establishments were not interested in visions of liberal democratic and socialist unity, any more than capitalist politicians were interested in the idea of peaceful coexistence with the USSR. On 7 August 1945, the day after the dropping of the Hiroshima bomb, Carter contributed to the *Toronto Star* a signed front-page article on the peacetime uses of atomic energy. By November, however, he was writing in the *Canadian Tribune* to attack the United States for its practice of "atomic bomb blackmail" against the USSR. Shortly afterward he wrote a public letter to LPP leader Tim Buck, "Dyson Carter Explains: Why I've Joined the LPP," which was published in the *Tribune* of 15 December 1945. "I have long been convinced that capitalism is now obsolete and that socialism is a higher form of society," Carter declared. "Like science, literature in Canada today writhes under the dirty hooves of capitalism."

In publicly announcing his membership in the LPP, Carter was marking the end of his association with the mass media. In a note on the author included in one of his later books, Carter wrote: "Because he refused to give up a belief that is basic in his writings—the view that all peoples, in their own interests, need to be informed about the achievements of Socialism—when the Cold War developed Carter was banned by publishers who had welcomed his work" (*Science and Revolution* n. pag.). But his restriction to the progressive media did not lessen Carter's output. In 1946 he began contributing to the *Canadian Tribune* a "Science Today" column which was reprinted in the weekly magazine section of the New York *Daily Worker*. In 1947 he revised and updated his successful *Sea of Destiny* under the title "Open Sesame!: The Story of the Hudson Bay Route," for serialization in the Winnipeg Communist weekly *Western Tribune*. In 1948 he and his wife moved from Winnipeg to Toronto, where he continued his writing for left-wing publications.

Carter briefly revived his involvement with the mass media in 1949, when the New American Library of New York bought the paperback rights to his novel *Night of Flame,* although as a self-declared Communist Carter was obliged to avoid trouble with the American government by having the reprint appear under the pseudonym "Warren Desmond." Encouraged by this access to a lucrative market, he churned out a novel under this pen-name for Export Publishing of Toronto, a pulp house that issued pseudonymous potboilers by several Canadian writers, including Hugh Garner and Raymond Souster. *The Governor's Mistress* was an old-fashioned bodice ripper, but it was also a historical novel that made use of some of the material accumulated for the 1947 revision of *Sea of Destiny*. The autocratic power of New France, centralized in the sinister Governor Frontenac, is related to monopoly capitalism and identified as the basis of economic exploitation. Pierre Radisson and his bush-rangers are, conversely, portrayed as brave revolutionaries who pit themselves against imperialist power.

But Carter was not really interested in hack writing, even if he could make such writing serve a Marxist purpose. In 1950 he published with Progress Books under his own name a serious novel of socialist realism, *Tomorrow Is with Us*. Set in a vaguely identified city that could be in either Canada or the United States, the novel conveys the anxieties of the Cold War through a story with overtones of both the Gouzenko case and the espionage investigations and trials currently under way in the United States that were to culminate in the executions of Ethel and Julius Rosenberg. Carter's main character, physicist Alan Baird, is not the sinister foreign agent the government and capitalist press accuse him of being, but merely an idealistic scientist. Baird is falsely suspected of dealing in "atom" secrets for the Soviet Union, a suspicion mainly arising from the scientific ignorance of the police and politicians who accuse him. Baird eludes the police with the help of Communist activists, who are presented as sacrificing their domestic tranquility to their belief in justice and world peace. The enormity of the forces opposed to the progressive movement is emphasized in the ambiguous conclusion which leaves Baird under indictment with little hope of righting the wrongs against him. But as the title suggests, the progressive movement is vindicated by the reliability of scientific socialism's promise of a better future.

Carter followed this novel with a polemical travel book, *We Saw Socialism* (1951), written jointly with his wife Charlotte Carter, and published by the Canadian-Soviet Friendship Society. The C-SFS had been established in 1943 at the height of Canadian enthusiasm for the Soviet war effort, with major federal politicians as patrons, and with such culturally distinguished figures on its councils as poet E.J. Pratt, painter A.Y. Jackson, and university professor Barker Fairley. By 1950, however, the Society had fallen victim to the Cold War, its liberal supporters had backed away from it and its executive and membership were dominated by members of the LPP. In 1950 Carter was elected president of the National Council of the Society, and in May of that year he and his wife were invited to make a month-long visit to the USSR, sponsored by Volks, the Russian All-Union Society for Cultural Relations with Foreign Countries. *We Saw Socialism* is a somewhat hastily prepared compendium of travel notes, written in a casually colloquial style presumably directed to working-class readers. Avoiding all technical language—and often thereby excluding specific detail that might have strengthened its arguments—the book emphasizes the USSR's remarkable recovery from wartime devastation and its recent achievements in medicine, housing, urban renewal, human rights, theoretical and practical sciences, culture, and education. In response to Western newspapers and politicians who denounce Soviet hypocrisy in preaching peace while pursuing imperialist policies, the

Carters remind readers that some of the most horrific battles of the war were fought on Russian territory, and that the Russian people now want only to build a stable and secure society. But in defending Soviet attitudes and achievements, *We Saw Socialism* goes too far and paints a Utopian picture of a relentlessly cheerful, optimistic, and ideologically homogenous populace. The book ends up being too much an anti-capitalist, anti-US counterpart to the equally unrestrained anti-USSR diatribes of American capitalist apologists.

But in the early 1950s Carter was especially eager to adapt his political ideals to fiction. To this end he began researching and writing his most ambitious novel. Published by Progress in 1955, *Fatherless Sons* was the first of his serious fictions to use an explicitly Canadian setting, and to convey the political and personal experience of working-class Canadians in the early years of the Cold War. As the verbal echo in its title suggests, *Fatherless Sons* may have been partly inspired by the Communist reaction against Hugh MacLennan's popular novel *Each Man's Son* (1951). A reviewer in the *Canadian Tribune* complained that MacLennan ignored the poverty and strife-ridden labour conditions of industrial Cape Breton to concentrate on a sentimental and pseudo-psychological scrutiny of the main characters (Don Fraser, rev. of *Each Man's Son*). *Fatherless Sons*, by contrast, portrays working-class struggles for survival against capitalist exploitation and militarism. Set in the Northern Ontario mining community of Sudbury (fictionalized as "Deep Rock"), the novel exploits a political background of major Cold War developments up to the end of hostilities in Korea. The central character, Dave Nelson, a third-generation miner, returns in 1945 from service in the Canadian army to take up his family obligations, especially to the widow and children of his brother who has been killed in the war, and to face his public responsibilities in the struggle against the anti-union policies of the mining company. Like other works of socialist realism, Carter's novel sometimes makes its point through mechanical plot contrivances. For three generations, the author reveals, from the time of the Boer War through the two world wars, the Nelson family has consisted of two brothers, one of whom has been killed in war. This artificial historical pattern serves to suggest how capitalism, in its reliance on war to stimulate industrial activity, has wasted the lives of workers and destabilized a basic unit of working-class solidarity, the family.

*Fatherless Sons* also extols Canadian nationalism. In the 1920s and 1930s socialist realist fiction, like the Communist movement in general, exalted international working-class unity. But by the 1950s the Stalinist ideal of "socialism in one country" served to authorize militant nationalism as a Communist strategy. Carter especially emphasizes the Canadian identity of his characters by means of a vehement anti-Americanism. The United States appears in the novel as a mad empire that threatens to annihilate its economic rivals by the suicidal means of nuclear war. This insanity is personified in the sinister figure of the American chairman of the board of Trans-World Alloys (the International Nickel Company), Chester Lee Nolles (a thinly disguised John Foster Dulles, who was in fact a director of International Nickel). Americans are criticized throughout the novel in a descending scale from the darkly evil Nolles through the toadyish managing director of Trans-World and the lampoon figure of a pompous army officer who comes to lecture Canadian workers on US defence strategies, down to a clownish, Shriner-like parade of visiting businessmen that degenerates into a riot. Carter conveys his anti-Americanism further through a fictionalized version of an episode in Sudbury's labour history, when the United Steelworkers of America raided the International Union of Mine, Mill and Smelter Workers after Mine Mill was expelled from the Canadian Congress of Labour in 1949 because of allegations of Communism (Saarinen 194). In Carter's version, the US-based United Metal and Mill (the Steelworkers) attempts an unsuccessful raid on General Mine and Mill, represented in the novel as an independent Canadian union. Carter extends his anti-American criticisms to encompass the social democratic CCF, a recurrent antagonist of Canadian Communism since the 1930s. In *Fatherless Sons* the CCF member of parliament for Deep Rock joins forces with the Americans behind United Metal and Mill to serve as local leader in the raid.

Like *Tomorrow Is with Us*, *Fatherless Sons* ends ambiguously. The union battle is won by General Mine and Mill, and the Americans have been unable to achieve military victory in Korea, but Dave Nelson is killed in a mining accident and the rapacious American-owned company still controls the economy of Deep Rock. As at the end of the earlier novel, however, the author affirms his confidence in the future and in the ultimate triumph of the Communist movement under the leadership of the USSR. Both of Carter's novels give priority to ideology over psychological subtlety, as socialist realism was usually inclined to do. As unapologeticallly Communistic statements, the two novels were ignored by the Canadian mainstream media, although the Party press gave them full review coverage. According to the *Canadian Tribune, Tomorrow Is with Us* was published in translation in the USSR and several of the Soviet-bloc countries of eastern Europe ("The Author"). In spite of bourgeois hostility, *Fatherless Sons* also fared well, gaining an underground reputation among working-class Canadian readers. One commentator in the *Tribune* even made a case for *Fatherless Sons* as an important contribution to Canadian literary history. Complaining that by extolling the novel as unique the *Tribune* reviewer had taken the cosmopolitan view that denies the existence of a Canadian literary tradition, V.G. Hopwood insisted that "*Fatherless Sons* belongs with those finest works of Canadian literature such as Charles Mair's *Tecumseh* and F.P. Grove's *Master of the Mill*, which deal with the forces shaping Canada's destiny" ("Review Missed Full Import").

In a review in *New Frontiers* (Fall 1955) Margaret Fairley approved Carter's emphasis on the social theme and avoidance of the narrowly personal introspections that increasingly dominated the bourgeois fiction of the 1950s. In contrast to Dorothy Livesay's insistence that "the artist must stand above the struggle" and concentrate on "knowing himself," Fairley agreed with the implication of *Fatherless Sons* that "there are no 'private lives.' Every life is lived in a particular place at a particular time. Carter is in the first rank of novelists in making us realize this." But Fairley goes on to criticize Carter for his emphasis on authorial explanation. He is "too quick to tell us instead of leaving us to find out for ourselves." She also objects to his pejorative generalizations against whole collectivities of people, such as the US and the CCF. "This is unpardonable," says Fairley, "not so much because it may alienate readers as because it reflects an attitude based on false generalizations which may produce race prejudices" ("Mining Town" 41-42). Other Communist readers shared Fairley's reservations about the novel. Some letters to the *Tribune* praised its treatment of working-class characters and its condemnation of US capitalism, but others criticized its extreme anti-Americanism and its stereotyped characterizations. These conflicting responses led to a discussion of the novel at an LPP conference on literature, and a follow-up public discussion in which Carter participated ("Open Forum on 'Fatherless Sons'"; "Author Meets Readers"). The debate over *Fatherless Sons* was probably the most substantial controversy over a purely literary topic to take place within the Party. Although *Fatherless Sons* went on to critical and sales success in the USSR and other Communist countries in Europe and Asia, Carter did not publish another novel for thirty years. Perhaps the Canadian objections to *Fatherless Sons* had something to do with his prolonged neglect of fiction, but a more obvious reason was his commitment to other projects. For most of the next three decades Carter devoted himself to work deriving from his involvement with the Canadian-Soviet Friendship Society, especially the writing of articles and books extolling the political and scientific achievements of the USSR.

# 8

# After Stalinism
## Decline and Achievement

In the larger non-Communist literary community the post-war popularity of social realism, as reflected in the work of such writers as Christine van der Mark, Henry Kreisel, Joyce Marshall, and Selwyn Dewdney, did not continue into the 1950s. These vestiges of the 1930s were being pre-empted by fiction in which the emphasis moved away from a socio-economic context toward individual psychology, or interactions between character and regional landscape. The new writers of mainstream Canadian literature in the 1950s were more interested in introspection than in political didacticism, and in conflicts of character rather than of social forces. Thus the acclaimed novels of the 1950s included Morley Callaghan's psycho-sexual study *The Loved and the Lost* (1951); Ethel Wilson's narrative of female self-discovery and liberation *Swamp Angel* (1954); Ernest Buckler's combined pastoral idyll and portrait of the (failed) artist *The Mountain and the Valley* (1952); Mordecai Richler's tragi-comic urban satire *The Apprenticeship of Duddy Kravitz* (1959); and Sheila Watson's symbolic prose poem *The Double Hook* (1959). The novelists of the 1950s had turned, as Northrop Frye said of the poets, toward a "disembodied anarchism, in some respects a reversion to the old artist-versus-society theme." Much of this fiction was indeed a reversion, for behind it were the influences of the early-twentieth-century international modernist experimentalism of James Joyce, Virginia Woolf, William Faulkner, and Thomas Wolfe. This kind of fiction, with its intensely individualistic vision and its technical subtleties, rejected social realism as a stagnant vestige of outdated political and artistic ideals. Two novels published in Canada in the mid-1950s reinforced the Canadian repudiation of pro-Communist themes and artistic forms. *The Fall of a Titan* (1954), a vehement attack on Stalinist Russia attributed to Igor Gouzenko, was selected as winner of the Governor General's Award for fiction for 1955. Also in 1955, McClelland and Stewart—the same company that three years earlier published *The Scalpel, the Sword*—released a wickedly satirical anti-Stalinist novel, Earle Birney's *Down the Long Table*.

Gouzenko's debut as a novelist was something of a surprise. Soon after his defection he published what purported to be his autobiography, *This Was My Choice* (1948). A preface to a 1968 paperback reprint indicated that the book was translated from Russian then rewritten by Montreal journalist A.W. O'Brien (ix). *The Fall of a Titan* was described on the title page as "translated from the Russian by Mervyn Black," who was the interpreter assigned by the RCMP to the debriefing of Gouzenko in 1945. After Gouzenko's death in 1982, journalist John Sawatsky presented testimony in *Gouzenko: The Untold Story* (1984) that Gouzenko's literary efforts were to a great extent attributable to translators, editors, and ghost writers. Whoever should be credited with the authorship, *The Fall of a Titan* was an ambitious attempt to produce a novel in the grandiose Russian style. Based on the promising historical and literary theme of Maxim Gorky's ambivalent relationship to Stalin, the novel is set in the years between the Revolution and the late 1930s, with particular emphasis on the period of forced collectivization in the USSR during the 1920s. The action is seen mainly through the eyes of the fictional Feodor Novikov, who enters the revolutionary era as an intellectually curious young romantic, and is transformed by subsequent experience into a cynical and opportunistic servant of the new regime. The novel purports to be a critical study of the status of the artist and intellectual under Stalinist Russia, but its main purpose is obviously to reveal the evils of Communism. According to Gouzenko, the majority of the Russian people under Stalin are ill-housed and ill-fed as a result of unsuccessful social experiments; mutual suspicion and life-and-death struggles for power are everywhere in a society dominated by police spies and self-interested bureaucrats. The picture of the USSR between the two world wars may well be accurate in many details, but the malevolence of Soviet officialdom and the cynical attitudes of the supposed victims of the system end up conveying a relentlessly one-dimensional image of the USSR, an inverse and equally incredible counterpart of Dyson Carter's idyllic *We Saw Socialism.*

Critical responses to the novel were polarized according to the political inclinations of the reviewers and publications. In the opinion of the *New York Times*, it was "a novel of substantial merit," but the *New Yorker* found it "as heavy as lead." To the *Atlantic Monthly* it was "a most impressive...work of fiction," but to the *New York Herald-Tribune* it was "not a novel, but a tract" (*Book Review Digest* 1954: 368-69). The Canadian Communist literary community was at first inclined to ignore *The Fall of a Titan*, but the awarding of the Governor General's Award provoked an angry response from Margaret Fairley in the Summer 1955 issue of *New Frontiers*. As Fairley reported, two of the three judges regarded *Fall of a Titan* as unworthy of the prize. The award, she insisted, was "not the recognition of genuine literary merit, but a reward for political services" ("Cold War Award" 2).

The publication of Gouzenko's novel was followed within months by another work of fiction offensive to the LPP literary community, Earle Birney's *Down the Long Table*. Birney (1904-95) had flirted with the CPC during the 1930s, but rejected Stalinism in favour of the political and cultural ideals of Leon Trotsky. His *Down the Long Table* is a fictionalization of one Canadian's journey from political naiveté, through Stalinism and Trotskyism, to disillusionment. Non-Marxist social realists like Marshall, Van der Mark, and Kreisel had begun the literary enterprise of re-evaluating from a post-war perspective the experiences of Canadians during the 1930s, but Birney's novel was the first of this kind to be written by an author who had been a Marxist-Leninist radical at the time. The re-examination of the 1930s might have been a promising subject for Stalinist socialist realism in the 1950s, but the appearance of a Trotskyist exposition of this theme was a particularly bitter pill for LPP members to swallow. *Canadian Tribune* editor Charlie Sims, in a letter of 7 February 1956 to *Pacific Tribune* editor Tom McEwen, reported that he had been assigned the unwelcome task of reviewing the book for *New Frontiers*. "I finished my first reading of it last night and it is an evil thing" (CPC/LPP papers, NAC). Apparently Sims was unable to bring himself to write about the book at all, for no review of *Down the Long Table* appeared in either of the two final (Spring and Summer) issues of *New Frontiers*.

As a novel about the ideological controversies and factionalism that plagued the Communist movement in the 1930s, *Down the Long Table* is in part a roman à clef. Birney introduces as characters the two earliest leaders of the Communist movement in Canada, Jock MacDonald ("MacCraddock") and Maurice Spector ("Leo Sather"), who were expelled from the CPC in the late 1920s by the Stalinists and, as Birney chronicles in the novel, served briefly as leaders of the Trotskyist movement in Toronto during the early 1930s. But the author is more interested in his fictional protagonist than in the prominent personalities of the radical community. *Down the Long Table* chronicles the experience of a naive intellectual, Gordon Saunders, who is drawn toward radical activism but impeded by his emotional immaturity and by his attraction to the secure life of the academic world. Like Birney himself, Saunders at first dabbles in the CPC, then drifts toward the Trotskyist Communist League of North America. In the League he becomes involved in the quixotic project of "the founding of the first branch in northwestern North America of what was to be the great regenerated Third International, or if necessary even the Fourth, which would bring at length to this whole weary globe that true socialism which the Third had so far missed bringing even to one-sixth of the land-mass" (183).

Like Birney's earlier novel of the Second World War *Turvey* (1949), *Down the Long Table* exposes both the absurdity and the tragedy of the historical context in which the protagonist moves. Birney treats Stalinists and Trotskyists with equal irreverence. Besides emphasizing the pretentiousness of the Trotskyists' political aims, the deviousness of the Stalinists' methods, and the remoteness of both movements from the actualities of Depression-era North America, Birney exposes the ambivalent motives of the would-be revolutionary intellectual. Saunders accepts his mission to found a Trotskyist group in Vancouver only as a summer job—his ultimate purposes are to marry his sexually alluring but empty-headed political comrade Thelma Barstow, and settle down in a supposedly secure middle-class life as a professor of English. Although he sympathizes with the sufferings of the unemployed people he encounters, his sympathies do not extend to a full-time commitment to the Revolution. The shallowness and inconsequentiality of this kind of commitment are underscored by the novel's frame story, in which Saunders, as a university professor in the United States of the 1950s, ends up, like many other American academics who dabbled in leftist politics in the 1930s, facing the inquisitions of the House Committee on Un-American Activities. Having failed in his opportunity to help bring about a revolution, the radical of the 1930s finds himself twenty years later trapped by totalitarian capitalist institutions that have flourished partly as a result of his own indolence.

The novels of Gouzenko and Birney were literary indications of the extent and nature of the hostility within Canada against the political and cultural views of the LPP in the 1950s. But the fact that only two such novels appeared perhaps indicates that the bourgeois literary community was no longer even interested enough in Communism to criticize it. In the 1920s and 1930s, Morley Callaghan had satirized the Communist movement in his fiction; in *The Loved and the Lost* he ignored the subject as irrelevant to the kinds of topics and perspectives that now engaged his imagination. The collapse of *New Frontiers* in the fall of 1955 was the most visible sign of the failure of the initiatives so enthusiastically proclaimed by the LPP's cultural commission in 1947. The end of the magazine was also part of the general decline of the Communist movement in Canada, a decline earlier manifested in the disastrous showing of the LPP in the federal election of 1953, in spite of the Party's attempt to promote an image of liberal democratic nationalism. Then in 1956 the whole international Communist movement suffered fresh disasters when Nikita Khrushchev denounced Stalin, and Russian tanks suppressed the anti-Soviet uprising in Hungary. The intervention in Hungary alienated many LPP members of Eastern European ethnicity, but the attack on Stalin was the traumatic experience for most members of a Party that for almost thirty years had been devoutly pro-Stalinist. The political debate that followed the reprinting of the text of Khrushchev's speech in the *Canadian Tribune* of 18 June 1956 resolved into a power struggle between hard-liners led by Tim Buck who advocated unquestioning loyalty to Moscow and reformers who believed that the end of Stalinism could mean a looser and more democratic Party structure with fraternal rather than hierarchical ties to the USSR.

The victory of Buck and his followers led to a veritable hemorrhage of members from the Party, including some of the leading intellectuals. One of the most notable exceptions to this reaction, however, was Stanley Ryerson, who came out on the side of the hard-liners and retained his position on the Central Committee. The LPP's decision in 1959 to revert to its original name of the Communist Party of Canada was a public declaration of the Party's opposition to the winds of liberal change within the international Communist movement. Although in 1962 the seventy-two-year-old Buck was removed from his position as General Secretary and given the ceremonial position of Chairman, the Party remained for most of the next quarter-century— in spite of its continued decline in membership and influence—loyal to its Russophile Leninist revolutionary roots. Most of the best-known writers of the older generation, including Margaret Fairley, Joe Wallace, Dyson Carter, and Oscar Ryan, followed Ryerson's lead and stayed with the Party. But the writers' groups and cultural clubs withered away in the 1960s, and few new writers emerged. The Party's youth paper, *Champion*, expired in 1958, and although the *Tribune* carried on into the 1990s, for its cultural content it relied on the old Party faithful like Wallace and Ryan. No new attempts were made at creating a culture periodical, although a new theoretical journal, the *Marxist Quarterly* (1962-69; renamed *Horizons* in 1966), under Ryerson's editorship devoted some space to literary topics.

The decline in the cultural and political fortunes of the LPP by the end of the 1950s was underscored by a novel that exposed the vagaries of both the post-war Party and Canadian society as a whole, in a manner analogous to Birney's satire of radical activity in the 1930s. Although emphasizing the many unique aspects of Quebec politics and culture, Pierre Gélinas's *Les Vivants les morts et les autres* (1959) also conveys elements of the national and international contexts. Gélinas (b. 1925), like several other writers who were Party members, has eluded biographical research. Of no known relationship to the playwright Gratien Gélinas, he was a self-taught writer of working-class background, who served briefly as a journalist for *Le Jour* and Radio-Canada before joining the LPP around 1948. He served on the cultural commission of the Quebec wing and as editor of the monthly newspaper *Combat* until 1956, when he resigned from the Party in the aftermath of the Khrushchev anti-Stalin revelations. His first novel was followed by a second, *L'Or des Indes* (1962), after which he fell literarily silent, and seems to have vanished from the public record. In the 1980s Jacques Pelletier found him working in the publications department of the Université de Québec à Montréal, but Gélinas proved reluctant to talk about his past or his literary career. In 1996 he finally published a third novel, *La Neige*, the first volume of a proposed trilogy (Pelletier 8-9).

Set between 1952 and 1956, *Les Vivants les morts et les autres* is enacted against a background that includes the later Duplessis era in Quebec, the Korean War, and the expanding anti-war movement as dramatized especially by the Canadian Peace Congress held in Toronto in May of 1952. The historical context also includes the hockey riot at the Montreal Forum in March 1955, the 1955 strikes against Dominion Textiles and Dupuis Frères department store in Montreal, and the Khrushchev revelations of 1956. Like most socialist realism, Gélinas's novel is concerned with various forms of alienation. A prologue introduces the central character, Maurice Tremblay, who has deliberately alienated himself from his bourgeois family to join the working-class struggle against capitalism. Tremblay's rather dilettantish commitment is contrasted to the involuntary alienation of proletarians like union activist Réjeanne Lussier, who toils in the Montreal plant of Dominion Textiles under the kind of sweatshop conditions that Stanley Ryerson describes in his *French Canada*. The bourgeoisie, as one early scene set in Ottawa emphasizes, is characterized by political and moral corruption, narrow French-Canadian nationalism, and neo-fascism. The organized Communist movement, however, is little better: most of the Party bureaucrats are more interested in the exercise of internecine power than in the struggle against capitalism.

The novel effectively delineates the activity and atmosphere of the 1952 Peace Congress where, at a rally in Maple Leaf Gardens, the former United Church missionary James Endicott accused the Canadian government of complicity in the US millitary's use of chemical weapons in the Korean War. As a union delegate to the Congress, Tremblay experiences the seductive allure of public oratory and mass action, but he also glimpses the Party's rather sinister bureaucratic machinery at work behind the scenes. But Gélinas does not suggest that the working class might be able to achieve liberation by rejecting both capitalist exploitation and Communist manipulation. Later in his narrative the author contrasts the Peace Congress episode with another historic incident set in and around a sports arena, the Montreal Forum riot of March 1955, when the anglophone president of the National Hockey League suspended Maurice Richard for assaulting an opposing player. Here, Gélinas suggests, is the mass action of the Canadian proletariat, not united in righteous anger against economic exploitation or political corruption, but aroused to hysterical frenzy by a supposed insult to a popular sports hero. Even mass action in a more worthy cause is represented as pointless. In the Dominion Textiles strike—which concluded in the same spring as the Montreal Forum riot—the strikers are betrayed by an American representative of their union who denounces the local strike leaders as Communists, and the remnants of picketers are beaten into submission by police.

Finally, Tremblay discovers the hypocrisy of Communist political motives when he runs as an LPP candidate in the provincial election of 1956. Although he expects the experience will only gain publicity for the Party, not electoral victory, he is dismayed by the apparent indifference of local Party officials to the whole election. In the aftermath of Khrushchev's anti-Stalin speech, the Party has turned its energies entirely to assuring rank-and-file subservience to the internationalist line. Rather than follow the archaic orthodoxy of this line, Tremblay quits the Party. At the end of the novel, nothing has really changed. There is no suggestion of even a small step forward in the difficult progress toward a better world, as there is at the end of Richard's *Le Feu dans l'amiante*. The Union nationale is still in power in Quebec; the LPP is still obsessed by its internecine struggles; honest workers like Réjeanne Lussier struggle for survival under the negligent and exploitative policies of both capitalists and Communists. Other members of the proletariat live by their wits or, like the farmer's widow who sells her land for use as an army artillery range, sell out to the rapacious military-industrial complex.

But not all politically concerned, anti-capitalist creative writers shared Gélinas's disillusionment with Russian-style Communism. In the late 1950s the *Tribune* began to feature occasionally the work of a poet who was new to the Communist cultural comunity, although his literary career went back to the 1920s. Best known for his work in the nature lyric tradition of Bliss Carman, Wilson MacDonald had turned to socially critical, explicitly anti-capitalistic satire with his *Caw-Caw Ballads* (1930). But although his socialism came to have a definite Marxist tinge, MacDonald's opposition to Stalinism led him into the democratic socialist CCF. After the death of Stalin, however, he became more sympathetic to Russian Communism. In 1957 he was one of several foreign writers invited to the USSR to participate in cultural activities commemorating the fortieth anniversary of the Bolshevik revolution. In his memoir of the excursion, *On My Own in Moscow* (1958), he explained that he had decided to go because of a sneering remark made by an official of the Canadian Broadcasting Corporation that he was not one of Canada's "accepted poets." "If my sixty years' contribution of beauty and truth to Canada had meant nothing more to her than this," MacDonald complained, "I finally realized it would be useless to look for any approval, love or gratitude from my country any longer and that I must seek an audience elsewhere" (3). Like Joe Wallace, MacDonald found an enthusiastic audience in the Soviet Union, and was in turn very impressed by the friendly reception he received, and by the apparent contentment of the Russian people under their political system. "I am not a communist," he wrote to Bertrand Russell soon after his return from Russia, "but I prefer that brand of government to American capitalism" (n.d., MacDonald Papers, NAC).

Although MacDonald did not join the LPP/CPC, over the next few years the aging author contributed to the *Tribune* several lyric and satirical poems that more or less followed the Communist line on such subjects as the militaristic and imperialistic foreign policies of the

United States and the Canadian tendency to passively endorse these policies. Like Wallace, MacDonald relied on simple rhymed quatrains or couplets, and on rhetorically exaggerated expressions of belief in a coming revolution and a socialist millenium. His short poem "Blood and Oil" (18 August 1958) condemns western military intervention in the Middle East and the hypocrisy underlying it:

> Don't say our honor's at stake;
>     Hypocrisy makes evil doubly vile;
> Just say: "We do this for petroleum's sake"
>     And men will like your candid words and smile.

"Old Samuel Cashswigger" (22 September 1958) features a broad caricature of the capitalist who ghoulishly looks to war as a means of creating new markets when international trade enters one of its regular periods of stagnation.

> For old Sammy Cashswigger had only one obsession—
> That spilling guts
> With rifle butts
> Could stave off a depression.

Again, MacDonald emphasizes the hypocrisy of capitalist morality:

> ...if anybody says
> He is tricking the people
> He'll supply his church with a brand new steeple.
> So, whenever you hear old Sammy sing psalms
> You know he has sold some accessories for bombs.

Some of his poems, like "Big Hound-Dog" (12 June 1961), satirize both the United States and the Canadian tendency to truckle to American political policies:

> Don't call Americans
> "gawd-damn Yanks."
> They have feet like ours
> and teeth and shanks.
> They're a Big-Hound-Dog
> and we are the tail,
> and when Dog says "wag"
> Do we ever fail?

"The Ballad of Promising John" (21 August 1961) ridicules the campaign promises of "old Johnny Diefendumber," whose Progressive Conservative government, elected in 1958 with a huge majority, ignored its own election promises and did nothing to improve the lot of the Canadian working class. "The Song of the Makers" (27 June 1960) is MacDonald's tribute to socialist revolution, and specifically to countries like the USSR, China, and Cuba, where the "Makers" have overthrown the "Takers," where the working class has attained power and banished the Diefendumbers and Cashswiggers.

But although MacDonald provided an enthusiastic contribution to the Canadian radical literary tradition, his poetry obviously added nothing new to the tradition. Sharing Joe Wallace's admiration for Victorian poetry, his work relied almost entirely on the lyrical conventions and the extravagantly militant anti-capitalist rhetoric that had been characteristic of radical literature in Canada since the time of Alexander McLachlan. One younger and more promising literary light emerged from within the CPC in the early 1960s. Myrtle Bergren, born Myrtle Howkey in England in 1919, grew up near Kelowna, BC. After serving in the women's division of the RCAF during the war, she married Hjalmar Bergren, an organizer and executive of the International Woodworkers Union, and settled with her husband in the logging town of Lake Cowichan on Vancouver Island. Following her husband into the LPP, she was an unsuccessful candidate in the provincial election of 1953. Meanwhile, she had begun to write short stories for newspaper supplements and magazines. In 1964, Progress Books brought out a collection of her stories under the title *A Bough of Needles*, with a foreword by Margaret Fairley.

As Fairley observed, the strength of Bergren's fiction lies in her ability to invoke with sympathy the lives of ordinary workers. Also in line with Fairley's conception of socialist realism, Bergren in her most effective stories avoids political didacticism in favour of non-committal narration of recognizable experience and emotions that allows the reader to infer the political lesson from the characters and situations. Most of the stories emphasize a woman's point of view, with a concomitant stress on class solidarity rather than an introspective and defensive gender-based individualism. The best stories are probably autobiographical in origin. In "When I Was Seventeen" a woman nostalgically recalls her development through adolescence to early maturity, her growing awareness of sexuality, and her more comprehensive awareness of the larger socio-political world and her place in it. The setting is the farming region of southern British Columbia where Bergren herself grew up. The time is the late 1930s, and the narrator, while working as a farm "chore girl," becomes simultaneously aware of romance and politics, of popular songs and international conflict in Spain and Eastern Europe. Temporarily aroused to a stronger sense of her womanhood by a flirtation with the son of the family she works for, she ultimately rejects her would-be suitor because "I had just begun to see what the world was all about" (27). The story, with its working-class woman protagonist and class-constructed romance, is reminiscent of Dorothy Livesay's "In Green Solariums," but Bergren develops her character's growth to political and sexual consciousness more subtly than Livesay does in her early poem.

"The Christening" emphasizes the emergence of an adolescent girl's sense of her own identity and her potential place in a class-structured society. The story focuses with gentle humour on the self-consciousness of a thirteen-year-old girl who is the oldest in a group christening of the children in a poverty-stricken working-class family. The conclusion of the narrative briefly suggests the girl's growing understanding of the social meaning of her situation and the importance of having faith in the future, although this faith and understanding are still limited in her immature mind by her parents' astrology books that are almost the only reading available to her. "She knew she was going to have to leave school and do housework for other people. But they would see! She sat up presently, and reaching out she drew the fortune book toward her with her future in it, and held it fast" (87). Other stories in the collection, dealing with mature male workers in working-world situations, are more detached in their perspective and more explicit in their political message. "A Hard Pull" portrays both the tensions and the affinities between Euro-Canadian and Sikh pulp-mill workers who are gradually recognizing their class unity. "The Swedes Who Never Went Back" is another story of immigrants to Canada, who demonstrate a more conscious determination to develop through class and personal relationships their sense of social cohesion. "Some People's Luck" depicts loggers struggling doggedly to work in bad weather with the ominous possibility of lay-offs hanging over them, while the narrative briefly switches to anony-mous American corporate powers: "'Canada is a great country for investment,' they are saying in New York, as they work on the balance sheets and the computers spew forth figures" (79).

Bergren turned aside from fiction after the publication of this vol-ume, to compile an oral history of the Woodworkers' Union, *Tough Timber: The Loggers of British Columbia–Their Story* (Progress, 1967). In 1972 her literary career took a promising step forward when she won a Canada Council grant to write a novel about the log-ging industry. Unfortunately, Bergren was killed in an automobile accident only months after receiving the grant. Her literary reputa-tion must rest on the unjustly neglected *A Bough of Needles,* which demonstrates that Marxist-inspired working-class creative writing could still have relevance in the changing cultural milieu of the 1960s. Bergren's work is especially significant as an early postmodern literary attempt to expand the Communist emphasis on the class struggle to include issues of gender and ethnicity.

But while Bergren was developing what might have been a prom-ising literary career within the CPC, other writers, including the Montreal poet and activist Louise Harvey, left the Party in disillu-sionment. Harvey's breakup with Milton Acorn coincided roughly with Khrushchev's denunciation of Stalin and the beginnings of the great schism in the international Communist movement, the Sino-Soviet split. Harvey's closest Communist friend, Dorise Nielsen, went to live in China to work as a teacher in 1957, and although she remained in friendly correspondence with Harvey over the next decade, she became an outspoken opponent of the USSR and of the pro-Russian LPP/CPC. In Montreal, the Party writers' group lan-guished, and Harvey found herself cut off from the communal cul-tural milieu to which she had long been accustomed. While enter-taining false hopes of the revival of *New Frontiers,* she acknowledged to Margaret Fairley in a letter of 11 April 1957 that "our own writ-ers' group is barely functioning" (Fairley Papers). Although she claimed that she was busy with various attempts at poems and sto-ries, she published nothing between 1955 and 1958. She prepared a book of poems, tentatively scheduled to be issued by the Quebec LPP provincial committee, but the project collapsed and the volume never appeared.

In 1958 she began to publish two or three poems a year in the *Tribune*, mostly on the subjects of feminism, peace, and the world-wide struggle against capitalist imperialism. Her poetic responses to international politics include "Night in Algeria" (5 May 1958), on Algerian anti-French resistance and "Assassination in the Congo" (27 February 1961), on the murder of Patrice Lumumba. "Beloved Country" (30 June 1958) salutes what Canadian Communists had been calling "Canada Day" since the early 1950s; the anniversary of the October Revolution of 1917 as well as the launching of Sputnik II in November 1957 are commemorated in "1917-1958–A Tribute" (24 November 1958). "A Tribute: March 8 1959" (9 March 1959) and "To the Unborn Girl–Children of Tomorrow" (6 March 1961) mark International Women's Day; "After Liberation" (16 November 1959) praises the status of women in post-revolutionary China. "A Monologue for May Day" (1 May 1961) marks the ninetieth anniversary of the Paris Commune. "The Beautiful People" (12 October 1964), her last poem to appear in the *Tribune*, is a memorial to civil rights workers murdered in Mississippi. All Harvey's *Tribune* poetry is in a socialist realist idiom that avoids modernist indirection and complexity in favour of clearly expressed political didacticism. "Night in Algeria," for instance, is an explicit pictorial invocation of the French imperialist suppression of the Algerian independence movement, which recognizes both the capitalist underpinnings and the violence of French colonial policy ("Gold has chained France, set Terror loose through the byways of Algeria"), but resolves toward an expression of confidence in ultimate revolutionary victory. In her feminist poems, especially her annual tributes to Women's Day, she relates her belief in women's power to free themselves from past social restrictions to her confidence in the coming socialist millenium of peace and equality throughout the world.

Harvey clung to the CPC long after many of her contemporaries had fallen away, finding an outlet for her activism in a Party-sponsored Peace Council that survived feebly in Montreal from 1959 until 1963. In 1964 she reluctantly resigned from the Party, convinced that it was no longer committed to bringing about the reign of peace and equality. Like many other former Communists of long service, she found the sudden alienation from her ideological community disorienting. Anxious to re-establish her sense of social purpose, she joined a peace group associated with the Unitarian Church and eventually— to the bemusement of Dorise Nielsen—became a fervent Christian. Plagued by severe arthritis and other serious medical problems, she was forced to curtail her public activities. By the 1970s, her literary career had come to a complete end. After a visit to Nielsen in China in 1979 her medical problems worsened, and she died in 1983 at the age of seventy-one.

● ● ● ● ●

The most significant literary activity within the CPC after 1960 came from the little circle of longstanding Party faithful that included Margaret Fairley, Stanley Ryerson, Joe Wallace, Oscar Ryan, and Dyson Carter. Fairley, freed from the responsibilities of *New Frontiers*, was able to turn her full-time attention to the proposed edition of writings by William Lyon Mackenzie that she had taken on as part of the "People's History" project she and Stanley Ryerson had initiated through the National Cultural Commission back in 1947. Interested especially in establishing Mackenzie's reputation as a journalist and essayist and demonstrating how his writings became a principal catalyst for the Upper Canada Rebellion, she rediscovered and brought together material from Mackenzie's various newspapers and from his manuscripts in the national, provincial, and Toronto archives. By the summer of 1959 she had ready for the press *The Selected Writings of William Lyon Mackenzie 1824-1837*. With its positive image of Mackenzie's career as a revolutionary, the *Selected Writings* provided an illuminating contrast to William Kilbourn's recent biography, *The Firebrand* (1956), which portrayed its subject as an eccentric and sometimes ludicrous exception to the placidly bourgeois course of early-nineteenth-century Canadian history. Although it emphasized by implication the prefigurations of Marxism in Mackenzie's populist attacks on class and money privilege, Fairley's edition was much less obviously partisan Communist than most of her literary work. Published by the Canadian branch of Oxford University Press, it was distributed and reviewed internationally, and brought Fairley, at the age of seventy-five, recognition from the non-Communist literary and scholarly communities.

Reviewers either failed or declined to see Marxist connotations in the book, for the reactions were uniformly favourable. Robert Fulford, in the *Toronto Star*, hailed it as a "worthy companion" to Kilbourn's biography. In a Toronto *Globe and Mail* review, Kilbourn welcomed "this first readily available anthology of Mackenzie's writings," and offered a restrained mea culpa for his own contemptuous dismissal of Mackenzie's literary abilities by admitting that Fairley's "intelligent selection" showed Mackenzie "more a patient and methodical collector of factual evidence than a man of passion and prejudice" ("Many-Sided Character"). Carl Klinck, writing in the *Canadian Forum* (1961) and later in the *Literary History of Canada* (1965) suggested that the *Selected Writings* revealed Mackenzie's importance as a "man of letters" and that his "powerful popular style made him a Canadian Cobbett." The poet and anthologist John Robert Colombo was inspired by the rhythmic and aphoristic qualities of Mackenzie's prose to take brief selections from the edition and rearrange them in rough metrical or free verse lines to create an exercise in "found poetry," *The Mackenzie Poems* (1966). In England, the *Times Literary Supplement* admired the "well-edited and handsomely produced selection." In August 1961, after being ignored for years by the city, provincial, and national cultural establishments, Fairley was an invited guest of the Toronto Historical Board at an open house to commemorate the hundredth anniversary of Mackenzie's death (clipping, Fairley Papers).

Stanley Ryerson likewise produced important writings in the 1960s. As a member of the Central Committee and editor of *National Affairs Monthly* and its successor the *Marxist Quarterly*, his time was as usual much committed to Party work. In the late 1950s, however, he embarked on what became his most ambitious literary and scholarly endeavour, a two-volume history of Canada from the aboriginal era to the late nineteenth century. *The Founding of Canada: Beginnings to 1815* (1960; rev. 1962) surveyed the development of the country from the geological emergence of the American continents to the end of the War of 1812. *Unequal Union: Confederation and the Roots of Conflict in the Canadas, 1815-1873* (1968; 2nd ed., 1973) takes the story down to the aftermath of 1867. His work, Ryerson explained modestly, was intended as "a preliminary breaking of ground, suggesting a line of approach to a re-interpretation of this country's history" (*Founding* vii-viii). *The Founding of Canada* and *Unequal Union* remain the most ambitious Marxist expositions of Canadian history ever attempted. In contrast to his earlier work, the new books are more scholarly in style and documentation, addressed less to a working-class readership and more to academic historians and other well-informed readers. Specifically, they represent the challenge of historical materialism to what Ryerson describes as the prevailing historiography of "metaphysical idealism" in Canada, i.e., the notion that events are propelled by a "disembodied Idea"—such as the "idea of unity" represented by the Confederation movement, or the "idea of allegiance" represented by the Imperialist movement (*Unequal Union* 425). Such abstractions of bourgeois historiography are opposed by the Marxist assumption set forth in the postscript to *The Founding of Canada* that it is not ideas but people in their material relations to nature and to each other that make history.

Ryerson also condemns the tendency to represent Canadian history as a chronicle of the achievements of politicians and entrepreneurs, while ignoring the selfish and destructive impulses of capitalists and bourgeois governments towards nature, aboriginal people, and the working-class majority of the population. Non-Marxist historians, Ryerson insists, often present a deceptive picture of the explorers, entrepreneurs, and colonial administrators in early Canada, by emphasizing their curiosity, love of adventure, courage, and idealism. Ryerson draws especially on Gustavus Myers's *History of Canadian Wealth* to demonstrate that the main motives of these people were greed and lust for power. "The weight of 'official' historiography has hitherto been heavily on the side of efforts to smother the facts of exploitation," Ryerson argues. "The idyllic patriarchal picture" of colonial New France "is a piece of flagrant deception" (*Founding* 109, 162). Similarly, the bourgeois interpretation of the British conquest as the advent of "rational and ordered liberty" is contradicted by the clear historical facts of official British efforts to withhold free institutions and civil rights from the masses of the Canadian people (*Founding* 199-200).

If the idealist historians have indulged in over-simplifications and distortions, similar accusations might be made against Marxists. As non-Communist reviewers complained about all of Ryerson's historical writings, *The Founding of Canada* emphasizes the class struggle theme at the expense of a more comprehensive exposition of the profuse and contradictory forces at work in Canadian history. But as Ryerson indicates, historiography is not a documentary report of objective reality; it is a process of mediation that involves abstraction, synthesis, and authorial bias, but in the end achieves instructive communication. "My concern is not to claim exemption from a point of view," he declares in his prologue to *Unequal Union*, "but to be understood" (20). For Ryerson, the Marxist emphasis on class conflict is a much more comprehensible way of representing the complexities and contradictions of Canadian history than the idealistic theses of most bourgeois historians. Throughout the two volumes, Ryerson continually emphasizes how both French and English colonial administrators and landed proprietors attempted to keep aboriginal and colonist populations in a state of subjugation. The French converted the Hurons to Christianity and used religious discipline as a means of maintaining a docile work force for the fur trade. The church in combination with the seigneurial system likewise kept the small immigrant population of New France tied to the land as virtual serfs. Both human nature and economic evolution opposed these efforts: many colonists insisted on defying authority to take to the woods and follow the more lucrative independent fur trade, while many Hurons resisted the missionaries' attempts to convert them to Christianity.

But the struggle was not merely between feudal authoritarianism and a New World instinct toward freedom. When the landowners and colonial administrators allied themselves with the increasingly monopolistic resource capitalism of the fur trade and fishery, the resulting neo-feudal power soon found itself in conflict with the emerging industrial and mercantile capitalism. In order to keep wages low, the manufacturers and merchants needed a surplus of labour; the fur trade and the seigneurs, however, opposed mass immigration because large-scale agricultural and urban development interfered with their control and exploitation of the wilderness. The emergence of industrial capitalism led to conflicts between manufacturers and the seigneurs in alliance with the resource monopolies; the establishment of factories also led to new conflicts between employers and wage earners. The class struggle in the New World thus repeated in a more compressed time frame the struggles that emerged in Europe over the centuries of the decline of feudalism and the rise of capitalism. As in Europe, the North American situation was complicated further by wars of commercial rivalry between feudal nations, and by an emerging militant revolutionary spirit expressed by both the bourgeois and the proletariat. *Unequal Union* emphasizes the struggles for responsible government and for the legislative union of the British North American colonies. Ryerson retells the story of the Upper and Lower Canada insurrections, closely following his own *1837*, with occasional expansions and corrections. Although he sees the rebellions primarily as expressions of the bourgeois struggle for political power, he also emphasizes the importance of the proletariat in the military struggle, and attributes the defeat partly to "the still embryonic character of the working class, its lack of organization and political consciousness" (82). Challenging the idealist thesis that "colonial self-government was the spontaneous gift of a generous imperial power" (137), Ryerson insists that self-government was the consequence of the struggles of the colonial bourgeoisie, first in a militant alliance with the proletariat and subsequently through political and economic influence.

The period from the defeat of the rebellion to Confederation Ryerson sees in terms of the emergence of bourgeois democratic institutions and a rigidly stratified class society based on economics. "Democracy in a business society was perforce a class democracy" (203). Following Myers again, Ryerson finds the climax of nineteenth-century bourgeois economic ascendancy—and of all the exploitation and chicanery that accompanies the establishment of a "business society"—in the great era of railway construction. "The transition from an economy dominated by the old mercantile-landowner, Family Compact ruling group to that of the new industrial-railroad oligarchy is the main content of the bourgeois revolution in British North America" (281). Ryerson accepts in part the "staple" theory of economic historian Harold Innis, according to which the Canadian economy was established in the nineteenth century primarily as a supplier of raw materials. But Ryerson also

emphasizes the remarkable growth at the same time of small manufacturing and commodity production, which some historians dismiss
as "unimportant" (268). The emergence of Canadian manufacturing
is important to Ryerson because it brings Canada closer to the kind of
socio-economic model that underlies most of Marx's theories about
the class struggle and the inevitability of revolution. Although he is
confident that capitalist power will eventually be overthrown by the
political action of the industrial working class, he envisages a long
and difficult struggle in which localized and partial resolutions will
lead to new conflicts. The continuing course of this struggle is
emphasized in the conclusion of *Unequal Union*. Unlike the metaphysical idealist historians who would regard 1867 as an appropriate
epilogue to the evolution of responsible government and centralist
aspirations in nineteenth-century Canada, Ryerson takes the story
beyond Confederation, to the emergence of new conflicts involving
anti-centralist nationalist movements in Quebec.

The bourgeois newspapers continued the practice of ignoring publications from Progress Books, but several academic journals took
notice of Ryerson's histories. The response to the earlier *Founding of
Canada* was generally hostile. Gustav Lanctot in the *Canadian
Historical Review* accused Ryerson of misinterpretations and inaccu-
racies, and of basing his conclusions on ideological preconceptions
rather than evidence. G.E. Wilson complained in the *Dalhousie
Review* that "the Marxist candle sheds very little new light on the
well-known facts of early Canadian history." Robin Winks in the
*American Historical Review* compared the book unfavourably with
Donald Creighton's *The Story of Canada*. Ryerson responded rather
peevishly to these negative reviewers in an article in the *Canadian
Tribune* of 28 August 1961, but there was justification for his complaint that non-Marxist reviewers were unwilling—and, he might
have added, probably unqualified—to engage the Marxist historical
perspective seriously. The reviews of *Unequal Union* a decade later,
although also brief and limited to a few scholarly periodicals, were a
little more enlightened. Ramsay Cook in the *American Historical
Review* agreed with Ryerson about the importance of economic
themes in Canadian history, although he felt that the author overworked the class struggle thesis. According to F.W. Park in the

*Canadian Forum, Unequal Union* provided "material for a fruitful discussion"; the reviewer for the library journal *Choice* agreed that the book had "many penetrating insights that question some of the traditional views of Canadian historians." Bourgeois reviewers were still inclined to be wary of Ryerson's application of Marxism to the problems of Canadian history, but at least they were acknowledging that its scholarly bias pointed in new and suggestive directions.

Like Fairley and Ryerson, the poet Joe Wallace in the post-Stalinist period entered upon the busiest and most successful stage of his literary career. All through the 1950s his poems were regularly published in periodicals in the USSR, Eastern Europe and Asia. In 1957 he embarked on a ten-month visit to the Soviet Union and China, at the invitation of the writers' unions of the two countries. The trip was part cultural tour and part rest cure for the ailing sixty-six-year-old poet, as he reported in a *Tribune* column entitled "On My Way," but it ultimately became a literary triumph. After spending a few months at a sanitarium on the Black Sea, Wallace embarked on a busy round of readings, lectures, and meetings with writers in Moscow, Beijing, and smaller centres in the two countries, where he was greeted as a major literary ambassador from the English-speaking world. Early in 1958, after his return to Canada, the Foreign Languages Publishing House in Moscow issued English, Russian, and Chinese editions of *The Golden Legend*, an anthology of Wallace's poems incorporating new work plus abundant selections from all his previously published volumes.

Wallace's conception of poetry had not essentially changed for forty years, as he declared in his introduction to *The Golden Legend*. Poetry, he insisted, had become a "lost art" in the English-speaking countries, "because the poets are writing to poets, to critics, to professional intellectuals" instead of to the common working people (19). He believed as thoroughly as he ever did that the purpose of poetry was to inspire the proletariat with faith in the possibility of a world far better than that of the strife-ridden, greed-driven capitalist societies. Wallace still inclined to blend Christian with Marxist imagery, as he indicates in the title poem of *The Golden Legend*, in which apocalyptic images pour profusely forth in vigorous couplets, building toward a phantasma of transcendent life that merges abruptly with a moral vision of a post-revolutionary Utopia:

> Great beasts went by, celestial whales,
> That splashed the sky with swishing tails
> And shook the ships with golden bales
> That furrowed through the purple seas
> Flashing with phosphorescent gleams...

The poet, absorbed into the dream vision, follows the leviathan procession toward a new world:

> There self survived, like all things good,
> But based itself on brotherhood
> And all was measured by one test
> Not who has most but who does best.

The vision ends, in socialist realist fashion, with a bridge between the fantasy and the poet's confidence in the ability of Marxism to build this new Jerusalem in the real world:

> How could I help but dream like this
> Where all around the substance is? (*JW Poems* 99)

"On the Road to Martyrs' Hill," written in China, uses more restrained and natural images to construct a similar vision of the new world to come. Imagining himself out walking in the countryside in the early morning, the poet is at first intimidated by his lonely surroundings. But he soon gains confidence and expresses a cheerfulness that has been latent from the beginning in the jingling rhythms:

> Here a buffalo is staring. Am I first to come this way?
> No, the road is red and rutted from the years and yesterday
> There is Falling Flower Mountain where we went to look
>     for stones
> Others soon will gather better: time may take but time atones.

In the conclusion the pronoun shifts from "I" to "he," suggesting that the experience of the poet is the experience of universal man:

> Early in the morning while the eastern sky was wan
> And the birds were hardly stirring he went out and found
> the dawn. (*JW Poems* 40)

Wallace's second volume published in Moscow, *A Radiant Sphere* (1964), is significant for its inclusion of a collection of poetic renderings into English of the work of eleven Soviet poets. Wallace could neither read nor speak Russian, but working from prose translations prepared by others he produced lyrics that incorporated the Russian poetic thought into simple English idioms and conventional metric forms which reconfirm Frye's observation of his skill as a versifier. A few of the poems deal with militant political themes, but most are lyrical expressions of romantic love or of nature, as in this excerpt from his version of Andrei Voznesensky's "Mountain Springs":

> A mountain girl
> Comes to a fountain
> Falling near
> Flicking her heels
> Like a forest deer
> Dips and quaffs
> Slips and laughs
> Under a cascade of water
> Dances the mountain's daughter.... (*A Radiant Sphere* 105)

His adaptation of Andrei Malyshko's "Winged Words" combines romantic love with suggestions of commitment to an infinite and arduous journey:

> I thought I would gather
> Luxury fare with you,
> Luxury fare for our lovely abode
> But I have nothing
> Nothing to share with you,
> Only my life
> And this lengthening road. (*A Radiant Sphere* 97)

In contrast to the gratification of his success in Eastern Europe and China, Wallace felt that he was unappreciated in Canada, even within the Communist community, as he complained to the leader of the CPC, Leslie Morris (letter 20 May 1963, CPC/LPP Papers, NAC). It is true that his sales in Canada came nowhere near the thirty thousand copies of one of his books in China, but he was gaining some recognition, even outside Communist circles. In 1957 he was praised by

F.W. Watt in his dissertation on "Radicalism in English-Canadian Literature" as the "only consistently dedicated and genuinely proletarian poet" the country had produced (261). Wallace had a notable talent for comic epigrams, as F.R. Scott and A.J.M. Smith acknowledged by including three of his best in their anthology of Canadian satirical verse, *The Blasted Pine* (1957). In 1960 Wallace was the subject of an interview by John Robert Colombo, which was published in the University of Toronto student newspaper the *Varsity* and reprinted in the July *Canadian Forum*. Milton Acorn, a rising star of post-modern anti-establishment poetry through the 1960s and 1970s, praised Wallace's work at every opportunity. But by the early 1970s, Wallace's poetry was seen only occasionally even by *Tribune* readers, and his reputation and influence continued to wane with the declining fortunes of the CPC.

Another faithful long-time member, Oscar Ryan, similarly remained loyal to the old Party through the decades of decline. Besides writing articles and book and theatre reviews for the *Tribune*, Ryan produced in the 1970s two ambitious literary works that attempted to pay tribute to the glory days of the Party. *Tim Buck: A Conscience for Canada* (1975) is an official biography of the sort written by press agents or friendly journalists about prominent political leaders. "The purpose of these pages is to set the record straight" (3), Ryan claims in his opening chapter. More precisely, he seeks to present Buck as a respectable Canadian statesman, in contrast to the caricatures of him as a wild-eyed fanatic which the bourgeois media have perennially suggested. In line with the Party's continuing attempts to present Communism as an ideology appropriate to working-class Canada, Ryan's book devotes a good deal of attention to the proletarian elements of the subject. The author details Buck's immigrant roots, his experience as a common labourer and machinist, and his efforts to acquire on his own the education his poverty-stricken family could not give him.

But these attempts to emphasize the commonplace human qualities of his subject ironically contribute to the impression of Buck's life as a rather improbable myth. As other political biographers have done to defend the controversial ideologies and activities of their subjects, Ryan emphasizes Buck's struggles against formidable barriers: his childhood poverty, his efforts to educate himself, his persecution by police and government bureaucracies. There is no basis for doubting Ryan's account of Buck's early life in England, but his narrative makes Buck's beginnings sound like the strive-and-succeed stereotypes of the Horatio Alger books. Besides presenting Buck's life in clichés, Ryan's biography tries to create an image of larger-than-life heroism, just as Allan and Gordon do in their representation of Bethune. The longest-serving leader of a Communist Party in a capitalist country, Buck was identified closely with the CPC/LPP for almost forty years. Ryan attempts to identify Buck as the virtual personification of the CPC, but the attempt takes on ironic implications, because it makes Buck appear like a Canadian counterpart of Stalin, the leader he had to repudiate after thirty years of conscientious devotion.

Even though Ryan writes out of a context of post-Stalinist ideology, his methods suggest even further parallels with biographies of the Soviet dictator. Like the writers of official lives of Stalin, Ryan seeks by means of questionable tradition and outright misinformation to reinforce the legitimacy of his subject's claim to perennial leadership. To emphasize his ideological orthodoxy, he offers the unsupported claim that Buck in 1917 was a member of the Socialist Party of North America, the one Party that "gave full support to the Russian revolution" (66). He suggests also, without proof, that Buck immediately recognized the Marxist orthodoxy of the Bolsheviks amid the competing Russian revolutionary movements. Although he does not go so far as to claim that Buck took part in the Winnipeg General Strike, he uses Buck as narrator and commentator in summarizing the story of the Strike, to create the impression that Buck was present at the events described. Ryan also repeats Buck's claim to have attended the famous organizational meeting of the CPC in Guelph in 1921, although evidence refuting that claim has been presented by historians William Rodney (37 and n. 182), Ivan Avakumovic (21) and Ian Angus (86).

In writing about the years after Buck's election as General Secretary in 1928, Ryan has no need to manipulate the facts. There is no reason to challenge the record of Buck's immense energy and zeal, his personal courage in facing police harassment and hostile crowds, his patience and dignity through almost three years of imprisonment in the Kingston penitentiary, his loyalty to the cause in the early years of the Second World War when the Party was illegal and during the Cold War when war-time détente with the USSR gave way to extreme anti-Communism, or his dogged belief in the legitimacy of Marxist-Leninist doctrine even after the repeated failure of the Party to break out of its marginalized position in Canadian politics. But again, Ryan's methods incline toward myth-making rather than realistic portraiture, as indicated by the suggestion of the allegorization of Buck in Ryan's subtitle, "a conscience for Canada." Through the whole narrative there is no intimation of weakness, of any duplicitous act or ambiguous motive, of momentary regret or disillusionment on the part of the hero. The book as a whole does little to reveal the flesh-and-blood human being who actually led the Communist movement with varying degrees of success through a crucial era in Canadian history.

As if to demonstrate the cliché that fiction can convey a more authentic kind of truth than allegedly factual narrative, Ryan produced a more convincing retrospective on the Canadian Communist movement in a novel, *Soon To Be Born* (1980). Like Dyson Carter's *Tomorrow Is with Us*, Ryan's novel suggests in its title the socialist realist emphasis on faith in the Communist millennium. But in his narrative, Ryan focuses like Carter on the episodic defeats and disappointments in the immensely difficult task of bringing the new world into being. *Soon To Be Born* is also in part an autobiographical bildungsroman, in which Ryan divides aspects of his own background and experience between two characters. Although concerned with Canadian history from the first decade of the twentieth century to the beginning of the Second World War, the author focuses particularly on the early 1920s—the years when the CPC came into being, and when he himself came to adulthood and to progressive political commitment.

To add to the historical verisimilitude, various actual Communists appear as minor characters in the story, including Tim Buck; Tom McEwen, Party organizer and journalist; Leslie Morris, a contemporary of Ryan in the Young Communist League, who was to follow Buck as leader of the Party; and the novelist and activist Trevor Maguire. But *Soon To Be Born* focuses mainly on two fictional characters, who suggest aspects of Ryan's own personality and experience. The frame story, concerning the aftermath of an anti-war demonstration in the fall of 1939, establishes a climax of hope and tragedy in the lives of the two protagonists. As one of the two lies critically wounded by a police bullet, the narrative moves backward and forward through the years in which the two men have lived. To the wounded Arthur Meller, Ryan gives much of his own personal background: born into a Jewish immigrant family, raised on St. Urbain Street in Montreal, forced by poverty to abandon formal education at the end of high school. But while Ryan himself joined the YCL soon after the founding of the CPC, Meller resists radicalization and tries to avoid the political conflicts of his generation, until he is drawn, half-comprehending, into the imperatives of history. The conscious radical side of his life Ryan assigns to Fred Shaughnessy, son of a veteran of the 1916 Irish uprising. Like Ryan, Shaughnessy joins the YCL and serves as a Party organizer; going beyond the author's experience he serves in Spain, is severely wounded, and returns to resume his radical activity, in spite of the government's suppression of the Party in 1939.

In effect, the two characters represent the two possible courses of action available to Ryan and all young men of his generation. They can suffer through the arduous conditions of commitment and struggle with the hope of seeing the Marxist promise of the new world fulfilled; or they can retreat into the self-indulgent illusions of capitalist society, only to be drawn violently into the struggle without the strength and knowledge to enable them to survive. Ryan elaborates his point further through his characterization of Gabrielle Lajeunesse, Arthur Meller's French-Canadian lover who, in spite of her humanism and social awareness, falls prey to the fallacy of self-reliance. Proud of her ethnic and family heritage, she is determined to follow the example of her grandfather and make her own life. In the crisis of the brutal police attack on Meller, however, and with the friendship and tutelage of Shaughnessy, her self-reliance is giving way to a new sense of class unity. It is revealed at the end of the novel that she is carrying Meller's child, and like all those who seek genuine freedom, she awaits the new world soon to be born.

Ryan's novel and biography were part of an effusion in the 1970s of retrospective writing from older Communists, of which Dorothy Livesay's *Right Hand Left Hand* (1977) is the best known. But Livesay's book is written by a lapsed Party member, and her conceptions of Communist politics and literary theory are coloured by her ultimate rejection of them. Among other memoirs of the 1930s, Ron Liversedge's *Recollections of the On to Ottawa Trek* (private publication 1961, commercial publication 1973) tells a plain tale with no literary pretensions, but the author's evocation of the events of 1935 and of the surrounding ambience of personal experience of poverty and unemployment through the late 1920s and early 1930s raises the book to the forefront of progressive autobiographical writing. Tom McEwen's *The Forge Glows Red* (1974) is the autobiography of a journalist and activist whose career as a Communist, like Buck's, reflects fanatical partisan belief and commitment. Harold Griffin, for many years McEwen's associate on the *Pacific Tribune*, produced three collections of verse, *Confederation and Other Poems* (1966), *Now and Not Now* (1973), and *Paul Bunyan and Other Poems* (1977), reflecting more than thirty years of poetic response to crises of Depression, war, and Cold War. His book *Soviet Frontiers of Tomorrow* (1982), based on a recent tour of Siberia, provided a suggestive complement to his *Alaska and the Canadian Northwest* (1944).

• • • • •

Of the older literary Communists who continued to write into the 1970s and 1980s, by far the most prolific was Dyson Carter. After the publication of his novel *Fatherless Sons* in 1955, Carter turned most of his energies to the Canadian-Soviet Friendship Society, of which he had been elected president in 1950. In 1955 he established his own company, Northern Book House, to publish a magazine promoting Canadian understanding of the USSR, *News-Facts*, which was transformed a year later into the glossy picture magazine *Northern Neighbours*. The magazine was not primarily devoted to culture, although it included articles on literature and the arts, along with such topics as family life, youth, morality, and science and medicine in the USSR. The fact that *Northern Neighbours* survived for thirty-three years supports Carter's claim that the magazine was relatively successful in attracting subscribers. Northern Book House was also able to develop a flourishing business with a small annual list of books and pamphlets on science, medicine, and the USSR. Carter himself wrote several Northern monographs, mostly in collaboration with Charlotte Carter, including *Science of Health and Long Life in the*

*USSR* (1956), *Cancer, Smoking, Heart Disease, Drinking: In Our Two World Systems Today* (1957), *The Future of Freedom* (1962), *Science and Revolution* (1966) and *Worker Power* (1970). In the early 1960s Carter moved his publishing operation from Toronto to Gravenhurst, Ontario, where he carried on a mail-order business in Canada and abroad, until declining sales, the imminent collapse of the USSR, and Carter's own failing health forced the end in 1989.

Among his various books dealing with scientific and political questions from a Marxist perspective, one of the more interesting is *Science and Revolution*. Carter wrote an early version of this work in 1947, but Progress Books declined to publish it because of its overemphasis on science as a determining factor in the evolution of Communism. According to orthodox Marxism-Leninism, the revolution that would lead to world Communism is to be brought about through political and economic forces, not through science and technology. The 1966 revision seems to have been inspired by the recent successes of the USSR's space program, from Sputnik 1 in 1957 to the Luna 9 soft moon landing in January 1966. Carter's tone throughout the book is jubilant: the Soviet Union has shown that there are no limits to what science, under socialism, might achieve in the future. Science in the West is advancing, he admits, but at a cost inflated by non-producing profiteers. If science and technology can be liberated from the profit motive, the Americans may even be persuaded to enter into cooperation with the USSR to conquer the global problems of over-population, disease, and mass starvation. As in the first version of the book, Carter remains determined to elevate the physical sciences to a position of priority in Marxist-Leninist theory and Soviet history. As far as he is concerned, it is scientific progress, rather than either economic developments or outstanding political leadership, that controls socialist history.

In 1986 Carter published through Northern Book House an autobiographical novel, *This Story Fierce and Tender*. A long and very subjective work, it repays careful reading, if not for its ambiguous artistic achievement, at least for its record of Carter's early life and its revelation of the growth of a unique sensibility. The work is a Communist political apologia, but it owes much less to the socialist realist tradition than to the bildungsroman. In its emphasis on the

sensuous experiences of childhood, *This Story* bears some resem-
blance to the 1929 novel *Look Homeward Angel*, by the American
Thomas Wolfe, whose name Carter once included in a list of writers
who influenced him (Thomas 20). Like Wolfe's, Carter's novel is the
story of a hypersensitive male growing from childhood to young
adulthood in the early twentieth century. In narrative method,
Carter's novel also resembles another bildungsroman, Samuel Butler's
*The Way of All Flesh* (1903). Like Butler, Carter distributes his own
experience between the young protagonist and an older observer
through whose eyes the development of the other character is presented. *This Story* traces the efforts of a biographer named "Dyson
Carter" to reconstruct in the 1970s the life of "Elgin Morley" from his
birth in 1910 to age thirty-five. Since Morley is both a victim of
osteogenesis imperfecta and an aspiring writer who becomes a
Communist, the book can be seen, like Butler's, as an attempt on the
part of the aging author to reassess his younger self.

Like most bildungsromans, *This Story* emphasizes the importance
of childhood: almost half the book's more than five-hundred pages
focus on Morley from ages seven to ten. Early in the novel, the narrator articulates the hypothesis that in "stricken individuals"—victims
like Morley of severe genetic diseases—the development of the brain
is accelerated to counteract the "course of self-destruction" that seeks
to dominate the physiological system. In people with such a powerful
will to live and to realize the potentialities of life as early as possible,
childhood, according to this hypothesis, is virtually "bypassed" (20).
Morley's extraordinary precocity, besides being evident in his hyper-
active intellect, is expressed in romantic feelings directed toward a
young woman who serves as his attendant while he is incapacitated
by bone fractures. Although these feelings are expressed in sentimental, immature terms, the novel is unambiguous in its assertion of the
sexual dimension of the child's feelings. Sexuality is associated with
love, and explicitly distinguished from "pornography," which is an
expression of hatred. Child pornography, says the adult Morley to his
biographer, is "disgusting" and "inhumane," "not because children
shouldn't experience sex," but because it "crushes love" (134). This
idea is developed into the basis of Morley's political beliefs, in a commentary reminiscent of Carter's idealization of "love and heroism" in

his wartime pamphlet *Russia's Secret Weapon*. "I didn't come to the truth by laboring through Capital, volumes one-two-three. For me the class struggle was beautifully simplified....Life reduced the whole thing to simplicity, for me. Divided the world into those who love people and those who hate them!" (135)

Throughout the novel, Carter demonstrates the experiences and thought processes—sexual, emotional, scientific, and political—that express his protagonist's commitment to the ideal of love. The longing of the child to achieve a life free from physical pain and to experience an ideal romantic/sexual relationship is paralleled with the politicized adult's vision of a world where universal happiness is possible (59). Happiness, furthermore, is to be achieved through the interaction of love and science. In the childhood chapters, the science that can make happiness possible is, of course, medicine. With Elgin Morley's maturity and gradual freedom from the worst effects of disease, the science that comes to the forefront is the socialism of the USSR. "Stalin is a scientist," declares Morley in the early 1940s. "Making socialism is a science. The whole Soviet Union is science applied to human life....Stalin will apply scientific socialism to wipe the Hitlerites off the face of the earth" (524).

As the latter passage indicates, Morley's pursuit of happiness is enacted against a backdrop of allusion to the great public events—international, national, regional, and local—of the decades from 1917 to 1945. Particular emphasis is placed on events directly related to the historical development of "scientific socialism": the First World War, the Russian Revolution, the Winnipeg General Strike, the activities of the Communist Party in Winnipeg in the 1930s, the outbreak of the Second World War and the internment of Canadian Communists, the formation of the Labor-Progressive Party, and Canadian Communist support for the war effort of the USSR. Unlike his earlier novels, which used traditional narrative methods, *This Story* uses discontinuous chronology, divided narrative perspective, and other literary techniques derived from avant-garde fiction of the early twentieth century. Chapters describing the interviews of the biographer "Dyson Carter" in the 1970s are interspersed with chapters focusing on Morley's childhood, and others dealing with his early adulthood and the beginnings of his political activities and literary career. Key characters and influential experiences are introduced briefly, often cryptically, then elaborated gradually and intermittently, as if to reproduce the actual process of the biographer's growing familiarity with the events and ideas that shaped his subject's life.

If *This Story Fierce and Tender* is not an entirely successful novel, it is a memorable one, if only for the boldness of its narrative methods and its approaches to public as well as personal themes. The novel is a forceful account of the interaction of influences and experiences that are derived from Carter's own life: his struggle with disease, his education as a Communist, his zealous commitment to both Marxism and science, and his development as a literary artist. *This Story* covers, however, only the first thirty-four years of the author's life. The novel ends in 1945, when the fortunes of Carter/Morley, and of the Canadian and international Communist movements, were at their height. According to a note appended to the conclusion, Carter planned a sequel which was to bring the story to the 1980s. Such a sequel, should it ever emerge some day from Carter's unpublished papers, would be a narrative of falling action, chronicling the author's decline into old age and his aggravated health problems, as well as the decline of influence and popularity of the Communist movement in Canada.

Such a sequel might be an appropriate reflection of the historical and biographical records, but perhaps the optimistic ending of *This Story Fierce and Tender* provides a more memorable conclusion to what appears to be the last significant literary work to come from the old-generation Communist movement. The literary activity begun so confidently in the 1920s and 1930s, like the political movement from which it sprang, fell prey to the inevitable processes of time and change. A few writers remained doggedly loyal to the movement they had joined in the years when the Soviet Union and its political-economic ideology seemed to offer new hope for dealing with the crises that plagued the capitalist world. But by the time Carter published his autobiographical novel, most of his contemporaries in the Party were gone. The oldest, Margaret Fairley, had died in 1968 at the age of eighty-three. Joe Wallace maintained his Party membership and continued to write militant poetry expressing his faith in the coming revolution until his death at age eighty-five in a Vancouver nursing home in 1975. Oscar Ryan continued as a journalist and theatre reviewer for Party publications almost until his death in 1988. Thanks to flexible retirement laws in Quebec, Stanley Ryerson continued to expound the Marxist view of history as a professor at the Université de Québec almost until his death in 1998, but he had withdrawn from the Party in 1971. As the twentieth century drew to a close, the literary flowering of the Communist Party of Canada, like its political influence, appeared to be over.

# 9

# The New Left

Creative writers influenced by Marxism did not disappear from the Canadian literary scene with the passing of the older generation of Communists. A great many young writers in the 1960s and subsequent decades, acting inside and outside various formal and informal organizations including the old CPC, or pursuing their own individualistic impulses, joined the attack on capitalism and the quest for socialistic and/or revolutionary solutions to the inequities of modern industrial and post-industrial societies. Some older writers who left the Party in the late 1950s or early 1960s continued to write in socially conscious, politically radical idioms. The work of both the younger and older writers stands in ambiguous relationship to the tradition of radical writing that flourished during the heyday of the CPC. Some New Leftists were directly inspired by the concepts of proletarian literature and socialist realism developed from the 1920s to the 1950s. Others, although still committed to the attack on capitalistic economic and political structures, developed methods and themes adapted from postmodernism.

Among writers who left the Party in the 1950s, Milton Acorn especially profited from his interaction with such people in the non-
Communist literary community as Louis Dudek, Al Purdy, and
Gwendolyn MacEwen. His poetry became more formally complex and
more thematically varied, but much of it continued to be devoted to
attacking capitalism and expressing solidarity with the working class
and admiration for revolutionary heroes. At the same time, however,
he revealed his second thoughts about partisan communism, especially in his revisions of poems written while he was a member of the
LPP. In a 1969 edition of his selected poems, *I've Tasted My Blood*, he
included a new version of a work originally published in *New
Frontiers*, "Of Martyrs." The revision retains the free verse form and
most of the original wording, but omits three stanzas that emphasize
the solidarity among past victims of capitalist persecution. The
revised poem presents political martyrdom as a self-sufficient expression of individual courage, rather than as a manifestation of the collective commitment of Party members. Similarly, in *The Island Means
Minago* (1975) he included an extensive revision of another of his
*New Frontiers* poems, "Norman Bethune, Died Nov. 13, 1939."
Whereas the original poem was inspired by the ideological perspective and dramatic techniques of Allan and Gordon's *The Scalpel, the
Sword* (1952), the new version reflects the influence of Roderick
Stewart's more scholarly and politically liberal biography, *Bethune*
(1973). Where the dying Bethune of the 1953 poem is a poignant
Christlike spectacle of "worn-out gentleness" who feebly urges his
followers to carry on the struggle, twenty years later he is a defiantly
"cranky" human being whose challenge to his followers to work out
their own destinies suggests that his own view of Communism, like
Acorn's, was ambivalent.

Acorn's ambivalent attitude toward old-line Communism is evident
in the completely new poetry he wrote in the 1960s and 1970s. Many
of the important political poems in his collection *More Poems for
People* (1972; rev. 1973), written while he was under the influence
of the ultra-nationalist Canadian Liberation Movement, emphasize
the nineteenth-century roots of the radical tradition in Canada, the
legacy of British colonialism, and the new imperialism of the United
States. "Rabbie Still Be With Us," an ostensible tribute to Robert Burns,

is a review of Canadian heroes including Mackenzie, Louis Riel, and Gabriel Dumont, as well as "our poets" from "MacLauchlin [i.e., Alexander McLachlan] to Bisset." Acorn compares Canadians to both the people of Scotland and the North American "Indians," as victims of imperialism. While the native people at least maintained the virtues of their affinity with nature and their sense of community, the white colonists of Canada became enslaved to the US conception of a progress that exploits nature and is devoted to anarchistic individualism. The Canadians, like the Scots, suffered not conclusive military defeat, but betrayal to imperial power:

> They [the Scots] were never defeated. And neither were we.
> Their leaders were bought—ours sold from the first. (*More Poems* 14)

If "the people" recognize their history as a chronicle of both heroism and betrayal, says Acorn in his rather formulaic conclusion, they may yet be able to rise against their oppressors and create a new society.

In his "Poem on Life Insurance and Combat Aviation," Acorn ridicules the monopolistic multinational corporations who pretend to an aggressive rivalry among themselves while in fact using their monolithic power to victimize the people and subvert their democratic institutions. An insurance company advertisement depicting First World War aerial combat as a supposed symbol of business competition represents, in reality, says Acorn, "the Ontario Medicare plan going down in flames," under attack from the corporations who would turn social services into profit-making enterprises. Acorn redoubles his emphasis on capitalist cynicism by quoting, or pretending to quote, from the advertisement, adding his own editorial pun:

> "But that's the way it goes sometimes
> In a free [sick] economy." (17)

In "To the Canadian Ruling Class" he denounces business entrepreneurs as "claim-jumpers" who mark off territory

> So you can sell it later
> At a profit which
> 				Is
> 				Actually

A hundred percent
Since you never owned it. (46)

But if Acorn still hates capitalism, he is also critical of the failure
of old-line Communist parties to maintain the ideals of Marx and
the leaders of the Russian revolution. In the brash and irreverent
elegy "Hey You Guevara," he complains that the hero of the Cuban
revolution died "doing a piece of non-Bolshevik stupidity," and
refers sarcastically to the collapse of "the Communist Party of
Glorious Memory of Canada." But he has not entirely abandoned the
idea of partisan collective action as an ideal, for he still uses the
phrase "we Communists" as he denounces the capitalistic "bourgeois
ministers of death" (36-39). He is also willing to retain a favourable
memory of the Party to which he belonged for a few years in the
1950s, and to regard some of the poetry he wrote in that period as
still relevant. In *The Island Means Minago* he included "Callum,"
which originally appeared in the *Tribune* in 1957, and which he was
willing in the 1960s to describe to his friend and fellow poet Al
Purdy as one of his two or three best works. The poem appears in *The
Island* virtually unchanged, except for additions of punctuation, cap-
italization, and exclamation marks that probably reflect Acorn's
vehement style of public reading and emphasize the anger and defiance underlying the poem.

Poems of anger and defiance feature prominently throughout *The
Island Means Minago*. The volume focuses especially on the land-
lord/tenant struggles in early nineteenth-century Prince Edward
Island, which Acorn describes as one of the "Canadian revolutions...
which historians solemnly state never happened, but actually took up
most of the nineteenth century" (9). Many of the poems in this collection Acorn also adapted to a stage play, with music composed by
Cedric Smith, *The Road to Charlottetown* (produced 1977, published
1998), which reveals through political caricatures and stage artifice
reminiscent of 1930s agitprop the continuing influence on Acorn of
the partisan Communist conception of creative literature. The play
also reflects the more specific influence of Acorn's first editor,
Margaret Fairley, for his search for the revolutionary spirit in Prince
Edward Island history resembles Fairley's own exploration of the rev-

olutionary tradition in the Canadian past, especially in the political dissent of William Lyon Mackenzie.

Like Acorn, George Ryga continued throughout his writing career to exploit many of the literary themes and formal strategies he learned as a member of the Party. In 1956 he dropped out of the LPP, partly in opposition to the Soviet intervention in Hungary, and partly because like Acorn he wanted to move on to new literary challenges. But his writing remained rooted in the tradition of social and socialist realist political art he had learned in his days as a student under the Marxist instructor Burton James at the Banff Centre, and as a member of the National Federation of Labor Youth. Again like Acorn, his loyalty to certain basic Marxist ideas of literature and society can be demonstrated by reference to works he originally conceived when he was a Communist, and prepared for publication or revised after he had left the Party. He began work on early drafts of his novels, *Hungry Hills* (1963) and *Ballad of a Stonepicker* (1966), for instance, while he was still a member of the LPP; both were republished in slightly revised editions, in 1974 and 1976 respectively. From early drafts to revised editions, Ryga maintained certain ideological inclinations and artistic techniques that are consistent with Communist conceptions of literature. As one commentator on the political dimension of his art has noted, Ryga combines individual psychology with a public message by frequently focusing on the persona of an outsider who is persecuted for his political convictions (Innes 15). Although both *Hungry Hills* and *Ballad of a Stonepicker* place a strong emphasis on individual character through the use of first-person narration, both also focus on a sense of hopelessness among its working-class characters that recalls much of the social and socialist realist fiction of the 1920s and 1930s. And both novels eventually make explicit through the speeches and actions of the characters a Marxist conception of the social struggle.

In his representation of this struggle, Ryga focuses on the people he knows from his own background, the rural poor. Like some of the Canadian social realist novels of the late 1940s and early 1950s, *Hungry Hills* is set in the period that was especially bad for these people, the Great Depression. Ryga begins with emphasis on the individualist perspective: the main character, having been battered and rejected by a poverty-stricken rural society, returns to his family's farm after some years, determined to assert by fair means or foul his right to the materialistic comfort of a permanent home. The struggle merely sinks him deeper into the degradation of poverty and vice until, near the end of the novel, his elderly aunt tries to encourage him by telling how some of the farmers of her generation discovered the power of collective action. She remembers how a farmers' protest against low prices for farm produce merely provoked brutal oppression from the government and police. But, says the aunt, this was the beginning of change:

> "For one thing, the whole community started to work and think together—not like here, where one neighbour don't know another, an' every family is afraid of itself. They really got through—used to come together into the schoolyard on Sundays, and everybody would talk and argue about how we needed better roads an' fertilizer for the fields, weed killer, and all that sort of thing. Then the Ukes [Ukrainians] used to sing, playing their mandolins, an' the girls dancing....We were all poor as hell, but when you laughed it made it easier." (167)

The image of rural community is very similar to the setting and action of Dorise Nielsen's 1953 *New Frontiers* short story about rural Saskatchewan, "The Dance."

*Ballad of a Stonepicker* also emphasizes individual psychology through first-person narration, but sets up a social contrast through the farmer protagonist's attempts to explain to an apparently indifferent researcher from the city something of the struggles and sufferings involved in subsistence farming. The farmer's memories of his dead brother reveal the futility of the dream of transcending class imperatives through education, for the brother's suicide as a student at Oxford has demonstrated the virtual impossibility of escaping the confinement of class through the pursuit of individualistic initiatives. The persistence of a peasantry in a supposedly prosperous first-world society, the narrator indicates, is a national social problem sustained by the greed of the exploiting class and the indifference and shame of the victims. "How many people are there in Canada in the same boat as me? Living on a farm off which they'll never make a thousand dollars a year?...You don't know, because the poorer a man gets the less

he wants to talk about how little he's got" (93). Like the physician
who, the farmer recalls, pressed him rudely for payment of his
bill (94), Canadian society regards everything from farm produce to
medical services as market commodities to enrich the haves at the
expense of the have-nots. In the end, the rural poor are stripped of
everything but their sense of communal and family solidarity, and
their will to survive:

> People born generations to earth know about seed, water and sun
> without being told. They can suffer the kind of pain that sends a
> city-bred man to suicide, and they come out of it a little more
> bent and wrinkled, but still doing those things that give food and
> shelter to themselves and their children. (110)

If Ryga's fiction is indebted to social and socialist realism of the
1930s, 1940s and 1950s, the stage plays with which he eventually
made his most prominent artistic mark can be related to another
artistic form from the same decades: agitprop. His most famous and
successful work, *The Ecstasy of Rita Joe* (first produced 1967, published 1971), for example, use the choric characters, ritual movements, and stylized repetitive speeches and scenes common to the
political plays of the 1930s. But if Ryga saw performances of agitprop
drama in England, where he came in contact with Joan Littlewood's
theatre, or in Canada, where Communist drama groups made sporadic attempts to revive agitprop in the 1950s, he for the most part
avoided the comic and satiric elements so often characteristic of the
form. *The Ecstasy of Rita Joe,* like most of Ryga's fiction and drama, is
a relentlessly grim testament to the poverty, injustice, and human misery imposed by an irresponsible system on the weakest members of
society. *Rita Joe* singles out the most marginalized group of all, the
native people. And as their suffering is intense, Ryga suggests, so is
their capacity to survive. Like the oppressed Japanese farm workers in
Louise Harvey's 1953 *New Frontiers* story "Oh My Lovely Kimi,"
Ryga's native people try to sustain each other by love and a recognition of their communal heritage. The world of white middle-class
officialdom, by contrast—the commodifying world of courts, police,
social workers, and even of sympathizers like the choric folk singer
who represents the white conception of artistry—is much more inter-

ested in the solipsistic assertion of its own values than in reaching out to understand the lives and values of others. As in much of the radical writing of earlier decades, the world of the oppressed class is characterized by manifestations of confinement, entrapment, and sinister threats to their safety and security. Although nature and their own community offer Ryga's native people the illusion of freedom, in the end there is no release but in death.

• • • • •

Throughout the 1960s and 1970s numerous periodicals emerged (and often rapidly submerged) to provide literary outlets for the New Left. *Canadian Dimension* (1963-) and *This Magazine* (1967-) devoted themselves primarily to news and editorial commentary from a non-partisan leftist perspective, but both publications provided space for poets and literary reviewers. The *Canadian Jewish Outlook* (1963-) is a similar magazine of leftist social and political comment, with the ethnic specialization indicated in the title. The *Outlook* has occasionally included poems and short stories by radical Jewish writers, although its literary component more frequently features work from the United States and Europe. *New Canada* (c. 1970) was a newspaper for the ultra-nationalist Canadian Liberation Movement; Milton Acorn was associated in Vancouver with the little magazine *Blackfish* (1971-75), a literary journal committed to the same movement. In the early 1970s Dorothy Livesay tried her hand at a periodical that would establish continuity between current postmodern Canadian literary activity and the socially conscious writing of earlier decades. The same retrospective impulses that led her to compile the memoir/anthology *Right Hand Left Hand* (1977) prompted her in 1975 to establish *Contemporary Verse II* (*CVII*), a magazine supposedly concerned with the current state of Canadian poetry, but with its roots in the politically radical past. From the beginning, however, *CVII* was an ill-defined hybrid. Livesay had served as an assistant editor on the original *Contemporary Verse* (1941-52), established in Vancouver by Alan Crawley, which had been primarily intended as an outlet for the work of poets; *CVII* was described in the subtitle of the first issue as "a quarterly of Canadian Poetry Criticism." Expressing reservations about contemporary poetry of "introspection" and work that might be labeled "metaphysical" or "absurdist," she called for poetry "that best expresses our craving for confrontation with the real, with direct, day-to-day living" ("A Putting Down of Roots," 2). This appeal for a revived social realism she supplements by a declared intention to include in the magazine a series of "retrospectives," the first of which, in the same issue, is a transcript of a recent interview with Joe Wallace. The second issue includes the reminiscences of Merwin Marks, a Communist jailed in 1940 under the War Measures Act. The May 1976 issue is devoted entirely to the 1930s, and includes Livesay's own essay "Canadian Poetry and the Spanish Civil War," and an autobiographical memoir of a former member of the Young Communist League. But if Livesay intended to inspire a new "poetry of the real" and a critical tradition to go with it, this nostalgic fascination with the 1930s was not an effective means of achieving these aims. Although she attracted a few young Marxist poets and reviewers, many of the contributors and editorial associates ignored or resisted the radical element; by 1978 the magazine was dominated by the advocates and practitioners of a postmodern poetry of "introspection," and Livesay had given up the editorship.

By the mid-1970s a new generation of political radicals, born during or immediately after the Second World War, had emerged on the Canadian literary scene, but these new radicals often had little more interest in the Old Left than the young editors of *CVII*. These activists brought new vigour to the culture of political protest, but many of them also rejected or ignored the historical continuity of this culture. At their extreme, they espoused an anarchistic individualism emphasizing a right to self-expression and self-gratification that could be completely opposed to the communal ideals fundamental to traditional socialist movements. In creative writing, this centralization of the self was in contrast to the traditional Communist literary tendency—to be seen, for instance, in the poetry of Joe Wallace—to conceive the self as a source of weakness, which was to be overcome by a commitment to the collective struggle. The individualism of the New Left was in its worst forms derived from the self-obsession encouraged by American popular culture and entertainment of the 1960s. But it was also a sign of the new intellectual energy resulting from the rapid expansion of education, as new universities and enlarged campuses burgeoned across Canada and post-secondary education became accessible to thousands more young people than had been the case in the past. The new masses of university students brought new elements to Canadian progressive thought and action. In the United States and Britain, many of the most influential radicals of earlier decades came from university backgrounds, but in Canada, scholars like Margaret Fairley and Stanley Ryerson were exceptions in what was overwhelmingly a proletarian movement. By the mid-1960s, Canadian university students had followed the example of their counterparts in the US and, joining the protest against the US involvement in the Vietnam War, soon became the principal advocates of revolutionary change in Canadian society. To a great extent, however, their protests were directed not against the capitalists and politicians who wielded the real power, but against the teachers and university administrators who appeared as the immediate epitome of the authoritarianism that the students denounced as the great modern evil. By the late 1960s, many new revolutionary groups had emerged, most of them established on the university campuses. Students for a Democratic University, a more narrowly focused counterpart of the US-based Students for a Democratic Society, attempted to unify the protest movements on the campuses. In the wake of the Sino-Soviet split, the "Communist Party of Canada (Marxist-Leninist)" declared its loyalty to the ideological interpretations and practices of the China of Mao Zedong. The ultra-nationalist Canadian Liberation Movement protested the US economic and cultural domination of Canada, especially through the recent importation of academics and technocrats who were seen as the representatives of a new form of imperialism. These and many other organizations and publications, some of which appeared and disappeared with rapidity, competed for public attention as the new wave of radical revolution in Canadian society. As the international Communist movement failed to keep pace with this kind of change, the CPC found itself degenerating rapidly in the public perception as one fringe group among many.

The political agenda of the New Left, particularly as expressed on Canadian post-secondary campuses and through student organizations, was proclaimed by various spokespersons in a 1970 collection of essays, *The New Left in Canada*, edited by D.J. Roussopoulos. A comparable manifesto volume relating to the literary New Left, *In Our Own House: Social Perspectives on Canadian Literature*, edited by Paul Cappon, appeared in 1978. The contributors to *In Our Own House* were mostly university teachers and scholars, all with intellectual and some with partisan ties to established Marxist and Marxist-Leninist traditions, but as the subtitle of the volume suggested, the perspectives that most of them brought to Canadian literature derived not from literary theory, history, and criticism but from the social sciences. The book was, in the words of its editor and principal contributor, an attempt to develop a "sociology of Canadian literature," based on "a general theoretical position [of] historical materialism" (10). Concerned primarily with the social origins of works of art and how they propagate social meanings, the contributors seldom illustrated their generalizations with specific references to literary texts. Only the few literary scholars among the contributors were prepared to make detailed suggestions as to how creative works by both liberal bourgeois and politically progressive authors could be read in the light of current political concerns as works of art rather than merely as social documents. In "Marxist Literary Criticism and English-Canadian Literature" Robin Endres addresses readers presumed to have little familiarity with Marxist literary theory, but effectively applies the basic principles of that theory to various nineteenth- and twentieth-century Canadian texts. Focusing on the concept of "alienation" as a dominant unifying element in Canadian literature, Endres shows how the Marxist social meaning of the term contrasts to the meaning conveyed by non-Marxist writers who are only concerned with the psychological and emotional experience of individuals. Many nineteenth-century Canadian literary works condemn the alienation of workers within the capitalist system, as Alexander McLachlan's poems do, for instance, or create visions of ultimate transcendence of them in utopian unity, as Crawford's "Malcolm's Katie" or Oliver Goldsmith's "The Rising Village" do. The best twentieth-century Canadian writers, such as Dorothy Livesay, Raymond Souster, and Margaret Laurence, Endres goes on to suggest, have avoided the escapist elements of bourgeois literary modernism to make direct assaults on the pervasive experience of alienation. But Endres finds less reassuring qualities in the work of one of the most popular and influential of modern Canadian writers, Margaret Atwood. In her novels, and more explicitly in *Survival: A Thematic Guide to Canadian Literature* (1972), Atwood suggests that alienation in modern literature is more accurately represented as an internal condition that arises from the individual protagonist's weaknesses of character, and the solutions to this alienation lie in individual efforts of will. "Atwood's political position," Endres argues, "on the surface fashionably radical, is bourgeois individualism. Her solution to cultural oppression is not collective struggle, but 'the creative non-victim position'" (113). Atwood's literary criticism and fiction feature a renewed version of the blame-the-victim attitude to poverty and injustice found in some bourgeois social realist fiction of the 1930s.

Another literary scholar among the contributors to *In Our Own House*, Robin Mathews, expresses an equally emphatic opposition to the conception of Canadian culture expounded by Atwood and by Atwood's mentor, Northrop Frye. Mathews's essay on "Developing a Language of Struggle" is one of several polemical studies of US imperialism and the failures of Canadian cultural and political nationalism that he wrote, beginning in the 1960s. Not a doctrinaire Marxist, Mathews uses Marxist and other ideological concepts in the cause of liberating Canadian intellectualism from American capitalist and imperialist assumptions about the nature of individualism and society. Mathews sees the main task of Canadian literary criticism as "developing a language of struggle" to counteract the unreflecting acceptance of neo-colonial values by many twentieth-century Canadian writers. Authors such as Hugh MacLennan, Morley Callaghan, Margaret Laurence, and Adele Wiseman, says Mathews, have all treated "serious Leftist activity in capitalist Canada as a kind of whimsy or aberration" (140), and have never recognized the significance of Canada's subservience to British, French, and ultimately American imperial power. Such writers frequently express the desire for "harmonious community" as an elemental urge in the national character (143), but reject the class analysis of Canadian society that would reveal the ultimate means of achieving this community.

In a subsequent collection of his essays, *Canadian Literature: Surrender or Revolution* (1978), Mathews especially attacks the economic and cultural domination of Canada by foreign ideas and meth-

ods, especially those imported from the United States. Like Margaret
Fairley in the 1950s, Mathews identifies the resistance to imperialism
as a dominant theme in Canadian literature from the eighteenth century onward, and advocates critical strategies for the reading of literary texts in the light of this theme. Insisting on the importance of
developing a distinctive Canadian literary voice, Mathews criticizes
writers like Morley Callaghan and Hugh MacLennan for their acceptance of assumptions about society and literature that arise from for-
eign-dominated economic and cultural power groups. With particular vehemence he attacks Northrop Frye, "one of the worst—certainly
one of the most arrogant—critics of Canadian literature" (136). Frye,
says Mathews, denies the possibility of a national art whose principal
virtues lie in its uniqueness. Postulating a vague moral and political
liberalism that he assumes to be universally valid, Frye approves only
those literary texts that appear to be consistent with such liberalism,
and dismisses as parochial Canadian attempts to develop a national
literary expression. "Americanization" is for Frye merely a misnomer
for powerful trends of homogenization that are absorbing all societies,
including that of the United States. But for Mathews, Americanization
is a very real and sinister imperialist process carried out by the US
media, educational establishments, and colonizing representatives
who through the 1960s and 1970s have made a concerted effort to
seize control of Canadian culture and make it conform to US values
and assumptions.

Besides being a prolific essayist, Mathews is one of several
Canadian authors in the post-1960 era to use the drama as a means
of political protest. Like their predecessors of the 1920s and 1930s,
the dramatists of the New Left have inclined toward both social realism and a revival of something like agitprop. Among the realists, one
of the most prominent is David Fennario (b. 1947), who has drawn
on his own working-class background to create such plays as *On the
Job* (1976) and *Nothing to Lose* (1977), which present the language
and action of workers with mimetic fidelity, and place their lives in a
context of radical—and sometimes explicitly Marxist—political ideology. The agitprop revival, by contrast, as theatre historian Alan
Filewood has documented, has been a collective and sometimes
improvisational art like its 1930s counterpart, with the emphasis on

performance and on the variable judgements of the actors and director, more than on the fixed conceptions of the literary text of a single author. Directly inspired by *Eight Men Speak*, the agitprop plays of the 1960s and afterward have often served to express leftist ideas on the class struggle and Canadian history and nationalism (Filewood, 19-20).

Probably the best-known example of New Left agitprop drama is Rick Salutin's *1837*. First produced in 1973 as *1837: The Farmers' Revolt*, the play presented characters and events in exaggerated and often incongruous terms, emphasizing its own artifices by means of vaudevillian dialogue and sight gags, cross-gendered role playing, brief snapshot-like episodes, narrative speeches, direct orations to the audience, and songs. An example of the "documentary theatre" phenomenon that emerged in the 1960s and that Alan Filewood has effectively analyzed, the play was evidently a collective creation of the Theatre Passe Muraille company, based on improvisation from a flexible outline rather than a fixed script. For publication, however, Salutin prepared an authoritative text of the play combined with a virtually book-length historical essay, under the title *1837: William Lyon Mackenzie and the Canadian Revolution* (1976). In both the play and the essay Salutin takes an irreverent view of the rebellion. Although having carefully studied Margaret Fairley's edition of Mackenzie's writings, Salutin sees his subject in terms closer to William Kilbourn's representation of Mackenzie and the rebellion as ludicrous anomalies in Canadian history. Like Kilbourn and unlike Fairley, he has little praise for Mackenzie's strengths as a political thinker and writer. Nor does he share Fairley's orthodox Marxist view that Mackenzie's rebellion was a stage in the development of the liberal bourgeois democracy that Marx saw as a necessary antecedent to proletarian revolution. He rejects the view of modern liberal historians that Mackenzie contributed toward the evolution of responsible government, for he regards as an impossibility the whole idea of Canada achieving self-rule while remaining an appendage to an imperial power. Emphasizing Mackenzie's achievements and writings of the 1830s and especially his participation in the rebellion, Salutin insists that the 1837 rebellion should be regarded as an unsuccessful nationalist revolution. Like the Canadian nationalists of the 1960s and 1970s who sought their country's independence from the political, economic, and cultural domination of the United States, Mackenzie's chief goal was political independence. "The upshot of this argument," says Salutin, "must be...that Canada has never yet gained independence" (79). "Mackenzie was not our George Washington, our Gandhi or our Mao. He failed, but what can you do—he was the best we've had so far. When the country is finally free, it will be because we've had better heroes" (179-80).

In their emphasis on Canadian nationalism, writers like Mathews and Salutin have much in common with the Québec francophones of the so-called "quiet revolution." In his *Social Realism in the French-Canadian Novel*, Ben-Z. Shek has emphasized the continuity between post-1960 Quebec indépendentiste creative writers and earlier social realists such as Gabrielle Roy and Roger Lemelin. Analogies of technique and theme between these two groups can be readily discovered, just as they can be in the work of the new and old leftists in English Canada. But an understanding of Québecois indépendentiste creative writing in terms of its relevance to the evolution of New Left politics in Canada must also be based on the distinctive elements of post-1960s work. As Malcolm Reid has demonstrated in *The Shouting Signpainters* (1972), the young Québecois writers who emerged in the 1960s did not share their predecessors' fascination with European social realism, but they were radically politicized to a much greater extent than their predecessors. Although earlier writers like Roy and Lemelin condemned the autocratic power of the Church and corrupt governments in Quebec and lamented the province's colonial status, they seldom referred favourably to socialist solutions or had recourse to the kind of Marxist class analysis of Quebec society that Stanley Ryerson had used in his *French Canada*, for instance. The generation of the 1960s, on the other hand, did use Marxist revolutionary ideas and rhetoric. But this rhetoric was inspired by a narrowly nationalistic political base, rather than by the ideals of international Communism. The historical event that galvanized these young indépendentistes toward revolutionary ideology was not the Depression or the Spanish Civil War and anti-fascism, or even the concept of the international anti-colonial struggle, but a much more local event, the 1949 strike in the Quebec mining town of Asbestos.

As an anti-colonial movement focused on the economic disadvantages of Québecois vis-à-vis powerful industrial employers and foreign political institutions, the new Quebec revolutionary cause had a basis in class conflict. The novelists and poets, even though they mostly came from the university intelligentsia like their English-Canadian counterparts, frequently identified themselves with and wrote about the working class. Novelists like Jacques Renaud, in his novel *Le Cassé* (1964), attempted to elevate *joual,* the slang of the lower classes, to a literary language; Claude Jasmin and others turned the exploits of the terrorists of the Front de libération du Québec (FLQ) into existentialist images of the historical sufferings of the Québecois; poets and dramatists attempted to convey the esoteric qualities of Québecois life that distanced that life from the materialistic ideals of their foreign capitalistic exploiters. These postmodern nationalistic efforts were tentatively linked to earlier progressive literary activity when in 1965 *Parti Pris* editions undertook the publication of a new novel by the long-silent Jean-Jules Richard, *Le Journal d'un hobo.* Based on the author's experiences during the 1930s Depression, the novel superficially appears to belong to the same retrospective impulses that were to inspire Livesay's *Right Hand Left Hand* and other English-Canadian works in the 1970s. Like Richard's first novel, *Neuf jours de haine,* furthermore, *Le Journal* appears to be concerned with multi-regional and multicultural Canada: the central character, though a francophone, is from the maritimes, rather than Quebec, and the emphasis is on his reactions to all regions of the country. But as Malcolm Reid has pointed out, the novel can be read—as it undoubtedly was read by the *Parti Pris* editors—as a "grotesque allegory on French-Canadian alienation" in the context of an overwhelmingly "Anglo-Saxon" continent (194). The bisexual hero is neither one thing nor another, and belongs nowhere, like the fluently bilingual Québecois who tries vainly to function in both anglophone and francophone societies.

Ultimately, as the work of Richard and the younger *joual* writers demonstrates, the primary basis of the postmodern Quebec literary and political revolution is ethnicity, not class. Although proclaiming their leftist political orientation and often expressing sympathy with an exploited proletariat, the Quebec New Left most commonly regarded its conflict in the terms explicitly articulated by the critic Gilles Lefebvre in a 1962 essay, which defined the Québecois "proletariat" as having "an industrial relationship of inferiority vis-à-vis the Anglo-Saxons" (qtd. in Shek, 98). The Quebec literary New Left, like the pre-1960s francophone social realism, is best studied in its distinctive ethnic context. In rare instances, individual writers from one group might expressed solidarity with the other or adapt the other's historical and political circumstances to their own literary purposes. The Montreal Jewish novelist Herman Buller, for instance, found in Québecois historical and modern crises material appropriate to his interest in the alienated individual within an intolerant and politically corrupt society. His *Quebec in Revolt* (1965, rpt. 1966) exposes nineteenth-century ecclesiastical tyranny and bigotry not by reference to the 1837 Lower Canada rebellion, but by a retelling of the little-known Guibord affair, in which the church exploited its power over the Québecois mass population to persecute a religious dissenter. Buller's *Days of Rage* (1974), on the other hand, deals with a political fanatic within the modern FLQ, and shows how the extremism provoked by a corrupt and violent society can destroy the person who espouses it. Although Buller's novels might be dismissed as oversimplified political thrillers, they have provided English-Canadian readers with clear and very readable introductions to Québecois political issues.

This survey of Canadian creative writing of the New Left is offered only as a representative outline of some of the trends that emerged after 1960, with particular emphasis on major points of continuity and distinction between the new and old radical movements. But it is essential to include one of the most important developments, the emergence of literary activity that unites radical political ideology with feminism. Although this is another topic that could be extended to volume length, Canadian Marxist feminist writing will here be represented by only three writers, all of whom are important for their creative achievements in their own right as well as for their effective demonstration of the New Left feminist position: Pat Lowther, Sharon Stevenson, and Helen Potrebenko.

Pat Lowther (1935-75), born into a British Columbia working-class family, left high school in her teens for clerical employment. In 1963, after an early failed marriage, she married Roy Lowther, a very

minor poet who had belonged to the LPP in the 1950s and had contributed to *New Frontiers*. Possibly influenced by Lowther, but
inspired mostly by her own working-class background and by the
general atmosphere of the 1960s, she became involved in political
activism, for the most part through the left wing of the New
Democratic Party (NDP). While writing and studying creative writing
part-time, she published poems in various little magazines as well as
three volumes of her own work. Some of her most explicitly politicized—and arguably her best—poems appeared in the volume she
prepared for the press before her untimely death, *A Stone Diary*
(1977). Like Dorothy Livesay, who became a friend and promoter of
her work, Lowther demonstrates with effective clarity the interaction
of the personal and political sides of the poetic consciousness. A wide
and serious reader, her familiarity with Freud and Darwin, as well as
Marx, is reflected in her emphasis on dreamlike barren landscapes
that suggest emotional and spiritual desolation, geological and evolutionary concepts related to the vastness of time and the limitations of
human life, and allusions that point to such socio-political evils as
capitalist exploitation and the pervasiveness of neo-fascism in the
modern world. In "Rumors of War," for instance, historical political
evil is evoked by a memory of a child's vague nightmare impression
of German Nazism during the Second World War:

> ...I dreamed a black forest
> moving across a map,
> I and my rag doll
> caught on the coast edge
> of the country
> I was too young
> even to name
>
> . . . . . . . . . .
>
> and Raggedy Ann
> and I woke screaming
> out of the clutch of
> evil trees. (*A Stone Diary* 10)

In "Chacabuco, the Pit," a series of poems about the CIA-sponsored
overthrow of Allende's Marxist government in Chile, the tropical
landscape typically associated with holiday escapism is at first identi-

fied with unreal mystery and horror, like the sacrificial murders in old "1940s movies" (17). But this romantic image of Chile is superceded by the public reports of dungeons, blank-faced guards, starving prisoners, torture, and murder. The poem goes on to refer to the revolutionary dreamers who woke "to find all their good wishes/happening faster/than they could move" and to contrast them with the neo-fascists who moved quickly to dispel the new freedom with murder and torture. The conclusion of the poetic sequence includes a reminder not only of the reality of the unthinkable, but also of the need to recognize the universal responsibility for the unthinkable:

> ...the horrors of the mind
> are the horrors of
> what we allow to be done. (26)

In other poems, Lowther takes up public issues with comparable effectiveness. The strikingly titled "Leonard George and, Later, a Rock Band" juxtaposes native spiritualism to North American mass culture with its substructure of capitalist entrepreneurship and electronic gadgetry, and ends by questioning whether the native people achieve freedom by adapting technology to their own creative purposes or are merely made subservient to it. "The Earth Sings Mi-Fa-Mi" raises political evil to a cosmic level as the hopeful chants and mimetic movements of people protesting the Vietnam War are superceded by the imagined lamentation of a planet overwhelmed by misery and famine. Conversely, in "Face," evil is presented in terms of human weakness, through the description of a politician seen in the sweaty flesh as opposed to the cool distortions usually viewed on television. The insignificance of human ambition, greed, and lust for power is further exposed in "Coast Range." The mountains retain their transcendent importance in spite of attempts to subject them to selfish human purposes. Their presence is real, as opposed to the merely metaphorical significance of human action. Even if human beings "reduce them to slag,"

> the shapes they've made in the sky
> cannot be reduced. (37)

The high poetic point of *A Stone Diary* is probably the sequence of elegaic poems addressed to the dead Chilean poet Pablo Neruda. Conceiving Neruda as absorbed into nature as "an element imperishable in earth," and unified with geological antiquity as "the man who kisses stone," Lowther emphasizes the need for all poets to reach beyond the world of appearance, beyond the "metaphorical" world of human action with its characteristic patterns of hatred and cruelty. Both as a poet and as a spiritual presence, Neruda has achieved perfect affinity with Nature, and can decipher its meaning.

> Are you there
> always at the centre
> like Buddha contemplating
> the heart
> of the plural self? ("Letter to Pablo" 55)

In the "Last Letter to Pablo," Lowther emphasizes again how Neruda has transcended the world of atrocities and disease, to be reunited with "your substance," the earth. The poet stands finally for the ability to merge with all life forms, to find life everywhere:

> dark jewel of history
> the planet carries you
> a seed patient as time. (58)

In these poems Lowther goes far beyond mere political statement, to adapt her idea of the poet's function in a strife-ridden but ephemeral world to her vision of a noumenous existence where the creative element merges with the spiritual and eternal. In a comparable—though not similar—way, her ideas on women and the feminist movement move beyond the public political level. Avoiding a rhetoric of collective activism, Lowther's meditations on female psychological and emotional experience are reminiscent of those of the American poet Sylvia Plath, especially in the emphasis on violence and death. Her preoccupation with the primeval, through geological images and allusions, is evident in her title poem "A Stone Diary," but the continuing emotional element in her metaphysics of feminism appears to be woman's yearning for love and her awareness of the dangers of it. "Inheritance" relates women to time through an evocation of the continuity between generations. "To a Woman Who Died of 34 Stab Wounds" eerily prefigures Lowther's own violent death in a representation of women victimized by male jealousy of the female ability to endure time and change. "Kitchen Murder," by contrast, turns the tables on male violence in a fantasy of female empowerment comparable to Plath's "Lady Lazarus."

Sharon Stevenson (1946-78) is a much less metaphysical poet than Lowther, more directly concerned with public questions and with the specifics of her own political experience. At the same time, however, her poetry reflects techniques and preoccupations of postmodern creative writing that distinguish it from the poetry of earlier socialists and Communists. Born in Northern Ontario of a working-class family, Stevenson continued both her political and academic education in the 1960s, at the universities of Toronto, Alberta, and British Columbia. Although she joined the old-line CPC, she left it in the early 1970s to join the Maoist "Communist Party of Canada (Marxist-Leninist)." A frequent contributor to little magazines, she published only one book, *Stone* (1972) before her death by suicide. *Gold Earrings: Selected Poetry* was edited by a group of friends and published in 1984 with an introduction by Robin Endres. As the work in this posthumous volume suggests, many of her poems are meditations on historical moments or periods in her personal life, in working-class history, and in Canadian and international political history. A sampling of her work also suggests that Stevenson's early Marxist-Leninist education became complicated by many uncertainties: about the political power of the working class; the contradictions between Marxism and feminism; the conflict between the intuitive inclinations of the poetic imagination and Marxist linear rational and historical thinking; and about the Marxist-Leninist legitimacy of the Stalinist and post-Stalinist regimes in the USSR.

In the poem "Stone" (the title perhaps alluding to the proverbial substitution in response to an urgent request for bread), Stevenson recalls or imagines various historical moments in Communist history: the death of Stalin in 1953; the Khrushchev anti-Stalin revelations in 1956, including details about the prison camps that had apparently existed since the 1930s; and finally, her uncertainties of the present moment:

us still here
wondering what to do
1971
no models/no truths revealed (*Gold Earrings* 25)

Her personal memories could also provide her with a symbol of the
strength of the Marxist-Leninist tradition. In "The Third International"
she recalls from her childhood a birch tree that grew out of the rocky
ground in the Northern Ontario city of Sudbury. Blending the terminology of radical politics with romantic storybook images,

We called it the Third International
it grew shining white as
        any chivalrous knight's horse. (26)

The tree is also associated in the child's imagination with aboriginal
and geographical antiquity as well as with nature's imperviousness
"to men in power," and even "to the slag piling up/around its lower
branches." In the end, however, the tree is consumed by a fire started
by molten slag, and although its annihilation is described in the
imagery of a heroic funeral pyre, the "Third International" is still
destroyed by the power of industrial capitalism. "What Slag Is Made
Of" is a similar recollection of childhood, in which she recalls how
the ugly word is associated with the death of fathers killed in industrial accidents, and the exhaustion of working-class mothers. These
consequences, especially the life of the mother trapped in a prolonged
sequence of domestic labour, represent a dismal but clear factual
contrast to the dialectic of the radical socio-economic theory that
would purport to solve the problems of such people.

In other poems, Stevenson addresses specific political problems
from her own period of mature radicalization, the late 1960s and
early 1970s. "Closer to the Bone" is a poem about the October Crisis
of 1970, and the invocation of the War Measures Act. The poem for-
tuitously echoes Marcus Adeney's 1942 poem "Sirens," which
appeared in Margaret Fairley's *Spirit of Canadian Democracy*. Instead
of Adeney's concluding note of hope, however, Stevenson's poem converges on failure and loss, as the lives of young people in 1970 are
distanced by bureaucratic tyranny even further from the visions of
empowerment and independence they pursue. In the more personal

"Sometimes I Talk in American," the poet acknowledges the necessity of adopting the rhetoric that is the public language not only of bourgeois society, but of any context involving "leadership and power." The only times she does not "talk in American," in fact, are in those personal moments of romantic love, or of intellectual gratification, or of artistic creativity. "Poetry Too Has a Class Nature" similarly divides the personal and the political, but reveals the insidious aspects of the process, by suggesting that "the bourgeoisie" encourages writers to internalize their emotions about society and politics, to write meditative lyrics that will "help things stay as they are." But it is clear to Stevenson that "poetry too is part of the fight" against US neo-fascism and Soviet "social-imperialism." Women's empowerment is for Stevenson also part of the fight, and the prospects for such empowerment can sometimes inspire her to the hopeful rhetoric reminiscent of early Communist poetry. "Down with the Theory of Human Nature" is a criticism of liberals, academics, and journalists who persist in seeing class distinctions as mere reflections of "human nature." There is no preordained definition of what constitutes "human," Stevenson argues; throughout history there is only the tendency of the ruling classes to exploit the masses:

> & etched through all of this,
> Women have stood, turbulent property.

In modern times, both women and men are slaves to money power, which has reduced even love to a commodity. In the end, she appeals to her "dear sisters" to recognize the rising storm of revolution.

> & now at last down
> the long night of exploitation in history
> comes trundling freedom
> carried by class struggle to bright day (87)

Of all New Left Canadian writers, Helen Potrebenko (b. 1940) is the most explicitly and extensively committed to the conjunction of Marxism and feminism. Born in Alberta of Ukrainian working-class parents, Potrebenko attended the University of British Columbia, supporting herself by driving taxi in Vancouver. She has subsequently worked as a lab technician and most frequently, as a part-time office worker, while devoting much of her energies to writing. Her books have included the prose fiction *Taxi* (1975), *Sometimes They Sang* (1986) and *Hey Waitress and Other Stories* (1989); a history of Ukrainians in Canada, *No Streets of Gold* (1977), and the poetry collections *Walking Slow* (1985) and *Riding Home* (1995), as well as other volumes. A witty and original author, almost all her poetry and fiction involve the wryly recounted adventures of women attempting to survive in a male-dominated capitalist society that relegates women to economic and sexual inferiority. Well read in Marxism and the history of the labour movement, Potrebenko uses ideological concepts from her reading and experiences, while often emphasizing the limitations of formal partisan theory and practice.

Her first published book, the novel *Taxi* (1975), is both a satirical and grimly realistic episodic account of the experiences of a young woman named Shannon working as a cab driver in Vancouver. The opening scene, involving Shannon's futile attempt to help a drunken and battered woman derelict, establishes the ambience of the work. At first naively confident in the moral and rational patterns of social existence and inspired by her politically radical beliefs, Shannon aspires to intervene against the victimization of women, children, and the poor at the hands of the mainly male, economically dominant class. But her own exhausting struggles to survive economically, as well as the accumulated experience of arrogance and insensitivity in male-dominated society and of the fatalism of society's victims, are reducing her to cynicism. Her political rhetoric has become a passing reaction to routine inconvenience—"After the revolution we'll have public washrooms" (4)—and she regularly takes refuge in alcohol. Although she can look on and pity the miseries of the very poor from the slight social elevation of regular employment, her own life has been burdened by struggles to get an education and to survive on the inadequate income to which working-class women are still restricted in the 1960s and 1970s. By the early 1970s, as the transitory prosperity of the preceding decade recedes, the sufferings of proletarian women have become part of a general socio-economic degeneration:

> The streets acquired more people having nowhere to sleep. Despair and demoralization increased the crime rate and this

was blamed on police laxness. Drunkenness and dope addiction
increased by phenomenal numbers and more and more people
took their own lives....In Canada, there was the War Measures
Act. Canadians woke up one morning to find all their civil rights
had been taken away from them. English Canadians were
soothed back to sleep again with the assurance that it wasn't
meant for them, and that these laws would be used only on
French Canadians. (11)

The novel frequently features expository passages of this sort, sometimes attributable to the reflections of the central character, sometimes evidently the explicit ideas of the author. But Potrebenko, like
many of the socialist realists of earlier decades, is less interested in
such formal details of fiction as consistency of point of view than in
the importance of clarifying a novels's political implications. She is
especially anxious to establish that fiction, like all forms of commentary on human experience, must be understood in political and socio-
economic terms. As Robin Endres suggests about Atwood's fiction, the
bourgeois novel might pretend to be dealing with such terms, but its
real concern is with human weakness, the willingness to be victimized. If people have become passive in their victimization, says
Potrebenko, the real problem is the relentless and virtually irresistible
aggressiveness of the male-dominated power groups of business and
politics, who have decreed the myths of the inevitability of economic
imbalance between men and women and rich and poor. Apart from
strongly worded condemnations of such myths, Potrebenko offers
only brief and transitory glimmers of hope, as when her taxi driver
encounters a sanely exuberant working-class man who obviously
takes "pride in doing his job well. These are the people, and there are
millions of them, who will take power after the revolution" (103).

Potrebenko's poetry, like her fiction, is formally straightforward
and discursive, consisting usually of vocative appeals and aphoristic
observations in colloquial language on the themes of solidarity against
the social injustice, especially to women workers, perpetrated by
male-dominated government and corporate power. Like Joe Wallace
or Dawn Fraser, she aims to bring poetry to people who ordinarily
would not read poetry; but besides avoiding unnecessary obscurity as
they do, she avoids intimidating readers with self-conscious literary

technique. Her aims include directness, clarity, and simplicity without condescension, as can be seen in this excerpt from "Cheap Labour":

> Don't you hear them talking, sisters?
> Don't you hear them?
> They're talking about cheap labour.
> They're talking about you and me.
>
> When they say fiscal restraint,
> they mean cheap labour.
> When they decide on deficit financing
> they still mean cheap labour.
> When they talk about productivity
> they mean cheap labour.
> When they discourse on monetary reform,
> free trade, balance of payments,
> responsible management,
> wrestling inflation to the ground,
> revitalizing the economy,
> international competitiveness,
> optimum production,
> sound investment climate,
> maintenance of appreciable growth rates,
> they mean cheap labour. (*Life, Love and Unions* 61)

Potrebenko's aesthetic and political aims come together most effectively in *Sometimes They Sang*. Like *Taxi*, this novel reveals both the pervasive decadence of modern society and the possibilities of human revitalization, through the story of a sometimes naive but always vigorously adaptable woman struggling to make her way through the crumbling economic and moral environments of late-twentieth-century Canada. In many ways a latter-day Candide, Odessa Greeneway survives her encounters with the evils of society by means of her innocent determination to fulfill the goals she decides are most worthy of her status as a human being. Echoing the growth and fertility imagery of Candide's decision to "cultivate his own garden," Odessa decides that her main goal in life should be to have a child. She has established this goal at the beginning of her journey, however, as opposed to evolving it along the way, and it becomes the one stable factor in her progress through an unstable and often hostile environment. Her determination to have a child is like the confidence of the main character of *Taxi* in the coming of the revolution—except that the prospect of maternity is for a woman obviously the purest, most optimistic, and most literal of all birth visions, as opposed to the vision of destruction and rebirth that a social revolution conveys. It is both self-centred, like Candide's self-cultivation, and universal, in its fulfilment of the ultimate biological function of women, the propagation of the species.

The context of Odessa's journey toward self-fulfilment, furthermore, is not some vague inward image of individual or universal womanhood, but the materially and historically real world of late twentieth-century Canada. Raised on a farm but obliged to seek her living in cities, she is directly related by her personal background and experience to the novel's many reflections on farming, industrial labour, rural and urban poverty, the exploitation of women and of workers in general, the conflict between capital and labour, and the inequities of capitalist economics. In both its episodic structure and its frequent editorializing *Sometimes They Sang* is clearly in the tradition that can be traced back to the socialist realist and other anti-capitalist fiction of the 1920s and beyond. Potrebenko devotes particular attention to the plight of the rural worker in Canada. Odessa is both a victim and an observer of the expulsion of the farmers from the land and the evolution of so-called "agribusiness" in Canada. "Scientists and universities and conferences endlessly discussed the world food problem caused by overpopulation," the novel editorializes, "while in Canada, farmers were forced from the land and land was taken out of cultivation" (15). But Odessa also finds that movements of social reform and revolution are not prepared to address this particular iniquity of the capitalist system. Socialists, she discovers, "hated peasants just as virulently as did the capitalists" (19). The organized women's movement can be similarly selective in its attitudes and policies. In the 1960s "the personal had been declared political," so it became important to understand one's "personal oppression"; but Odessa soon learns "that she had almost no personal concerns which were also of concern to other women" (22).

When she abandons "rap group" feminism for the New Left, she finds a movement dominated by an overwhelmingly male perspective.

The heroes of the New Left, furthermore, are those who have opted out of society and cannot relate to the practicalities of day-to-day living, let alone the inequities of political economics that oppress workers and the unemployed. Odessa does find, early in the novel, what turns out to be a source of stability and solidarity in group activity, but this activity involves volunteering for a picket line in a seemingly endless and futile strike against a bookstore that has closed its business rather than give in to the demands of a union. Even in this situation, furthermore, she has difficulty making the human connections she seeks, for the other women picketers are enclosed in their own restricted concerns. Only briefly, when she participates in a "take back the night" protest march, does Odessa glimpse the potential power and unity of women. But this image is overridden by the characteristic struggles, failures, and disillusionments of day-to-day experience.

In the end, Odessa finds tentative companionship and feminist unity in the routine commitment of the picket line. Although she has come to realize that "there weren't and couldn't be any simple friendships or clean relationships" (87), she finds emotional strength in the intermittent human contact, the singing, the sense of shared experience. "Sometimes they sang, uncertain voices challenging the rain" (89). At the end of the novel, as at the end of *Taxi*, no changes in either the public or private circumstances of her life have overridden all the contradictions and uncertainties she sees around her. Not only has she not had a child, she remains in spite of many attempts unable to find the necessary prerequisite, a satisfactory relationship with a suitable man. Like the revolution, Odessa's maternity is still somewhere in the vague future, perhaps never to be realized. But as she has come to learn, life is not the achieving of goals but a journey toward a goal. "And she went forth into the world to discover what further adventures awaited" (102).

● ● ● ● ●

Writers like Helen Potrebenko, Robin Mathews, or Milton Acorn in his later years, although sharing the general anti-capitalist perspective and sometimes using socialist realist techniques, are in many ways remote from the partisan Communist writers of earlier decades. Most of the writers on the New Left rejected party politics, or regarded parties as loose democratic assemblages, not as sources of ultimate authority. Most of them accepted ideologies and literary forms that were more or less inspired by or related to Marxism, but they accepted other ideas and techniques as well. Above all, they were often more likely to regard literary activity as a process of raising questions and exploring possibilities, of expressing doubts and ambiguities, rather than of conveying fixed political positions. The New Left was potentially capable of carrying radical political literary activity away from the limitations that had too often characterized the work of writers of the Old Left, and toward many new possibilities. By thus opening out leftist writing, the younger writers of the 1960s and afterward might have more firmly established the anti-capitalist element as a legitimate theme in the Canadian literary tradition. But a precise and detailed evaluation of New Left literary efforts is beyond the scope of this book. This chapter has tried to illustrate merely that the efforts were made, and that they sometimes succeeded with impressive effectiveness. Progressive writing by the late twentieth century had moved far beyond the partisan politics of early decades toward unity with—or possibly absorption by—a larger context of literary modernism and postmodernism.

# Conclusion

In a series of lectures commemorating the centennial of Canadian Confederation, Northrop Frye again dismissed Marxist Communism and its cultural activities as false directions in the development of European-based civilization. *The Modern Century* (published in 1967) is a rumination on the place of art in a world characterized by many forms of conflict, including the conflict between capitalism and Communism. Frye's own loyalties are reflected in the fact that he avoids the words "capitalist" and "capitalism" and refers to the bloc of countries dominated by the United States and the investor-market corporate system as the "democracies," while he uses "Marxism" and "Communism" to describe the political and economic systems of the USSR, the People's Republic of China, Yugoslavia, and their satellites and allies. The main problem with Marxism, according to Frye, is its "optimistic" conception of progress that promises "deliverance from history as history [has] previously been" (44). Ideologies that seem to promise to transform the quality of life, he continues, are like the advertising of Western mass culture. In order to convey a simplified version of its theories to the largest number of people, Marxist Communism, like commercial advertising, relies on idioms and images that Frye calls "stupid realism" (61). These idioms and images, which pretend to offer accurate reflections of life as it is and as it can be, are actually derived from "worn-out Romantic and Victorian formulas" (55). They are parodies of the kinds of artistic realism that dominated much of the nineteenth century. "The 'social [sic] realism' of Communism," Frye concludes, "though much better in theory than [the stereotyped images of capitalist advertising], has in practice much in common with [them]" (61). What socialist realism produces, is "sentimental populism, of a the-people-keep-marching-on type" (75).

Frye's reduction of socialist realism to "sentimental populism" is as oversimplified and uninformed as his opinion expressed fifteen years earlier that proletarian literature was an obsolete vestige of the Depression. He employs the strategy of pseudo-criticism that Barbara Foley attributes to anti-Communist literary theorists and critics in the United States who characterize the allegedly stale formulas of proletarian fiction by reference to unnamed hypothetical novels (*Radical Representations*, chap. 1). Like the commentators that Foley cites, Frye does not produce a single example of the "people-keep-marching-on" literary work; nor does he offer reasons why literary themes and forms developed in the nineteenth century should be regarded as "worn out," or why the Communist adaptations of them should be considered "parodies." "Frye's comments on both the theory and practice of Marxism do no credit to his reputation as a scholar," V.G. Haines wrote with considerable justice in a review of *The Modern Century* in the Winter 1968 issue of the CPC theoretical journal, *Horizons.*.

Yet Frye's opinions were undoubtedly shared by a majority of literary critics in the "democracies," especially in view of the fact that by 1967 the Canadian and international Communist movements were beginning to show signs of a political and cultural debilitation that would continue for the rest of the century. By the mid-1970s some Canadian New Leftists had taken up the project of demonstrating that Marxist-inspired literature could be much more than "sentimental populism," but by the turn of the century the aging survivors of the New Left had lost ground to a younger generation of writers who lacked the political education and the imaginative inclination to continue the struggle. Like most of Canadian society, the fin-de-siècle literary milieu had followed the international trend of accepting capitalism as the self-evidently justifiable and inevitable socio-economic system. Writers and other cultural activists had been largely absorbed into a community that measured achievement in terms of fame and financial return. Politicians and bureaucrats began to refer to the complex of creative art and its administrative substructure as the "culture industries." Artists were encouraged to pursue success in the form of the best-seller or the literary award, just as every worker in the so-called new economy was encouraged to dream of rising to the top of the corporate ladder or, failing that, of winning a million-dollar lottery. Creative people who still professed a commitment to artistic ideals often applied those ideals to introspective, self-indulgent modes of writing that carefully avoided explicit political engagement. The kind of literary activity inspired by the Communist movement more and more appeared as an expression of ideas that were irrelevant to the modern world. If the collapse of the Soviet Union did not mark, in the extravagant phrasing of Francis Fukayama's book title, "the end of history," it certainly went a long way toward discrediting the political, economic, and cultural theories that the USSR had spent almost a century trying to turn into reality.

And yet it is much too facile to sweep the whole tradition of Marxist Communism and its cultural achievements into the dustbin of history. Even Frye goes on in *The Modern Century* to acknowledge that Communist ideology does not inevitably lead to bad art. Significantly, while he is unable to produce any examples of the "stupid realism" he despises, he is readily reminded that Communism can produce a higher form of artistic radicalism, "of the kind that helps to shape the dramas of Brecht and Gorky" (76). Frye was also willing to admit that a culture of opposition was needed to reinforce the values of the "liberal democracy" to which he was committed. As he wrote in a favourable review of Joe Wallace's latest book in 1953, "[it] is most important to keep the tone of genuine anger and contempt at hypocrisy alive in our poetry, no matter where it comes from or from what motives it is uttered" ("Letters in Canada" 1953: 261).

In the twenty-first century a culture of opposition is even more urgently needed, as multinational capitalism in conjunction with reactionary political regimes are consolidating their undemocratic power and treating both representative and participatory governmental institutions as well as the masses of population with contempt. If the ideal of fomenting an international armed revolution against capitalism no longer seems as feasible as it did in the times of Marx and Lenin, there is still a vital need for a creative literature that will help keep people aware of and resistant to the hypocrisy and injustice that are still characteristic of the private enterprise system. The specific social conditions against which the early- and mid-twentieth-century Canadian Communists rebelled may have changed, but this does not mean that the twenty-first century cannot learn from their experience and from the literary texts they produced, in the continuing struggle against new and even more sinister forms of capitalist evil.

This is not to say, as many Communist writers said, that all creative literature should be concerned with Marxist or politically revolutionary ideals. It is important to recall that the official Communist advocacy of a culture concerned exclusively with the theme of class struggle emerged mainly in the early 1930s. Although the doctrine of "socialist realism" continued to be expounded by cultural hard-liners for decades afterward, pluralists within the Communist movement were prepared to recognize that the moral and aesthetic obligations of creative artists could be fulfilled in a variety of ways. There is no really valid reason why Communist culture cannot exist simultaneously with non-Communist culture, or why the two traditions should not mutually influence each other. The idea that the two cultures should ignore—or actively work to obliterate—each other is as distasteful as the Cold War political antagonism that was dedicated to mutual intolerance and, in its worst forms, to mutual annihilation.

It is important that the work of all serious writers should be read and evaluated critically, and granted its appropriate position in literary history. This book has tried to suggest the literary significance of many Canadian writers who were unjustly ignored or condemned because of their political beliefs. The poetry of Joe Wallace, the novels of Dyson Carter, the early work of Dorothy Livesay and Milton Acorn, all the extensive and complex tradition of anti-capitalist creative writing in Canada, are part of the structure of this country's culture and should be read and written about with the same open-mindedness that is presumably applied to those writers who profess other political assumptions. If, furthermore, as some literary theorists have argued, all creative literature regardless of authorial intention fulfills a political purpose, where "politics" is defined broadly as the interaction of people within society and among societies, then surely it is as important to include in literary history creative writing with an explicitly partisan ideology as it is to include writing that presents its ideologies implicitly or indirectly.

One Canadian writer who understood the importance of inclusive-ness in the critical evaluation of literary history was Margaret Fairley. In 1967, Fairley wrote an article for *Horizons*, "The Cultural Worker's Responsibility to the People," which could be taken as a response to Frye's *The Modern Century*. The purpose of all artists in every era and culture, Fairley wrote, is "to enlarge the experience of the people, giv-ing them through thought and feeling a widening and deepening of their whole personalities" (4). The artist's responsibility is not to the private imagination, or even to a hypothetical reader constructed from the artist's own view of what art should be, but to the public social world. Fairley's argument is not about seeking the largest pos-sible audience and thereby courting popularity and financial success. As in all her writing, as in her edition of William Lyon Mackenzie, for instance, she is thinking in terms of creative art as a process of *teach-ing*—a process which people often resist, as all teachers, especially those who deal in unpopular ideas, know. Ultimately, says Fairley, the purpose of creative art is to help people "to look out upon the world, and understand and admit that what they see going on around them is far more important and far more exciting than what is going on, or failing to go on, in their own heads" (5). And what is going on around them is a struggle—not just a "class struggle," but a universal strug-gle that is part of the reality of being human. In other words, the artist teaches people to look outward, to abandon the inward, self-centred gaze which, as the experienced mother Margaret Fairley would know, belongs to the infantile stage of human development. "But the fashion of ignoring the outer world, of playing with colors or with words, is very powerful, and young artists and writers need all the help they can get to withstand it." They need above all to be encouraged to observe and record "real life": "writers and artists of the present day may well consider whether this is not still the best contribution they can make towards whole-hearted commitment...in present-day struggles" (6).

Fairley's argument is easily challenged, of course, on the basis of the meaning of her terminology, for instance. The inward world of Virginia Woolf is just as "real" as the outward world of George Bernard Shaw, as Fairley herself well knew, for she admired the work of both writers. But for Fairley, "reality" was commensurate with the moral commitment to making the world a better place, by whatever actions or literary strategies that could be found to advance that end. Hence the works of Canadian and world literature she admired included writings by Communists, non-Communists, and even anti-Communists. Her favourite literary quotation was from Joseph Conrad, a writer who certainly had no use for socialistic and radical revolutionary political ideas—although far from ignoring or dismissing such ideas contemptuously he wrote about them constantly. "It had come into her mind," Conrad wrote in *Nostromo*, "that for life to be large and full, it must contain the care of the past and of the future in every passing moment of the present. Our daily work must be done to the glory of the dead, and for the good of those who come after" (cited in Ryerson, "Margaret Fairley" n. pag.). These words summarize the aims of Fairley, of all Canadian progressive writers, and of all people who believe in progress toward a better world.

# List of Works Cited

## Manuscript Collections

Acorn, Milton. National Archives of Canada (NAC)

Baird, Irene. McMaster University

Carter, Dyson. National Archives of Canada

Communist Party of Canada/Labor-Progressive Party. National Archives of Canada

Communist Party of Canada, 1922-31. Public Archives of Ontario (PAO)

DeLury, A.T. University of Toronto

Fairley, Margaret. University of Toronto

Livesay, Dorothy. University of Manitoba

Nielsen, Dorise. National Archives of Canada

Sinclair, Bertrand. University of British Columbia

Stephen, A.M. University of British Columbia

## Periodicals

*Ontario Workman* (1872-74)

*Western Clarion* (1903-20)

*The Rebel* (1917-20)

*Canadian Forum* (1921-    )

*The Worker* (1922-36)
*Canadian Labor Defender* (1930-33)
*Masses* (1932-34)
*Clarté* (1935-39)
*New Frontier* (1936-37)
*Daily Clarion* (1936-39)
*Canadian Tribune* (1940-92)
*National Affairs Monthly* (1944-57)
*En Masse* (1945)
*Combat* (1947-60)
*Canadian Writing* (1950-51)
*Champion* (1951-57)
*New Frontiers* (1952-56)
*Marxist Quarterly* (*Horizons*) (1962-69)

## Primary Sources

Acorn, Milton. *I Shout Love and Other Poems*. Ed. James Deahl. Toronto: Aya, 1987.

_____. *The Island Means Minago*. Toronto: NC, 1975.

_____. *I've Tasted My Blood: Poems 1956-1968*. Toronto: Ryerson, 1969.

_____. *More Poems for People*. Toronto: NC, 1973.

_____. and Cedric Smith. *The Road to Charlottetown*. Hamilton, ON: Meckler & Deahl, 1998.

Allan, Ted. *This Time a Better Earth*. New York: Morrow, 1939.

Allan, Ted and Sydney Gordon. *The Scalpel, the Sword: The Story of Dr. Norman Bethune*. 1952. Toronto: McClelland and Stewart, 1989.

Allister, William. *A Handful of Rice*. London: Secker and Warburg, 1961.

*At the Mermaid Inn: Wilfred Campbell, Archibald Lampman, Duncan Campbell Scott in* The Globe *1892-3*. Intro. by Barrie Davies. Toronto: U of Toronto P, 1979.

Baird, Irene. *Waste Heritage*. 1939. Toronto: Macmillan, 1973.

Bergren, Myrtle. *A Bough of Needles*. Toronto: Progress, 1964.

Bethune, Norman. *The Politics of Passion: Norman Bethune's Writing and Art*. Ed. Larry Hannant. Toronto: U of Toronto P, 1998.

Beynon, Francis Marion. *Aleta Dey*. 1919. London: Virago, 1988.

Birney, Earle. *Down the Long Table*. 1955. Toronto: McClelland and Stewart, 1975.

Buller Herman. *Days of Rage*. Montréal: October Publ. [1974].

_____. *Quebec in Revolt*. 1965. Toronto: Swan, 1966.

Callaghan, Morley. "I Should Have Been a Preacher." Unpublished short story. 1923. Scribner's Papers, Princeton University.

\_\_\_\_\_. "'Radical Bill' Foster Urges Labor Revolt." *Toronto Daily Star* 7 August 1923: 5.

\_\_\_\_\_. *Strange Fugitive.* 1928. Edmonton: Hurtig, 1970.

\_\_\_\_\_. *Such Is My Beloved.* 1934. Toronto: McClelland and Stewart, 1964.

\_\_\_\_\_. *They Shall Inherit the Earth.* 1934. Toronto: McClelland and Stewart, 1969.

\_\_\_\_\_. "A Windy Corner at Yonge-Albert." *Toronto Star Weekly* 6 August 1921: 17.

Cappon, Paul, ed. *In Our Own House: Social Perspectives on Canadian Literature.* Toronto: McClelland and Stewart, 1978.

Carter, Dyson. *Fatherless Sons.* Toronto: Progress, 1955.

[\_\_\_\_\_] *The Governor's Mistress.* By "Warren Desmond." Toronto: General, 1950.

\_\_\_\_\_. *Night of Flame.* Toronto: McLeod, 1942.

\_\_\_\_\_. *Russia's Secret Weapon.* Winnipeg: Contemporary, 1942.

\_\_\_\_\_. *Science and Revolution.* Gravenhurst, ON: Northern, 1966.

\_\_\_\_\_. *Sea of Destiny.* New York: Greenberg, 1940.

\_\_\_\_\_. *This Story Fierce and Tender.* Gravenhurst, ON: Northern, 1986.

\_\_\_\_\_. *Tomorrow Is with Us.* Toronto: Progress, 1950.

\_\_\_\_\_. and Charlotte Carter. *We Saw Socialism.* Toronto: Canadian-Soviet Friendship Society, 1951.

Chapman, Ethel M. *With Flame of Freedom.* Toronto: Allen, 1938.

Colombo, John Robert. *The Mackenzie Poems.* Toronto: Swan, 1966.

Davis, N. Brian, ed. *The Poetry of the Canadian People 1720-1920.* Toronto: NC, 1976.

\_\_\_\_\_, ed. *The Poetry of the Canadian People 1900-1950.* Toronto: NC, 1978.

Dewdney, Selwyn. *Wind Without Rain.* 1946. Toronto: McClelland and Stewart, 1974.

Dumbrille, Dorothy. *All This Difference.* Toronto: Progress, 1945.

Durkin, Douglas. *The Magpie.* 1923. Toronto: U of Toronto P, 1974.

Endres, Robin. "Marxist Literary Criticism and English Canadian Literature." *In Our Own House.* Ed. Paul Cappon. 82-129.

Evans, Hubert. *Mist on the River.* 1954. Toronto: McClelland and Stewart, 1973.

\_\_\_\_\_. *The New Front Line.* Toronto: Macmillan, 1927.

Fairley, Margaret, ed. *The Selected Writings of William Lyon Mackenzie 1824-1837.* Toronto: Oxford UP, 1960.

\_\_\_\_\_, ed. *Spirit of Canadian Democracy: A Collection of Canadian Writings from the Beginnings to the Present Day.* Toronto: Progress [1945].

\_\_\_\_\_. "A Woman's Confession." *Canadian Forum* 1 (August 1921): 333.

Fraser, Dawn. *Echoes from Labor's Wars.* Expanded ed. Ed. David Frank and Don MacGillivray. Wreck Cove, NS: Breton, 1992.

Gélinas, Pierre. *Les Vivants les morts et les autres.* Le Cercle de livre de France, 1959.

Gouzenko, Igor. *The Fall of a Titan*. New York: Norton, 1954.

_____. *This Was My Choice*. Montréal: Palm, 1948.

Gregory, Claudius J. *Forgotten Men*. Hamilton, ON: Davis-Lisson, 1933.

Griffin, Harold. *Alaska and the Canadian Northwest: Our New Frontier*. New York: Norton, 1944.

_____. *Soviet Frontiers of Tomorrow*. Moscow: Progress, 1982.

Grove, Frederick Philip. *A Search for America*. 1927. Toronto: McClelland and Stewart, 1971.

Harrison, Charles Yale. *Generals Die in Bed*. 1930. Hamilton, ON: Potlatch, 1974.

Klein, A.M. *Complete Poems, Part 2*. Ed. Zailig Pollock. Toronto: U of Toronto P, 1990.

Kreisel, Henry. *The Rich Man*. 1948. Toronto: McClelland and Stewart, 1961.

Lampman, Archibald. ["Socialism"] *The Essays and Reviews of Archibald Lampman*. Ed. D.M.R. Bentley. London, ON: Canadian Poetry Press, 1996. 186-90.

Leacock, Stephen. *Arcadian Adventures with the Idle Rich*. 1914. Toronto: McClelland and Stewart, 1969.

Lemelin, Roger. *Au Pied de la pente douce*. 1944. Montréal: Editions de l'Arbre, 1948.

Leslie, Kenneth. "The Censored Editor." *New Frontiers* 2 (July/August 1937): 10-11.

_____. *The Poems of Kenneth Leslie*. Ladysmith, QC: Ladysmith Press, 1971.

Liversedge, Ronald. *Recollections of the On to Ottawa Trek*. Ed. Victor Hoar. Toronto: McClelland and Stewart, 1973.

Livesay, Dorothy. *Collected Poems: The Two Seasons*. Toronto: McGraw-Hill Ryerson, 1972.

_____. *Right Hand Left Hand*. Erin, ON: Press Porcepic, 1977.

Lowther, Pat. *A Stone Diary*. Toronto: Oxford, 1977.

MacDonald, Wilson. *Caw-Caw Ballads*. Toronto: MacDonald, 1930.

_____. *On My Own in Moscow*. Toronto: Northern, 1958.

Machar, Agnes Maule. *Roland Graeme: Knight*. 1892. Ottawa: Tecumseh, 1996.

Maguire, Trevor. "O Canada!: A Tale of Canadian Workers' [sic] Life." *The Worker* [Toronto], 19 February-3 September 1927.

_____. "Unemployment." *Canadian Labour Monthly* May/June 1928. *Eight Men Speak and Other Plays from the Canadian Workers' Theatre*, ed. Richard Wright and Robin Endres. 5-14.

Marshall, Joyce. *Presently Tomorrow*. Boston: Little, Brown, 1946.

Mathews, Robin. *Canadian Literature: Surrender or Revolution*. Toronto: Steel Rail, 1978.

_____. "Developing a Language of Struggle: Canadian Literature and Literary Criticism." *In Our Own House*. Ed. Paul Cappon. 135-46.

McArthur, Peter. *In Pastures Green.* Toronto: Dent, 1915.

McEwen, Tom. *The Forge Glows Red.* Toronto: Progress, 1974.

McKay, Colin. *Windjammers and Bluenose Sailors: Stories of the Sea.* Ed. Lewis Jackson and Ian McKay. Lockeport, NS: Roseway, 1993.

Myers, Gustavus. *A History of Canadian Wealth.* Intro. Stanley Ryerson. 1914. Toronto: James Lewis & Samuel, 1972.

Phillips, Donna, ed. *Voices of Discord: Canadian Short Stories from the 1930s.* Toronto: New Hogtown, 1979.

Potrebenko, Helen. *Life, Love and Unions.* Vancouver: Lazara, 1987.

_____. *Sometimes they Sang.* Vancouver: Press Gang, 1986.

_____. *Taxi.* Vancouver: New Star, 1975.

Richard, Jean-Jules. *Le Feu dans l'amiante.* Montréal: chezlauteur [sic] [1956].

_____. *Neuf jours de haine.* Montréal: l'Editions de l'arbre [1948].

Roy, Gabrielle. *Bonheur d'occasion.* 1945. Montréal: Beauchemin, 1947.

Ryan, Oscar. *The "Sedition" of A.E. Smith.* Toronto: Canadian Labor Defense League [1934].

_____. *Soon to Be Born.* Vancouver: New Star, 1980.

_____. *Tim Buck: A Conscience for Canada.* Toronto: Progress, 1975.

Ryerson, Stanley. *1837: The Birth of Canadian Democracy.* Toronto: Francis White, 1937.

_____. *The Founding of Canada: Beginnings to 1815.* 1960. Toronto: Progress, 1972.

_____. *French Canada: A Study in Canadian Democracy.* Toronto: Progress, 1943.

_____. *Unequal Union: Confederation and the Roots of Conflict in the Canadas, 1815-1873.* 2nd ed. Toronto: Progress, 1973.

Ryga, George. *Ballad of a Stonepicker.* Vancouver: Talonbooks, 1976.

_____. *The Ecstasy of Rita Joe and Other Plays.* Toronto: New Press, 1971.

_____. *Hungry Hills.* 1963. Vancouver: Talonbooks, 1974.

Salutin, Rick, and Theatre Passe Muraille. *1837: William Lyon Mackenzie and the Canadian Revolution.* Toronto: Lorimer, 1976.

Sinclair, Bertrand. *Big Timber.* Boston: Little, Brown, 1916.

_____. *The Inverted Pyramid.* New York: Burt, 1924.

_____. *North of Fifty-three.* New York: Grossett and Dunlap, 1914.

_____. *Poor Man's Rock.* Toronto: Ryerson, 1920.

Stephen, A.M. *Fascism: The Black International.* Vancouver: B.C. Clarion [1936].

_____. *The Gleaming Archway.* Toronto: Dent, 1929.

_____. *Hitlerism in Canada.* [Vancouver?] Canadian League against War and Fascism [1936].

_____. *Marxism: The Basis for a New Social Order.* Vancouver: B.C. Clarion, 1933.

Stevenson, Sharon. *Gold Earrings.* Vancouver: Pulp Press, 1984.

*The Stone, the Axe, the Sword, and Other Canadian Poems*. New Frontiers Pamphlet No. 1. Toronto: New Frontiers, 1955.

Thompson, T. Phillips. *The Labor Reform Songster*. 1892. Appendix to *The Politics of Labor*. Toronto: U of Toronto P, 1975.

_____. *The Politics of Labor*. 1887. Introduction by Jay Atherton. Toronto: U of Toronto P, 1975.

van der Mark, Christine. *In Due Season*. Toronto: Oxford UP, 1947.

Vulpe, Nicola and Maha Albari, eds. *Sealed in Struggle: Canadian Poetry and the Spanish Civil War*. La Laguna, Spain: Universidad de la Laguna, Center for Canadian Studies, 1995.

Wallace, J.S. *The Golden Legend*. Moscow: Foreign Languages Publ., 1958.

_____. *Joe Wallace Poems*. Toronto: Progress, 1981.

_____. *A Radiant Sphere*. Moscow: Foreign Languages Publ., 1964.

Wright, Richard and Robin Endres, eds. *Eight Men Speak and Other Plays from the Canadian Workers' Theatre*. Toronto: New Hogtown, 1976.

## Secondary Sources

Aaron, Daniel. *Writers on the Left: Episodes in American Literary Communism*. 1961. New York: Columbia UP, 1992.

Abrahams, Edward. *The Lyrical Left: Randolph Bourne, Alfred Stieglitz and the Origins of Cultural Radicalism in America*. Charlottesville: UP of Virginia, 1986.

Acorn, Milton. "I was a communist for my own damn satisfaction." *Evidence* 5 (1962): 32-38.

_____. "In Wry Memoriam: Joe Wallace." *Canadian Dimension* 4-5 (September 1977): 38-43, 51.

Adams, Rose. "Oscar Ryan." *Dictionary of Literary Biography 68: Canadian Writers 1920-1959*, First Series. Ed. W.H. New. Detroit: Gale, 1988. 318-23.

Anderson, Patrick. *Search Me: Autobiography–the Black Country, Canada and Spain*. London: Chatto, 1957.

Angus, Ian. *Canadian Bolsheviks: The Early Years of the Communist Party of Canada*. Montréal: Vanguard, 1981.

"The Author" [biog. note on Dyson Carter]. *Canadian Tribune* 8 August 1955: 10.

"Author Meets Readers." *Canadian Tribune* 17 October 1955: 8.

Avakumovic, Ivan. *The Communist Party in Canada: A History*. Toronto: McClelland and Stewart, 1975.

Baird, Irene. "Sidown, Brother, Sidown." The *C C Free Press* 16 July 1973. Clipping, Baird Papers, McMaster U.

Baldwin, H.W. Rev. of *Sea of Destiny* by Dyson Carter. *New York Times* 25 August 1940: 16.

Berger, Carl. *The Writing of Canadian History.* Toronto: Oxford UP, 1976.

Boire, Gary. *Morley Callaghan: Literary Anarchist.* Toronto: ECW, 1994.

Bothwell, Robert and J.L. Granatstein, eds. *The Gouzenko Transcripts.* Ottawa: Deneau, n.d.

Broadus, E.K. and E.H. Broadus. Preface. *A Book of Canadian Prose and Verse.* Ed. E.K. and E.H. Broadus. 1923. Toronto: Macmillan, 1926.

Brown, Edward J. *The Proletarian Episode in Russian Literature, 1928-1932.* 1953. New York: Octagon, 1971.

Brown, E.K. "Letters in Canada 1942: Poetry." *University of Toronto Quarterly* 12 (April 1943): 309.

Carter, Dyson. "Dyson Carter Explains: Why I've Joined the LPP." *Canadian Tribune* 15 December 1945: 7.

Cecil-Smith, E. "Propaganda and Art." *Masses* 2 (January 1934): n. pag.

_____. "The Workers' Theatre in Canada." *Canadian Forum* 14 October 1933: 68-70.

Cohen, Nathan. "Canadian Literature: Trends and Limitations." *National Affairs Monthly* 3 (April 1946): 118-20.

Commons, John R., ed. *History of Labour in the United States.* 1918. New York: Kelley, 1966.

"Communist Poet." *Saturday Night* 3 July 1943: 3.

*Creative Canada: A Biographical Dictionary of Twentieth-Century Creative and Performing Artists.* 2 vols. Toronto: U of Toronto P, 1972.

"Culture Sessions Center of Conflict of East and West." *New York Times* 27 March 1949: 1.

Davey, Frank. "Dorothy Livesay." *Oxford Companion to Canadian Literature.* 2nd ed. Ed. Eugene Benson and William Toye. Toronto: Oxford UP, 1997. 674-75.

Denning, Michael. *The Cultural Front: The Laboring of American Culture in the Twentieth Century.* New York: Verso, 1997.

Devanney, Burris. "Kenneth Leslie: A Biographical Introduction." *Canadian Poetry: Studies/Documents/Reviews* 5 (Fall/Winter 1979): 83-104.

Elliott, Robbins L. "The Canadian Labour Press from 1867: A Chronological Annotated Directory." *Canadian Journal of Economics and Political Science* 14 (1948): 220-45.

[Fairley, Margaret] "Cold War Award." *New Frontiers* 4 (Summer 1955): 2.

_____. "The Cultural Worker's Responsibility to the People." *Horizons* 25 (Spring 1968): 4-6.

_____. "*Jean Christophe*, by Romain Rolland." *The Rebel* 1 (March 1917): 5-8.

_____. "Mining Town." Rev. of *Fatherless Sons* by Dyson Carter. *New Frontiers* 4 (Fall 1955): 41-42.

_____. "Our Cultural Heritage." *New Frontiers* 1 (Winter 1952): 1-7.

_____. "Our Heritage Is Rich–But How Can We Find It?" *Canadian Tribune* 28 June 1954: 17.

_____. "Prof. A.T. DeLury–A Resolute Champion." *Canadian Tribune* 19 November 1951: 12.

_____. "Short Notices." *Canadian Forum* October 1931: 34.

_____. "Socialist Poet of Upper Canada." *New Frontiers* 4 (Spring 1955): 34-38.

_____. "Want Stories of People Who Built Canada." *Canadian Tribune* 27 February 1950: 8.

_____. "The Women's Party." *The Rebel* 3 (October 1918): 27-29.

F[airley], M[argaret]. "Young Canadian's First Novel Is Sound Working-Class Fiction." Rev. of *The Rich Man* by Henry Kreisel. *Canadian Tribune* 6 December 1948: 10.

Filewood, Alan. *Collective Encounters: Documentary Theatre in English Canada.* Toronto: U of Toronto P, 1987.

Foley, Barbara. *Radical Representations: Politics and Form in U.S. Proletarian Fiction, 1929-1941.* Durham: Duke UP, 1993.

Frank, David and Don MacGillivray. Introduction. *Echoes from Labor's Wars* by Dawn Fraser. ix-xxvi.

Fraser, Don. Rev. of *Each Man's Son* by Hugh MacLennan. *Canadian Tribune* 21 May 1951: 13.

Fried, Albert and Ronald Saunders, eds. *Socialist Thought: A Documentary History.* Rev. ed. New York: Columbia UP, 1992.

Frye, Northrop. "Conclusion." *Literary History of Canada: Canadian Literature in English.* Ed. Carl F. Klinck. Toronto: U of Toronto P, 1965. 821-49.

_____. "Letters in Canada" [1951]. Reprinted in *The Bush Garden.* Toronto: Anansi, 1971.

_____. *The Modern Century.* Toronto: Oxford UP, 1967.

_____. "Poetry; Letters in Canada 1953." *University of Toronto Quarterly* (1953-54): 260-61.

Fulford, Robert. "Books." Rev. of *Selected Writings of William Lyon Mackenzie.* *Toronto Star* 9 December 1960: 20.

Gornick, Vivian. *The Romance of American Communism.* New York: Basic, 1977.

Griffin, Harold. "J.S. (Joe) Wallace." *Canadian Tribune* 10 December 1975: 9.

_____. "An Outstanding Canadian Novel of Native Indian Conflict." Rev. of *Mist on the River* by Hubert Evans. *Canadian Tribune* 22 November 1954: 9.

Hannant, Larry. "Doctoring Bethune." *Saturday Night,* April 1998: 75-81.

Harrington, Lyn. *Syllables of Recorded Time: The Story of the Canadian Authors Association 1921-1981.* Toronto: Simon and Pierre, 1981.

Hoffman, James. *The Ecstasy of Resistance: A Biography of George Ryga.* Toronto: ECW, 1995.

Hopwood, V.G. "A Burns of the Backwoods." *New Frontiers* (Fall 1952): 31-38.

_____. "Review Missed Full Import of Carter Book." *Canadian Tribune* 22 August 1955: 8.

_____. "The Sage of Ekfrid and the Owl of Medonte." *New Frontiers* 3 (Spring 1954): 41-43.

Hughes, Kenneth J. and Birk Sproxton. "Malcolm's Katie: Images and Songs." *Canadian Literature* 65 (Summer 1975): 55-64.

Innes, Christopher. *Politics and the Playwright: George Ryga.* Toronto: Simon & Pierre, 1985.

Irr, Caren. *The Suburb of Dissent: Cultural Politics in the United States and Canada during the 1930s.* Durham, NC: Duke UP, 1998.

Kealey, Gregory S. "Stanley Bréhaut Ryerson: Canadian Revolutionary Intellectual." *Studies in Political Economy* 9 (Fall 1982): 103-31.

_____. "Stanley Bréhaut Ryerson: Marxist Historian." *Studies in Political Economy* 9 (Fall 1982): 133-71.

Keeling, Margaret A. Introduction. *Poems of Nature and Romance 1794-1897.* By Samuel Taylor Coleridge. Oxford: Clarendon, 1910. 7-49.

Kilbourn, William. *The Firebrand: William Lyon Mackenzie and the Rebellion in Upper Canada.* 1956. Toronto: Clark Irwin, 1964.

_____. "The Many-Sided Character of Our Rebellious First Mayor." *Globe and Mail* 25 March 1961: 22.

Kimmel, David. "The Spirit of Canadian Democracy: Margaret Fairley and the Communist Cultural Worker's Responsibility to the People." *Left History* 1 (Spring 1993): 34-55.

Kimmel, David and Gregory S. Kealey. "With Our Own Hands: Margaret Fairley and the 'Real Makers' of Canada." *Labour/Le Travail.* 31 (Spring 1993): 253-85.

Klinck, Carl F. "Literary Activity in the Canadas 1812-1841." *Literary History of Canada: Canadian Literature in English.* Ed. Carl Klinck et al. Toronto: U of Toronto P, 1965. 125-44.

_____. "Turning New Leaves." Rev. of *Selected Writings of William Lyon Mackenzie,* ed. Margaret Fairley. *Canadian Forum* April 1961: 20-21.

Lanctot, Gustave. Rev. of *The Founding of Canada* by Stanley Ryerson. *Canadian Historical Review* 42 (1961): 147.

Lemm, Richard. *Milton Acorn: In Love and Anger.* Ottawa: Carleton UP, 1999.

Lenin, V.I. *Selected Works.* 3 vols. Moscow: Progress, 1971.

Lindsey, Charles. *The Life and Times of William Lyon Mackenzie.* 2 vols. Toronto: Randall, 1862.

Livesay, Dorothy. "The Documentary Poem: A Canadian Genre." 1969. *Contexts of Canadian Criticism.* Ed. Eli Mandel. Chicago: U of Chicago P, 1971. 267-81.

———. Editor's foreword to "I Was a Young Communist" by Peter Hunter. *CVII* 2 (May 1978): 17.

———. "A Putting Down of Roots." *CVII* 1 (Spring 1975): 2.

Longpré, Daniel. "The Life of Bethune." Rev. of *The Scalpel, the Sword* by Ted Allan and Sydney Gordon. *New Frontiers* 1 (Fall 1952): 40.

Lucas, Alec. "Peter McArthur." *Oxford Companion to Canadian Literature.* 2nd ed. Ed. Eugene Benson and William Toye. Toronto: Oxford UP, 1997. 685-86.

Lukàcs, Georg. *Essays on Realism.* Ed. Rodney Livingstone. Trans. David Fernbach. Cambridge, MA: MIT Press, 1981.

———. *The Meaning of Contemporary Realism.* Trans. John Mander and Necke Mander. London: Merlin, 1963.

"Magazines Meet: A Symposium of Canadian Culture." *Canadian Tribune* 31 March 1952: 13.

"Makers of a Nation." Rev. of *Selected Writings of William Lyon Mackenzie. Times Literary Supplement* May 1961: 269.

McKay, Ian. "Colin McKay's Alternative Vision of the Age of Sail." *Windjammers and Bluenose Sailors* by Colin McKay. 21-29.

McLay, Catherine. "Irene Baird." *Dictionary of Literary Biography 68: Canadian Writers 1920-1959*, First Series. Ed. W.H. New. Detroit: Gale, 1988. 15-17.

"Meet the Staff." *Canadian Tribune* 29 March 1947: 10.

Murphy, James F. *The Proletarian Moment: The Controversy over Leftism in Literature.* Urbana and Chicago: U of Illinois P, 1991.

Nielsen, Robert F. Introduction to *Generals Die in Bed* by Charles Yale Harrison. Hamilton, ON: Potlatch, 1975.

"Open Forum on 'Fatherless Sons'." *Canadian Tribune* 19 September 1955: 9.

Paine, Thomas. *Rights of Man, Common Sense and Other Political Writings.* Ed. Mark Philp. Oxford: Oxford UP, 1995.

Pelletier, Jacques. Preface. *La Neige* by Pierre Gélinas. Montréal: Triptyque, 1996.

Penner, Norman. *Canadian Communism: The Stalin Years and Beyond.* Toronto: Methuen, 1988.

Reid, Malcolm. *The Shouting Signpainters: A Literary and Political Account of Quebec Revolutionary Nationalism.* New York: Monthly Review Press, 1972.

Repka, William and Kathleen M. Repka. *Dangerous Patriots: Canada's Unknown Prisoners of War.* Vancouver: New Star, 1982.

Roberts, Michael. "*Two Solitudes* Fine New Novel about Quebec." *Canadian Tribune* 14 April 1945: 14.

Rodney, William. *Soldiers of the International: A History of the Communist Party of Canada, 1919-1929.* Toronto: U of Toronto P, 1968.

Rosenthal, Henry M. and S. Cathy Berson, eds. *The Canadian Jewish Outlook Anthology.* Vancouver: New Star, 1988.

Roussopoulos, Dimitrios J., ed. *The New Left in Canada.* Montréal: Black Rose, 1970.

Ryan, Toby Gordon. *Stage Left: Canadian Workers Theatre 1929-1940.* 1981. Toronto: Simon & Pierre, 1985.

Ryerson, Stanley B. "Author of *The Founding of Canada* Writes Rejoinder to Criticisms." *Canadian Tribune* 28 August 1961: 8.

———. "Democracy and the Arts: The Need for Action." *National Affairs Monthly* 4 (December 1947): 376-80.

———. Introduction. *A History of Canadian Wealth* by Gustavus Myers. 1914. Toronto: James Lewis and Samuel, 1972. vii-xxx.

———. "Novel 'All This Difference' Seeks Roots of Prejudice Against the French Canadians." *Canadian Tribune* 22 September 1945: 12.

———. "Our Country's History Has Yet to Be Written." *Canadian Tribune* 11 January 1947: 7.

R[yerson], S[tanley]. "Out of the Frying Pan…" *Masses* 2 (March/April 1934): n. pag.

Saarinen, O.W. "The 1950s." *Sudbury: Rail Town to Regional Capital.* Ed. C.M. Wallace and Ashley Thomson. Toronto: Dundurn, 1993. 190-214.

Safarik, Allan and Dorothy Livesay. "Perspective: How I Began–Selections from an Interview with Joe Wallace." *CVII* (Spring 1975): 35-42.

Sandwell, B.K. Rev. of *French Canada* by S.B. Ryerson. *Canadian Historical Review* 25 (June 1944): 200-01.

Sawatsky, John. *Gouzenko: The Untold Story.* Toronto: Macmillan, 1984.

Schabas, Ann. Interview. 14 July 1993.

Scott, F.R. Preface to *New Provinces.* 1936. *The Making of Modern Poetry in Canada.* Ed. Louis Dudek and Michael Gnarowski. Toronto: Ryerson, 1970.

Sharpe, Errol. *A People's History of Prince Edward Island.* Toronto: Steel Rail, 1976.

Shek, Ben-Zion. *Social Realism in the French-Canadian Novel.* Montréal: Harvest House, 1977.

"Short Stories." *Canadian Forum* October 1932: 5.

Stalin, Josef. *Works.* 13 vols. Moscow: Foreign Languages Publ., 1955.

Suleiman, Susan. *Authoritarian Fictions: The Ideological Novel as a Literary Genre.* New York: Columbia UP, 1983.

Talbot, Emile J. "Literature and Ideology in the Thirties: Fictional Representations of Communism in Quebec." *International Journal of Canadian Studies* 20 (Fall 1999): 67-80.

Thomas, Clara. *Canadian Novelists 1920-1945.* Toronto: Longmans, 1946.

Thompson, Lee Briscoe. *Dorothy Livesay.* Boston: Twayne, 1987.

_____. "Dorothy Livesay." *Dictionary of Literary Biography 68: Canadian Writers, 1920-1959*, First Series. Detroit: Gale, 1988. 214-25.

"Toronto University Professor Barred by U.S. Border Guards." *Globe and Mail* 6 October 1949: 4.

"Trial of 12 Communists 'Major Test for Democracy,' Fast Warning to Canada." *Canadian Tribune* 17 January 1949: 2.

"A Tribute from His Old School to People's Poet Joe Wallace." *Canadian Tribune* 27 June 1973: 9.

Trotsky, Leon. *Literature and Revolution*. New York: Russell, 1957.

Waddington, Miriam. "The Cloudless Day: The Radical Poems of A.M. Klein." *Tamarack Review* 45 (Autumn 1967): 65-90.

Wald, Alan M. *Writing from the Left: New Essays on Radical Culture and Politics*. New York: Verso, 1994.

Watt, F.W. "Literature of Protest." *Literary History of Canada: Canadian Literature in English*. Ed. Carl F. Klinck. Toronto: U of Toronto P, 1965. 457-73.

_____. "Radicalism in English-Canadian Literature since Confederation." Diss. U of Toronto, 1957.

Weisbord, Merrily. *The Strangest Dream: Canadian Communists, the Spy Trials, and the Cold War*. Toronto: Lester and Orpen Dennys, 1983.

Whitaker, Reg and Gary Marcuse. *Cold War Canada: The Making of a National Insecurity State, 1945-1957*. Toronto: U of Toronto P, 1994.

Wilson, G.E. Rev. of *The Founding of Canada* by S. Ryerson. *Dalhousie Review* 41 (1961): 127.

Winks, Robin W. Rev. of *The Story of Canada* by Donald Creighton and *The Founding of Canada* by S. Ryerson. *American Historical Review* 66 (1961): 1075-76.

# Index